The Making of Modern Jewish Identity

This volume explores the processes that led several modern Jewish leaders – rabbis, politicians, and intellectuals – to make radical changes to their ideology regarding Zionism, Socialism, and Orthodoxy. Comparing their ideological change to acts of conversion, the study examines the philosophical, sociological, and psychological path of the leaders' transformation.

The individuals examined are novelist Arthur Koestler, who transformed from a devout Communist to an anti-Communist crusader following the atrocities of the Stalin regime; Norman Podhoretz, editor of *Commentary* magazine, who moved from the New Left to neoconservative, disillusioned by US liberal politics; Yissachar Shlomo Teichtel, who transformed from an ultra-Orthodox anti-Zionist Hungarian rabbi to messianic Religious Zionist due to the events of the Holocaust; Ruth Ben-David, who converted to Judaism after the Second World War in France because of her sympathy with Zionism, eventually becoming a radical anti-Israeli advocate; Haim Herman Cohn, Israeli Supreme Court justice, who grew up as a non-Zionist Orthodox Jew in Germany, later renouncing his belief in God due to the events of the Holocaust; and Avraham (Avrum) Burg, prominent centrist Israeli politician who served as the Speaker of the Knesset and head of the Jewish Agency, who later became a post-Zionist.

Comparing aspects of modern politics to religion, the book will be of interest to researchers in a broad range of areas including modern Jewish studies, sociology of religion, and political science.

Motti Inbari is an Associate Professor of Religion at the University of North Carolina at Pembroke. An expert in the study of Jewish Orthodoxy, his books include *Jewish Fundamentalism and the Temple Mount* (2009), *Messianic Religious Zionism Confronts Israeli Territorial Compromises* (2012), and *Jewish Radical Ultra-Orthodoxy Confronts Modernity, Zionism and Women's Equality* (2016).

Routledge Jewish Studies Series

Series Editor: Oliver Leaman

University of Kentucky

Jewish Studies, which are interpreted to cover the disciplines of history, sociology, anthropology, culture, politics, philosophy, theology, religion, as they relate to Jewish affairs. The remit includes texts which have as their primary focus issues, ideas, personalities and events of relevance to Jews, Jewish life and the concepts which have characterised Jewish culture both in the past and today. The series is interested in receiving appropriate scripts or proposals.

For more information about this series, please visit: www.routledge.com/middleeaststudies/series/JEWISH

The Making of Modern Jewish Identity

Ideological Change and
Religious Conversion

Motti Inbari

LONDON AND NEW YORK

First published 2019
by Routledge
2 Park Square, Milton Park, Abingdon, Oxon OX14 4RN

and by Routledge
52 Vanderbilt Avenue, New York, NY 10017

Routledge is an imprint of the Taylor & Francis Group, an informa business

© 2019 Motti Inbari

British Library Cataloguing-in-Publication Data
A catalogue record for this book is available from the British Library

Library of Congress Cataloging-in-Publication Data
Names: Inbari, Motti, author.
Title: The making of modern Jewish identity : ideological change and
    religious conversion / Motti Inbari.
Description: London ; New York, NY : Routledge/Taylor & Francis
    Group, 2019. | Series: Routledge Jewish Studies Series | Includes
    bibliographical references and index.
Identifiers: LCCN 2019006620 | ISBN 9780367135959 (hardback) |
    ISBN 9780429027390 (ebook) | ISBN 9780429648595 (epub) |
    ISBN 9780429645952 (mobipocket)
Subjects: LCSH: Jews—Identity. | Jews—Politics and government. |
    Jews—Social conditions. | Judaism—History. | Conversion—
    Judaism—History—20th century.
Classification: LCC DS143 .I53 2019 | DDC 305.892/4—dc23
LC record available at https://lccn.loc.gov/2019006620

ISBN: 978-0-367-13595-9 (hbk)
ISBN: 978-0-429-02739-0 (ebk)

Typeset in Times New Roman
by Apex CoVantage, LLC

To Aliza

Contents

Acknowledgements

This book is about ideological change. As I bring this project to an end, I must contemplate on what brought me to investigate this subject so deeply. With hindsight, I cannot but recall how I started my political journey as a young man, fascinated by the ideas of Socialism. As I investigated the biographies of the figures discussed in this book, I can truly identify with each and every one of these remarkable people, although not always in full agreement with their choices. Still, I have to understand it for myself, what brought me to change, why am I not a socialist anymore? Researching the chapters of this book helped me understand my own growth. Although I cannot offer clear answers, it probably has to do with the collapse of the prospects of peace in Israel, followed by my own immigration to the United States, which opened new perspectives in my life.

People tend to view ideological change in a negative way; we do not want our politicians to "zigzag," but I feel I must object. This research led me to appreciate open-mindedness and the ability of self-examination. I hope you would feel the same after reading this book.

The idea to investigate the subject of ideological and identity change came to me after spending several hours in conversations with Dr. Shalom Goldman in the fall of 2014. Goldman, who studied the biography of several prominent modern converts in and out of Judaism, suggested that I would explore the biography of Arthur Koestler. At that time, Goldman was studying Ruth Ben-David's conversion story, and the chapter in his book *Jewish-Christian Difference and Modern Jewish Identity* (Lexington Books, 2015) inspired me to research her story as well. Thank you, Shalom, for stimulating and challenging me to start this project. These conversations were truly inspirational.

The ideas for almost all of the chapters of this book came to me in conversations with colleagues and friends. My dear friend Dr. Menachem Keren-Kratz suggested that I investigate the biography of Rabbi Yissachar Shlomo Teichtel; Dr. David Ellenson proposed that I study the case of Avrum Burg; Dr. Jonathan Sarna and Dr. Dana Kaplan gave me the idea to focus on Norman Podhoretz. Thank you so much for your wonderful suggestions. I want to send a special thanks to Dr. Thomas L. Jeffers, the biographer of Norman Podhoretz, for allowing me to have access to transcripts of the interviews he took with Podhoretz for his research.

I am in deep gratitude to Dr. David Nikkel, my department chair at the University of North Carolina at Pembroke. Dr. Nikkel is such a wonderful person, and he always makes sure that I will have the time and resources needed for conducting research. Thank you, David, for your kindness and leadership. I want to thank also my dean, Dr. Jeff Fredrick, for being so considerate and generous over the years.

I want to thank dear colleagues and friends for their ongoing support. I am truly privileged to have Dr. Yaakov Ariel by my side. Dr. Ariel has been accompanying me from graduate school until today. I am so fortunate to have him as a mentor, and I have learned from him so much. Thank you, Kobi, for all that you are doing for me.

I want to thank Drs. Malachi HaCohen, Allan Arkush, Ilan Fuchs, and Yuval Jobani for reading sections of this book and suggesting excellent revisions. I want also to mention Drs. Robert Eisen, Ilan Troen, Reuven Firestone, and Mitu Ashraf for their friendship and collegiality. I want to express special gratitude to my editor and translator, Shaul Vardi. This is his fourth manuscript working with me.

Lastly, I want to mention the women in my life: my dear wife Aliza and my two precious daughters Shani and Shir. Although this book is about instability, disappointments, and change, my life has been rock-solid and it is all because of you. You were always there for me with comfort, support, and unconditional love. I love you back from the bottom of my heart.

Introduction

This book explores the process that led several modern Jewish leaders – rabbis, politicians, and intellectuals – to make radical changes to their ideological positions regarding Zionism, Socialism, and Orthodoxy. What leads a person to make fundamental changes in his or her ideology? What are the social conditions that affect change?

Any study of modern Jewry must take into account the historical crises that sparked such ideological changes. Over the course of the twentieth century, Jews experienced dramatic events: anti-Semitism, mass emigration, the Holocaust, the establishment of the State of Israel, and Israeli wars and victories. All these events left their mark on Jewish history and demanded ideological attention.

I selected six prominent individuals who underwent significant transformations. The figures are the novelist Arthur Koestler (1905–1983), who transformed from a devout Communist to an anti-Communist crusader following the atrocities of the Stalin regime; Norman Podhoretz (b. 1930), who as the editor of *Commentary* magazine moved from the New Left to a neoconservative position, disillusioned by liberal politics in the United States; Issachar Shlomo Teichtel (1885–1945), who transformed from an ultra-Orthodox anti-Zionist Hungarian rabbi to a messianic Religious Zionist due to the events of the Holocaust, which he did not survive; Ruth Ben-David (1920–2000), who converted to Judaism after the Second World War in France because of her sympathy with Zionism and the fate of the Jews during the war, but who eventually became a radical anti-Israeli advocate; Haim Herman Cohn (1911–2002), an Israeli Supreme Court justice who grew up as a non-Zionist Orthodox Jew in Germany but later renounced his belief in God due to the events of the Holocaust; and Avraham (Avrum) Burg (b. 1955), a prominent centrist Israeli politician who served as the Speaker of the Knesset and head of the Jewish Agency but who later became a post-Zionist, disillusioned by Israel's occupation of the Territories. I devote a separate chapter to each of these case studies, outlining the ideological transformation and the circumstances that led to it.

Until modern times, Jewish identity was understood as holistic, combining ritual and spiritual elements with a sense of peoplehood. This holistic view was broken during the 19th and 20th centuries as Jews developed new views of Judaism, mostly as either a religion or a nation. Each of the case studies discussed in this book represents a different position on the question of what it means to be Jewish in our time. The cases I chose may be examined according to an axis between two polar views: one pole argues that Jewish nationalism is the major pillar of Jewish identity, while the other asserts that Jewish nationalism is antithetical to this identity. The subjects of this book switched from one identity to the other, and their internal debates yielded different responses. Some found their identity in non-national universalism (Koestler); others found their identity in Israeli-Palestinian binationalism (Burg); some drew close to an anti-Zionist ultra-Orthodox ideology (Ben-David); others stripped Judaism of its religious content and viewed Judaism as national rather than spiritual (Cohn); some saw the horrors of the Holocaust as signs of imminent national messianic fulfillment (Teichtel); still others found their identity in political conservatism, viewing the support of the State of Israel as their main pillar of identity (Podhoretz).

I have chosen this group of people because they all changed their identity: this is not particularly common, and my options were limited. The individuals I have selected were not the only options available, however; other notable candidates included Israeli figures who moved from left to right, such as the poet Naomi Shemer or the novelist Moshe Shamir. Radical transformations can also be observed in the cases of Israeli journalist Uri Avnery and American political theorist Irving Kristol. However, in my selection of the case studies I was concerned to ensure that each case represents a different option of Jewish identity, so that the manuscript explores a broad spectrum of modern Jewish possibilities. The manuscript is divided into three main sections: Koestler and Podhoretz represent English-speaking intellectuals who became alienated from Socialism; Teichtel and Ben-David represent the debates over Zionism during and after the Holocaust among ultra-Orthodox Jews in Europe (Hungary and France); Burg and Cohn represent the debate over Jewish nationalism among German Jews living in Israel after the Holocaust.

The question of Zionism is extremely controversial in academic and non-academic circles today, and accordingly it is important and interesting to hear the voices of Jews who endorsed and condemned the Jewish national movement. This manuscript offers a broad overview of this debate among twentieth-century Jewish intellectuals.

The introduction includes four major sections: a discussion of the different options of modern Jewish identities, the theory of ideological change with regard to religious conversion, the view of modern politics as secular religion, and a description of the chapters of the book.

Jewish identities

The debate over what it means to be Jewish is a modern phenomenon: in pre-modern times, the meaning of being Jewish was clear. Prior to modernity, which brought Jews citizenship rights, Judaism was not a religion, and Jewishness was not a matter of culture or nationality. Rather, Judaism and Jewishness were all these at once: religion, culture, and nationality.

The basic framework of organized Jewish life in the medieval and early modern periods was the local Jewish community, an autonomous legal body that exercised jurisdiction over the Jewish population in a particular geographical area. In premodern Jewish societies there was no question that normative Judaism was defined by allegiance to the Halakhah (Jewish law). The autonomous Jewish communities had the power to keep law and order, collect taxes, offer education, and even to excommunicate the deviants.[1] The common ideological commitment went far beyond the established organizational units. According to social historian Jacob Katz, it was based on a strong identification with the idea of a Jewish nation, to which one belonged by birth and religious obligations and which created a demand for mutual responsibility. Teachers and preachers of this period drew the substance of their teachings from the Talmud and medieval sources, which were imbued with the notion of Jewish nationhood, its metaphysical origin, its religious implications, and its historical destiny. In this manner, the conceptualization of nationhood and the individual's allegiance to it, as expounded by philosophers and Kabbalists in the Middle Ages, was disseminated and absorbed.[2]

According to scholar of religion Leora Batnitzky, the idea that Judaism is a religion but not a nation emerged together with the modern nation-state. The German-Jewish invention of the idea of Jewish religion was also a cultural and political reaction to the gap between the ideal of full Jewish integration into the German state and a far more ambiguous and complex political and cultural reality. "Religion" as a distinct category of human activity was invented to separate it from other realms of the modern West, such as culture and politics. The transformation of religion into a private, universal, and apolitical realm came hand in hand with the rise of sovereign states in Europe. As the state strove for monopoly over the use of violence, it curtailed the power of the church and relegated religion to the status of personal piety.[3]

A movement away from the feudal and collective structure of medieval Europe toward a unified Prussian state went hand in hand with the German Enlightenment's argument for a universal, rational ideal. One may have expected sympathy for the Jews and demands for their full integration into such a unified state, but instead the Jewish community was increasingly accused of being a "state within the state" that could not, by definition, be integrated into Prussia.

As a result of this complex new reality, the Jewish philosopher Moses Mendelssohn (1729–1786) called for the adjustment of Jewish life in Germany in the eighteenth century. As Jews wished to join the newly established nation-states, Mendelssohn helped reshape their argument that Judaism does not strive for power and thus lacks a political dimension. This approach would enable the inclusion of Jews inside the political order of the modern nation-states, highlighting that there is no conflict between Jewish identity and loyalty to the state. Mendelssohn stressed that Jews should enjoy civil rights as individuals and not as a collective entity.[4] Both the Reform and Orthodox streams that emerged in Germany agreed with Mendelssohn's analysis that Judaism is not political.[5] Thus, for example, Reform Judaism's Pittsburg Platform (1885) declared: "We consider ourselves no longer a nation, but a religious community, and therefore expect neither a return to

Palestine, nor a sacrificial worship under the sons of Aaron, nor the restoration of any of the laws concerning the Jewish state." (I will discuss the later transformations in Reform Judaism below.)

The logic behind viewing Jews as members of a religion, a component of an identity that is confined to the private sphere of beliefs, was to enhance the assimilation and the acculturation of Jews into German society. According to this logic, the concept of Jewish peoplehood was to be abandoned and muted. This process went hand in hand with strong waves of secularization that dramatically reduced the level of observance of Jewish laws and customs. Historian Todd Endelman argues that although the Emancipation of Jews was supposed to weaken Jewish identity, this transformation was incomplete. Jews still constituted a well-defined and high-profile social group. The tribalism of the Jews created a dilemma for Jewish representatives and apologists in the West. Jews continued to insist that their Jewishness was a purely confessional difference, but they could not reject the idea that they maintained social cohesion and ethnic distinctiveness.

One way to solve this dilemma was by arguing that the Jews are a race. Endelman describes the racial definition as a "widespread, casual, everyday use of racial language to describe the Jews as a social unit."[6] By using this term, Jews sought to suggest a feeling of community with other Jews, a sense of a common historical fate, and a deep emotional bond. Endelman concluded that the emancipation of the Jews in Western Europe was not developing as planned. Although traditional faith and practices had been eroded and cultural distinctiveness blurred, social cohesion remained strong.[7]

Orthodoxy, which I will discuss at length in this manuscript, continued these tendencies with its own nuances. Orthodox thinkers did not reject the concept of Jewish collectivity and argued that all Jews are united as people. However, a central foundation of classical Orthodoxy was the principle of passivity. According to Jacob Katz, all three types of Orthodoxy that emerged in the late nineteenth century in Germany, Russia, and Hungary shared this principle, which had been a hallmark of Jewish society in the premodern era: "This was far reaching passivity with respect to long range planning for the future of the Jewish community." Following exile from its homeland, the Jewish people lost faith in its own capacity to engineer its redemption. This change could come only as the result of divine and miraculous intervention. The modern era brought new opportunities for Jews: emancipation, emigration, and in 1948 the establishment of a Jewish state. However, Orthodoxy – or more precisely, Haredi (ultra-Orthodox) Judaism – seemed reluctant to free itself from its premodern mentality and refrained from playing a leading role in any of these enterprises. In the case of the Jewish national movement, the Haredi leadership found theological justifications for its opposition. The dominant Haredi theological position preserved the tradition of passivity and rejected any possible affinity between the Zionist enterprise and the process of redemption. For the most part, rabbinic literature did not envisage an interim state between exile and redemption, and in this sense Zionism was regarded as an illegitimate deviation from the course of history. Moreover, the theological interpretation adopted by some of the most extreme Haredi elements, such as the Eda

Haredit and Neturei Karta, views Zionism as no less than the work of the Devil, designed to confuse the Jews and divert them from their path to redemption.[8]

While Western European Jews identified their Jewishness mainly as a religion, their Eastern European peers were more attracted to the view that Judaism is primarily a nation. Among the promoters of the national idea were the followers of the Zionist movement.[9]

Modernity was late to arrive to the Jewish masses in Eastern Europe. Moreover, in Eastern Europe Jews were not offered citizen rights as they were in the West. Indeed, their situation deteriorated due to the spread of anti-Semitism, including anti-Jewish pogroms such as those in Kishinev in 1903 and 1905. Anti-Jewish violence led many Jews to support the idea of Jewish nationalism.

Zionism is commonly recognized as a movement that rebelled against previous Jewish political and religious behavior. The Zionist message was indeed shockingly revolutionary: it was a rebellion against political passivity and against Jewish exile with its observant way of life.

For the first time, according to the newly created Zionist movement, Jewish identity was to be framed by nationality and not by religion. Whereas the traditional Jewish model of self-identity involved observing the Torah and its commandments as interpreted in the Oral Law, the Zionist message aimed to present a more holistic model: a return to the motherland, to power, to a "healthy" way of life, and to normality. These were all perceived as a substitute for religious law.[10]

The Zionist ideology argued that Jewish life in the Diaspora was illegitimate, and according to Zionist thinkers, the Jewish Diaspora would eventually be destroyed due to anti-Semitic violence. The Zionist concept of the "negation of exile" sought to create a new Jew – the diametric opposite of the Jew of the Shtetl. The new Jew, according to this image, would be proud and strong – a peasant who works the land, lives independently without reliance on gentile power, and creates a new Hebrew culture.[11]

In its attempt to acquire historical legitimacy, Zionism appropriated themes and myths from the Jewish past, but these were modified and selectively culled elements that suited the national allegory.[12] The Zionist sense of superiority over the Jewish Diaspora was justified, in some ways, by a renewed emphasis on the Bible, which was understood as the link between the mythological past and the present. The Bible enabled the creation of a national myth and the consolidation of a distinctive Zionist ethos around the ancestral land. Any national movement requires a foundation story, and the Bible served this function for Zionism. However, the religious lesson of the Bible was sterilized: the role of God as creator and the demand for faith and observance were ignored. The Zionist movement used the Bible from a secular perspective as Jewish national history was replayed in their lifetime. The Bible was viewed as a national asset, denuded of its faith-related aspects.[13]

Although predominantly Socialist, secularist, and verging on the anti-religious, Zionism developed a sense that it constituted a fulfillment of biblical messianic prophecies. Jewish collective memory carries a strong messianic message. From the rabbinical standpoint, the destruction of the Second Temple (AD 70) represents the beginning of exile. Rabbinical commentary argues that exile was imposed on the nation due to its sins, and only after its complete repentance can redemption begin, with the coming of the messiah. Thus exile serves a spiritual purpose: to prepare the Jews for their salvation.[14] According to biblical and rabbinical writings, the end of days will bring the national restoration of the Jews, the ingathering of exiles, the rebuilding of a Davidic kingdom, and the re-establishment of the Temple as the central site of worship.[15]

Many early Zionist thinkers, most notably David Ben-Gurion (1886–1973), the unchallenged leader of political Zionism and Israel's first prime minister, developed a sense of messianic fulfillment in their actions. They were gathering the Jewish exiles in the land of Israel; they were building a Jewish state (parallel to the Davidic Kingdom); they were redeeming the land from its Gentile occupants; they were reviving Hebrew as the Jewish language; and they were forced into military conflicts in defense of their national enterprise. At the same time, however, Ben-Gurion envisioned Zionism as a "light unto the nations" – a moral and universalist national movement that would set standards for the creation of a perfect society. This was therefore a secular messianism that blended humanism and nationalism. The Bible was the ancient model for national revival and for the social model expounded in the words of the prophets.[16]

Support for Zionism helped transform Jewish identity in America. Historian Jonathan Sarna argues that the idea of Zionism was very divisive among American Jews in the early twentieth century, due to the opposition of both Reform and Orthodox Judaism. However, the commitment of Louis Brandeis (1856–1941) to Zionism, and his prominent role among American Jews, transformed Zionism into a significant force. Sarna maintains that Brandeis was attracted to the concept of national Judaism because he was himself an agnostic secularist "who found in Zionism a way of synthesizing their (Brandeis and his supporters) progressive ideas with their hitherto latent Jewish attachment." Zionism became a form of civil religion for secular Jews: "This utopian vision offered Jews who had become disenchanted with the traditional beliefs, rituals, and practices of Judaism a sacred task that both linked them to other Jews and infused their own personal lives with meaning."[17]

Scholar Noam Pianko describes the term "peoplehood" among American Jews as a modern nationalist paradigm that introduces a secular definition of Jewish collectivity that went far beyond statehood, stressing national unity, shared essential characteristics, a common past and future mission, solidarity in the face of external persecutions, and a need for Jewish political engagement on the world stage to protect Jewish interests. Pianko connects these notions with the writings of Rabbi Mordechai Kaplan (1881–1983), and indeed argues that Kaplan was inspired by Zionist thinking when he formulated his worldview during the 1940s. The trauma of the Holocaust reinforced the conviction that the Jews must be united, and the common denominator of Jewish cohesion was the creation of the State of Israel, and especially the Six Day (1967) and Yom Kippur (1973) Wars. Pianko concludes that the concept of peoplehood came to be a tool to support Israel in the name of common destiny.[18] Thus concern for Israel united American

Jews and the new state became the central pillar of their identity (a pattern we will see in the case of Norman Podhoretz).

Between the two poles of secular nationalism or religious pietism, several hybrid movements had also emerged. Religious Zionism in Israel and Conservative Judaism in the United States are examples of these intermediate models. The idea of Jewish unity eventually influenced Reform Judaism as well, especially after the Holocaust and the establishment of the State of Israel.

Very soon after its emergence, Religious Zionism was forced to consider dialectical perspectives that seek to imbue the Zionist enterprise with covert messianic significance. These approaches are identified, in particular, with the religious philosophy of Rabbi Avraham Yitzhak HaCohen Kook (1865–1935). According to historian Dov Schwartz, many Orthodox Jews found it difficult to identify with the Zionist movement and to act within the classic Zionist parameters. Zionist rhetoric spoke of the need to "normalize" the Jewish people and make it "a nation like all the others." The essence of Zionism was described as being "to build a safe haven for the Jewish people." All these definitions are inconsistent with Jewish tradition, which emphasizes a distinction between Israel and the other nations and proclaims that the Land of Israel has a unique theological function. Accordingly, many of those who developed the Religious Zionist approach, led by Rabbi Avraham Yitzhak HaCohen Kook, integrate this religious purpose in the Zionist idea.

These thinkers used the traditional rabbinical technique of *pshat* and *drash* (literal meaning as distinct from exegetical meaning) to describe the Zionist act. While ostensibly adopting the general Zionist definition of the movement's purpose, this definition was imbued with specific religious meaning: the reinstatement of divine worship within the context of a theocratic national framework. The Zionist body acts in the material realm, but its innermost core aspires to an eternal spiritual life, and this constitutes the "real" foundation for its operations and aims, even if the movement itself is still unaware of this.[19] The long-awaited theocracy is about to arrive, and it will be realized once secular Zionism chooses the true path (i.e., the complete worship of God). Zionism will then advance to its second phase: the revival of the monarchy, the restitution of the sacrifices on the Temple Mount, and the re-establishment of the Sanhedrin.[20] Until these lofty goals were achieved, Religious Zionism saw itself as a bridge between secular Zionism and Orthodox Judaism.

Conservative Judaism is the only major American Jewish movement without any anti-Zionist past, and its liturgy has consistently engaged with the new reality of Israel, argues scholar of religion Daniel Gordis. At the same time, he continues, Conservative Judaism is at its core deeply American, and as such, a sense of comfort in America is one of its commitments. Gordis identified that the commitment to Zionism and Israel can be found in its liturgy, and its followers tend to support Israel in large numbers. However, there is much less interest among its followers in Aliya (immigration to Israel). As much as Conservative Judaism is committed to the idea of Jewish nationalism, it is also committed to a vibrant American Jewish community, he concludes.[21]

Reform Judaism has undergone several transformations regarding the question of Jewish nationalism. The movement initially rejected Zionism and indeed any manifestation of Jewish peoplehood. However, the influx of a new generation of Reform rabbis from Eastern Europe between the two world wars led the movement to amend its position. Influenced by the ideas of Mordechai Kaplan, Reform Judaism affirmed the concepts of Jewish peoplehood in its Columbus Platform, adopted in 1937. The Holocaust created a broad consensus, including within Reform Judaism, for political Zionism. In 1973, under the leadership of Rabbi Richard Hirsch (born 1926), the World Union for Progressive Judaism moved its headquarters to Jerusalem, and in 1970, the Hebrew Union College opened a campus in the city.[22]

Ideological change and religious conversion

Political theorist Leonard Williams argues that ideology is an essential part of modern political life: "It seems that we can no more do without ideology than we can do without breathing." Williams defines ideology as the primary means by which people relate to political life. Ideology provides the lenses through which we view political events, the conceptual framework through which we come to understand the political world we inhabit. Similarly, it supplies us with standards by which we evaluate the social and political order in which we live; it gives us a set of values and helps us construct a vision of better society.[23]

In his famous biography of young Martin Luther, psychologist Erik Erikson did not distinguish between Luther's religious and political views, combining both under the joint term of an *ideology*:

> At the most it is a militant system with uniformed members and uniformed goals; at the least it is a "way of life," . . . a world-view which is consonant with existing theory, available knowledge, and common sense, and yet it is significantly more: an utopian outlook, a cosmic mood, a doctrinal logic, all shared as self-evident beyond any need for demonstration.

Luther suffered from identity crisis, eventually rebelled against his parents and his church, and later led the Protestant Reformation. Ideology, said Erikson, offered Luther's peers the "overly simplified and yet determined answers to exactly those vague inner states and those urgent questions which arise in consequence of identity conflict."[24]

Luther's fusion of the political and the spiritual is consistent with our study. All the positions in the spectrum of modern Jewish identities presented above are ideological: they offer a perspective for viewing the condition of Jewish existence and a path to the future. This book will review a group of selected individuals who transformed as the result of identity crises not unlike that experienced by the young Martin Luther.

Leonard Williams, mentioned above, studied the transformations of political thoughts, especially in the case of American liberalism. He claims that ideological change is simply a fact of social and political life: when national circumstances change, ideologies adjust as well. This book aims to understand change, however, not on the level of political thought but in individuals. What leads people to change their political philosophy?

While researching the case studies discussed in the book, I realized that political change and religious transformations as in the process of conversion are actually very similar in terms of the course they entail in the individual's life. I found the sociological, psychological, and philosophical literature on conversion very illuminating to this research, as I discuss in greater detail in Chapters 1, 2, 4, and 5.

I devote particular attention in my study to the role of personal life events as major factors in creating ideological changes. This analysis is informed by several theories: (1) William James' *The Varieties of Religious Experience* describes the inner feelings of the convert and distinguishes between the "healthy minded" and the "sick soul," who needs to transform his identity in order to heal miseries and reach happiness.[25] (2) The *cognitive dissonance* theory seeks to explain the distress caused when two contradictory ideas or cognitions are held simultaneously. The theory argues that those involved will be strongly motivated to resolve the tension between the contradictory ideas. Ideological change is one solution to cognitive dissonance; however, it requires admitting lifelong ideological mistakes, which individuals are often unable or unwilling to do.[26] (3) Any process of change requires first shedding off old identities, thus before a conversion there is a process of *deconversion*, a loss or deprivation of religious faith or ideology. This process entails intellectual doubt, moral criticism, emotional suffering, and disaffiliation from the community. Deconversion may take the form of a sudden dramatic reversal, but the research suggests that in most cases it is a slow and gradual process.[27] (4) Chana Ullman's *The Transformed Self* explains the religious quest in the context of a search sparked by emotional distress. The converts in her study described the period preceding their conversion as fraught with negative emotions, and many reported that their conversion offered relief from this turmoil.[28] (5) Armand Mauss' theory of *religious defection* includes three parts. The first is the intellectual dimension, reflecting disbelief in one religious faith and the acceptance of an alternative. The second level is social: a defection can be on the communal or associational level, embodying an unwillingness to confirm to church, or as in our case, political norms. The third category is emotional defection, which is associated with emotional distress between parents and children or some negative event involving religion that causes people to deconvert.[29]

In *The Varieties of Religious Experience*, William James conceded that some people can never be converted, since religious ideas are not the center of their spiritual energy. He acknowledged, albeit only in a brief aside, that a similar course of obtaining happiness through conversion, which he called "unification," "can be intellectual in its process" in some cases, and not spiritual.[30] For our purposes, it would have been productive had James discussed this aspect in greater depth, since the cases discussed in this book lean more toward intellectual than spiritual transformation. Nevertheless, many of the cases presented in this book appear to follow similar patterns to those outlined by James and others. All the individuals discussed might be called "sick souls" – their self was divided and they sought healing. Their political change constituted their process of unification, and their conversion into a different political ideology brought them happiness and assurance. In this sense, they were indeed "twice born." James' analysis of converts, like the other theories presented in the book, may be applied in understanding ideological and political change, and this transfer in itself constitutes an example of the overlap between the spiritual and the political.

Political theology

Change, the concept that forms the heart of this book, is about shifting loyalties. Ideological change and religious conversions may seem to be two distinct phenomena: one is political while the other is spiritual. However, as this book argues, the similarities are striking. The seeming parallels require some introspection into the structures of modern politics, which, in my opinion, can be viewed as based on secularized religious structures.

Scholars and political theorists long ago noticed the similarities between secular political ideologies and religious ideologies. Scholars have also pointed out that even the aspects of modern politics that appear to be secular are in fact intrinsically theological. Locke, Hobbes, and other founders of modern political theory based their works on readings of the Bible and other religious texts.[31]

Political messianism is a term that came to define totalitarian ideologies in the twentieth century. In his 1922 *Political Theology: Four Chapters on the Concept of Sovereignty*, Carl Schmitt argued that political theology advances "all significant concepts of the modern theory of the state are secularized theological concepts ... the omnipotent God became the omnipotent lawgiver ... the exception in jurisprudence is analogous to the miracle in theology."[32] After the Second World War, intellectual critiques of the totalitarian states compared them to secular religion. Historians such as Jacob Talmon and Norman Cohn framed revolutionary politics as messianic and exposed the underlying millenarianism of the Marxist vision of history. Allegations of political religion and secular messianism became the preferred liberal tool for delegitimizing Communism.[33]

Talmon's *The Origins of Totalitarian Democracy* (1952) was the first major postwar critique of secular messianism. Modern revolutionaries' pursuit of rational order, argued Talmon, exemplified a messianic mentality akin to that of the premodern Christian revolutionaries. Secular messianism, he said, seeks worldly salvation and depends on collective transformation. Having removed all barriers to violence, modern secular religion unleashed a series of revolutions from France to Russia.[34] The replacement of the kingdom of God on earth with the kingdom of humanity on earth; the perception of the ideal of the End of Days as an achievable reality that must be brought about here and now through the actions of believers; the need for revolutionary political action by an informed vanguard in order to restore history to its proper path; and the construction of a new social, national, or world order – all these are the characteristic components of political messianism according to Talmon.[35]

In *The Pursuit of the Millennium* (1957), Norman Cohn argued that premodern millenarianism and modern totalitarianism are virtually synonymous: "The old symbols and old slogans have indeed disappeared, to be replaced by new ones; but the structure of the basic phantasies seems to have changed scarcely at all."[36] Surveying an area extending from northern France through the Low Countries to Germany and Bohemia between the late eleventh and the sixteenth centuries, *The Pursuit of the Millennium* found social unrest intermittently taking the form of millennial rebellion by the needy and discontented masses, moved by the prophecy of an approaching end to the world, an apocalyptic struggle between Christ and his enemies that will usher in a blissful millennium. Regarding the modern totalitarian movements, Cohn suggested that the ideologies of Communism and Nazism, dissimilar though they are in many respects, are both heavily indebted to that very ancient body of beliefs that constituted the popular apocalyptic lore of Europe.[37]

Political scientist David Apter argued that during the 1960s the regimes in some Third World countries, such as Ghana, China, and Indonesia, developed a political religion that attributed continuity, meaning, and purpose to individual actions. The attempts of the regimes to better the material status of the state made this goal sacred. The decline of religion has presented the Western democratic polity with the problem of how to substitute sources of meaning, faith, and spirituality that all humans need to some degree. New nations dealt with this problem by defining political and moral aims as one and the same. Political religion includes the representation of the state as a sacred value, the tendency of the state to provide direction in a variety of social and cultural realms, the demand of absolute loyalty from the citizenry to the state and its institutions, the mobilization of citizens on behalf of the state objectives, the identification of the state interest as superior to individual or subgroup interest, a tendency to charismatic leadership, and the effort to instill meaning and purpose into the lives of the individuals by virtue of their identification with the state and its objectives.[38]

In *The Broken Covenant*, Robert N. Bellah studied the motivations of the Puritans, who profoundly influenced the shaping of American democracy. In his analysis of the American civil religion, Bellah argues that religious moral understandings underpinned the American political structure and the cultural legitimization of society. Bellah suggests that the vision of the founding fathers included a biblical-like myth of origin with a vision of a covenant that was made between God and the Pilgrims, so that those who joined the covenant had to follow a "born-again" experience. The founders of the republic believed that their government was derived from a higher source, either God or nature. America was viewed as a promised land for the chosen people, while the establishment of a republic was viewed as akin to the coming of the millennium.[39]

Israeli political scientists Charles Liebman and Eliezer Don-Yehiya argued, based on Apter's and Bellah's insights, that the State of Israel has developed a similar system of civil religion. Israeli civil religion includes a system of sacred symbols, beliefs, and practices that consolidate society, legitimize social order, and mobilize the population in social efforts while transmitting the central values and worldview that dominate the society.[40] Historian David Ohana has shown that many Zionist thinkers saw Zionism as a secular religion and used the messianic myth to prove that Zionism is the fulfillment of messianic promises of redemption.[41] Philosopher Yotam Hotam maintained that Zionist secularization was actually a theology of heresy influenced by the gnostic ideas adopted by the German political school known as Life Philosophy. The Zionist secular and anti-Halakhic stand was an anti-theological theology founded in gnosis.[42]

I would like to add another layer to the comparison by discussing the concept of loyalty. The loyalty of the premoderns living in Christian Europe was to God and to the institutions God has established on earth. Being loyal to God, following a righteous life, and obeying God's laws and commandments guaranteed that God would be loyal as well – a barter agreement that both sides win. Placing one's trust in God and being loyal to His will was the guarantee for life after death. The promises of afterlife for the righteous or eternal damnation for the wicked had been strong motivators in premodern societies. The political institutions of premodern Europe built their power on the basis of this notion of loyalty. Thus, the idea of the divine right of kings was based on the assumption that God placed the monarch on earth, and accordingly loyalty to God also requires loyalty to the kings He crowned on earth. For example, Baruch Spinoza argued in his *Theological-Political Treatise* that obedience to God includes love of one's neighbor and blind obedience to political authority.[43] Given such a premise, it is not a surprise to read the following statement made by King James I from 1616: "The state of MONARCHIE is the supremest thing upon earth: For Kings are not onely GODS Lieutenants upon earth, and sit upon GODS throne, but even by GOD himselfe they are called Gods."[44]

What did it mean to be loyal to God? In extreme cases, loyalty was tested on the basis of a willingness to sacrifice one's life. Thus, the noblest thing that a man could do was to manifest his loyalty by offering his life for the honor of God. Every monotheistic religion has developed mechanisms that justified martyrdom for the sake of God, and this expression of loyalty usually granted the highest rewards in the afterlife. Praising martyrs is common among Jews, Christians, and Muslims, and those who gave their lives in this manner were revered and adored.

In modern times, God no longer crowns kings, and the focus of loyalty was transferred to the political institutions. Moderns have been expected to be loyal to their country, their party (in the case of the Soviet Union), or their race (Nazi Germany). These political institutions adapted the structure of loyalty: in order to be a good citizen, it is not necessary to be loyal to God; He is no longer important in this regard. However, martyrdom is still expected in certain situations. The willingness to die in the defense of the homeland is regarded as necessary and is regarded as an honorable and necessary sacrifice (another secularized religious structure). Thus, for example, one of the most famous Zionist slogans proclaims that "it is good to die for the sake of our country" (a statement that is associated with Joseph Trumpeldor, who arguably said these words just before he died while defending his settlement in the Battle of Tel Hai in 1920). Thus we can conclude that loyalty justifies martyrdom. In premodern times, martyrdom for God was viewed as honorable and noble, but in the modern era the concepts of loyalty and martyrdom have been transferred to the political institutions, which are viewed with appreciation and reverence (I will discuss these notions of loyalty in the case of Arthur Koestler).

The structure of the book

The data on the individuals discussed in this book were collected mostly from their own autobiographies and publications. Their narratives were written years after the events they describe took place, and it is important to take this gap into account. As psychological research has shown, personal narratives based on memory can be smoothed in order to make sense and to form a logical course of events; accordingly, scholars who study personal narratives must be cautious.[45] Therefore, I have not relied on the personal narrative alone, and I have tried as much as possible to crosscheck every fact with independent and external sources.

All the subjects of this research changed their ideology; I am inclined to believe their descriptions of why they decided to change. For the purpose of this research, their own testimony of their intellectual struggles, the dissonances between theory and reality as they saw them, and their emotions and feelings as they remember them have great importance.

Chapter 1 presents the novelist Arthur Koestler (1905–1983), who renounced his messianic beliefs in Communism in 1938 following the crimes of the Stalin regime. The chapter outlines Koestler's spirituality against the background of his deconversion and highlights the role of cognitive dissonance in his actions. Koestler's case illustrates the impact of a spiritual awakening he experienced while imprisoned in a Spanish jail in 1936.

Chapter 2 describes the path that led Norman Podhoretz (b. 1930) to transform as the editor of *Commentary* magazine from the New Left to a neoconservative position – a change that took place in the late 1960s in the United States. My discussion of Podhoretz contains previously unpublished sources clarifying the spiritual nature of his political transformation, which included a mystical and life-changing experience in the early spring of 1970.

Chapter 3 discusses how Yissachar Shlomo Teichtel (1885–1945), the head of the rabbinical court (*av bet din*) and chief rabbi of Pishtian in Slovakia, transformed his opinions during the interwar period and the Holocaust regarding the theological role of Zionism in the messianic drama. In my discussion of Teichtel, I show how he departed from the anti-Zionist ideology of Hungarian radical ultra-Orthodoxy by comparing his views to those of Chaim Elazar Shapira ("the Munkacser Rebbe," 1871–1937), the leader of the Orthodox community in Hungary. Teichtel was a follower of the Munkacser Rebbe and initially supported his anti-Zionist approach. However, he changed his position following the rise of the pro-Nazi state in Slovakia and its persecution of the Jews. In 1942 he began to write the book *Em HaBanim Semekhah* (A Happy Mother of Children), in which he refuted his rebbe's position and offered a justification for Zionism.

Chapter 4 explores the course taken by Madeleine Lucette Ferraille (1920–2000), who was born into a Roman Catholic family in France and converted to Judaism after the Second World War because of her identification with Zionism and with the fate of the Jews during the war (she changed her name to Ruth Ben-David after her conversion). In the early 1960s she was involved in the kidnapping of Yossele Schumacher, a seven-year-old boy, as part of her transformation into a radical anti-Israeli advocate. The chapter on Ruth Ben-David is largely based on her unpublished autobiography and includes some discoveries concerning the kidnapping, a saga that shook Israeli society during the early 1960s.

Chapter 5 summarizes the life story of Haim Herman Cohn, a central figure in the shaping of Israel's judicial system, who served as consultant to the state, as attorney general, and as a Supreme Court justice. One of the main chapters of his life was the process of abandonment of faith, a traumatic process entailing disappointment and grief. Cohn was born into a non-Zionist, strictly Orthodox household in Germany and was descended from a distinguished rabbinical family. He had planned to continue the traditions of his grandparents and to become a rabbi himself, but unusually strong intellectual capabilities pushed him outside of the religious world. The story of how Cohn fell out of faith may sound typical of many young men of his generation who abandoned the Orthodox lifestyle. Still, Cohn's story is different. During his lifetime as a nonbeliever, one of the main missions he took upon himself was to adjust Jewish law to the reality of a liberal and modern state so that it could be incorporated in the Israeli statute book.

Chapter 6 follows Avraham (Avrum) Burg (b. 1955), a prominent centrist Israeli politician who served as the Speaker of the Knesset and head of the Jewish Agency but later became a post-Zionist. The chapter begins by discussing his first ideological change, when he departed during the 1970s from Religious Zionism, the ideology of his upbringing. Later, in the 2000s, at the height of his career as an Israeli politician, he decided to quit politics, leaving mainstream Zionism to become a post-Zionist. The chapter places Burg in the broader context of the identity crisis of German Jews in the twentieth century and highlights Burg's complex relationship with his father, who was a prominent Religious-Zionist politician, as the key to understanding his many transformations.

Notes

1 Jacob Katz, *Out of the Ghetto: The Social Background of Jewish Emancipation 117–1870*, Cambridge, MA: Harvard University Press, 1973, 21.
2 Ibid., 22.
3 Leora Batnitzky, *How Judaism Became a Religion*, Princeton: Princeton University Press, 2011, introduction (e-book).
4 Ibid., chapter 1.
5 Yaakov Yadgar, *Sovereign Jews: Israel, Zionism and Judaism*, Albany: SUNY Press, 2017, 39–44.
6 Todd Endelman, "Jewish Self-Identification and West European Categories of Belonging," in: *Religion or Ethnicity? Jewish Identities in Evolution*, edited by Zvi Gitelman, New Brunswick, NJ: Rutgers University Press, 2009, 122.
7 Ibid., 104–130. On the question of Jews and race, see Mitchell Hart (ed.), *Jews and Race*, Waltham, MA: Brandeis University Press, 2011.

8 Motti Inbari, *Jewish Radical Ultra-Orthodoxy Confronts Modernity, Zionism and Women's Equality*, New York: Cambridge University Press, 2016.

9 Followers of the Bund, the socialist movement, also viewed their Jewishness as national. I will not address this type of identity here in this book.

10 Anita Shapira, "The Bible and Israeli Identity," *AJS Review* 28 (1) (2004): 11–42.

11 Ruth Shamir, *Who Are We?* Herzelia: Milo, 2012, 48–58.

12 David Ohana, *Nationalizing Judaism: Zionism as a Theological Ideology*, Lanham, MD: Lexington Books, 2017, 1.

13 Uriel Simon, *The Status of the Bible in Israeli Society: From National Commentary to Existential Literalism*, Jerusalem: A. Hess, 1991 (in Hebrew).

14 Ella Balfar, *The Kingdom of Heaven and the State of Israel*, Ramat Gan: Bar Ilan University Press, 1991 (in Hebrew).

15 See, for example, Maimonides' *Laws of Kings and Wars*, chapters 11–12.

16 David Ohana, *Political Theologies in the Holy Land: Israeli Messianism and Its Critics*, London: Routledge, 2010, 17–53.

17 Jonathan Sarna, *American Judaism: A History*, New Haven, CT: Yale University Press, 2004, 203–205.

18 Noam Pianko, *Jewish Peoplehood: An American Innovation*, New Brunswick, NJ: Rutgers University Press, 2015, 14–67.

19 Dov Schwartz, *Faith at a Crossroads – A Theological Profile of Religious Zionism*, Leiden: Brill, 2002, 156–192.

20 Motti Inbari, "Religious Zionism and the Temple Mount Dilemma: Key Trends," *Israel Studies* 12 (2) (2007): 29–47.

21 Daniel Gordis, "Conservative Judaism, Zionism and Israel: Commitments and Ambivalences," in: *Israel, the Diaspora and Jewish Identity*, edited by Danny Ben-Moshe and Zohar Segev, Portland: Sussex Academic Press, 2007, 67–80.

22 Michael Livni, "The Place of Israel in the Identity of Reform Jews: Examining the Spectrum of Passive Identification with Israel to Active Jewish-Zionist Commitment," in: *Israel, the Diaspora and Jewish Identity*, edited by Danny Ben-Moshe and Zohar Segev, Portland: Sussex Academic Press, 2007, 86–101.

23 Leonard Williams, *American Liberalism and Ideological Change*, DeKalb: Northern Illinois University Press, 1997, 15.

24 Erik Erikson, *Young Man Luther: A Study in Psychoanalysis and History*, New York: W. W. Norton, 1962, 41–42.

25 William James, *The Varieties of Religious Experience*, New York: Modern Library, 1902.

26 Leon Festinger, Henry W. Reicken and Stanley Schachter, *When Prophecy Fails: A Social and Psychological Study of a Modern Group That Predicted the Destruction of the World*, Minneapolis: University of Minnesota Press, 1956.

27 John Barbour, *Versions of Deconversion: Autobiography and the Loss of Faith*, Charlottesville: University Press of Virginia, 1994; Heinz Streib, Ralph W. Hood Jr., Barbara Keller, Rosina-Martha Csöff and Christopher Silver, *Deconversion: Qualitative and Quantitative Results from Cross-Cultural Research in Germany and the United States of America*, Germany: Vandenhoeck @ Ruprecht, 2009.

28 Chana Ullman, *The Transformed Self: The Psychology of Religious Conversion*, New York: Plenum Press, 1989.

29 Armand L. Mauss, "Dimensions of Religious Defection." *Review of Religious Research* 10 (3) (1969): 128–135.

30 James, *The Varieties of Religious Experience*, 201.

31 See, for example, Eric Nelson, *The Hebrew Republic*, Cambridge, MA: Harvard University Press, 2010; Michael Allen Gillespie, *The Theological Origins of Modernity*, Chicago: University of Chicago Press, 2009.

32 Carl Schmitt, *Political Theology: Four Chapters on the Concept of Sovereignty*, trans. by George Schwab, Cambridge, MA: University of Chicago Press, 1985, 36.

33 Malachi HaCohen, "The Liberal Critique of Political Theology: Political Messianism and the Cold War," in: *Die helle und die dunkle Seite der Moderne*, edited by Werner M. Schwarz and Ingo Zechner, Vienna: Turia and Kant, 2014, 38–50.

34 Jacob Talmon, *The Origins of Totalitarian Democracy*, London: Secker & Warburg, 1952.

35 Anita Shapira, "Zionism and Political Messianism," in: *Walking Toward the Horizon*, Tel Aviv: Am Oved, 1988, 11–13 (in Hebrew).

36 Norman Cohn: *The Pursuit of the Millennium*, London: Secker and Warburg 1957, xiv.

37 Ibid.

38 David Apter, "Political Religion in New Nations," in: *Old Societies and New States*, edited by Clifford Greetz, New York: Free Press, 1963, 57–104.

39 Robert N. Bellah, *The Broken Covenant: American Civil Religion in Time of Trial* (2nd edition), Chicago: University of Chicago Press, 1975.

40 Charles Liebman and Eliezer Don-Yehiya, *Civil Religion in Israel: Traditional Judaism and the Political Culture in the Jewish State*, Berkeley: University of California Press, 1983, 1–25.

41 David Ohana, *Zarathustra in Jerusalem – Friedrich Nietzsche and Jewish Modernity*, Jerusalem: Bialik Institute, 2016.

42 Yotam Hotam, *Modern Gnosis and Zionism: The Crisis of Culture, Life Philosophy and Jewish National Thought*, London: Routledge, 2013.

43 Yuval Jobani, *The Role of Contradictions in Spinoza's Philosophy: The God-Intoxicated Heretic*, London: Routledge, 2016, 13–43.

44 Quoted from: Glenn Burgess, "The Divine Right of Kings Reconsidered," *English Historical Review* 107 (425) (1992): (837) 837–861.

45 Donald Spence, "Narrative Smoothing and Clinical Wisdom," in: *Narrative Psychology*, edited by Theodore Sarbin, New York: Praeger Special Studies, 1986, 211–232.

1 Moving away from Communism

The case of Arthur Koestler[1]

Arthur Koestler was born in 1905 in Budapest and died in 1983 in London when he committed suicide together with his wife Cynthia. Over the course of his life he lived in Vienna, Tel Aviv, Berlin, Paris, and finally London; the many changes in his national identity caused critics to describe him as a "homeless mind." This instability also characterized his personality and his ideological identity. Koestler was born a Jew, but he turned his back on Judaism. He was a Zionist, but he became disillusioned, became a Communist, and later underwent yet another change and became an anti-Communist. He was interested in astronomy, evolution, and neuroscience but eventually became a fan of parapsychology (after his death, he bequeathed all his wealth, over one million pounds, to a British university that would establish a chair of parapsychology, but no university was willing to take the money according to the conditions of the will). Koestler published over 20 books, including six novels, four autobiographies, four scientific works, and four collections of essays, as well as hundreds of articles published in the press.

Arthur Koestler is considered one of the most important authors of the twentieth century, and he wrote on political, scientific, philosophical, and historical themes. His early books, which won him world fame, focused on the totalitarian experience. By the end of the century his name appears to have been largely forgotten, partly due to the end of the Cold War, but during the first half of the century he was considered one of the most important critics of the Soviet Union. His book *Darkness at Noon* (1941) has been called one of the most influential novels of the twentieth century.[2] Anne Appelbaum said that *Darkness at Noon* was one of the books that helped turn the tide on the intellectual front line and ensured that the West prevailed during the Cold War.[3]

During the show trials held in Moscow in the 1930s, many Communist leaders confessed crimes against the Soviet Union by joining and assisting anti-Communist powers. Intellectuals all over the world, some of whom had been attracted to Communism, were astonished by these confessions, and many believed that they were obtained by force. Koestler's main contribution to the public debate over these trials lay in his ability to explain the inner logic behind these confessions, which in reality probably were not taken by force. In *Darkness at Noon* (1941), Koestler explained the confessions as an act of loyalty to the party and its will. These Communist leaders, headed by Nikolay Bukharin, were requested to confess for crimes they had not committed, and they agreed to do so as their last act of service to the party. In the novel, Koestler described the detention of Robashov, one of the party's main leaders, who decided to confess in order to protect the revolutionary idea and to offer service to party with his execution.

The book was published during a period in which the Soviet Union was a closed state, and much of the information about the country came through the propaganda mechanisms of Communist parties all over the world that maintained contacts with the Comintern. During his Communist period, Koestler was one of the party's main propaganda agents in Europe. He visited the Soviet Union during the 1930s and he was in contact with Soviet intellectuals. In 1938, however, he resigned from his membership of the party. When he published his book, he was able to bring another level of understanding to the totalitarian mechanisms that were labeled as "progressive." His genius lay in his ability to present in a creative way the power of the party to maneuver its most committed supporters to confess treason and to volunteer to be executed as a service to a goal – a type of modern martyrdom. The head of the party wished the death of his political rivals, and they – out of commitment to obey the party's orders – agreed to offer their head to the executioner, just as any believer might offer his head to the executioner if he received a direct order from God. Koestler described loyalty to the party as a religious commitment, and indeed during the Cold War several Western intellectuals identified Communism as a secular religion (as mentioned in the introduction).

Koestler wrote on politics for two decades after he left the Communist Party before later moving on to other subjects. Ben Redman described his political writing as a continuing dialogue with his biography, a description of his conscience on different historical moments, and a description of how the revolutionary utopia had turned into a totalitarian tyranny. In his books, Koestler expressed nostalgia for a faith that was lost, deep pride in his revolutionary past, and an expectation of a new political path.[4]

Koestler analyzed the psychology of the totalitarian ideology in further books such as *The Yogi and the Commissar* (1945), *The God That Failed* (1949), and *The Trail of the Dinosaur* (1955). All these books were described by Michael Scammell as major contributions to an understanding of the political thought of our times.[5] His two books on Zionism, *Thieves at Night* (1946) and *Promise and Fulfillment* (1949), were considered major works for understanding the success of the Zionist enterprise. Although these books may seem outdated today, in these books he was able to convey sensitively the complexities of the Zionist activities while looking deeply into the unresolved Arab-Israeli conflict. Near his death, Koestler published *The Thirteenth Tribe* (1976), in which he developed a thesis regarding the Khazar origins of most European Jews. This book contradicted his previous support for Zionism.

Since Koestler's main contribution to the intellectual discourse of the twentieth century stemmed from his personal experiences as a disillusioned Communist who stood before the executioner but was able to survive, in this chapter I will try to examine his entrance and exit from Communism as an expression of conversion and prophetic failure. In order to review Koestler's narrative, as presented in his own very detailed autobiographical work, the research uses psychological theories on what happens when prophecy fails, and the influence of disillusionment on exit.

Arrow in the blue

Koestler was a great admirer of Sigmund Freud, and perhaps because of this he has left us with a detailed narrative of his innermost emotions and intentions.[6] He explained at length the way he was converted into the Communist faith, employing religious language to describe his attraction to that ideology. Later he became disillusioned, again providing a detailed description of the psychological path that led him to resign from the party.

Koestler began to publish his memoirs in 1949 in an article in the collection *The God That Failed*. He later published his autobiography during 1952–1953. These materials were written some ten years after the events he described, and it is important to take this gap into account. As psychological research has shown, personal narratives based on memory can be smoothed in order to make sense and to form a logical course of events; accordingly, scholars who study personal narratives must be cautious.[7] Nevertheless, one cannot write 1,100 pages of autobiography without having a strong memory, quite possibly refreshed on the basis of diaries and notes he kept from the period; accordingly, I am inclined to believe that Koestler's accounts of his feelings and emotions are reliable. Koestler's personal history is well-known; it has been the subject of several biographies, and I crosschecked some of the facts he mentions in his autobiographies in several different biographies written by independent authors.

So far, research on prophetic believers has centered mainly on those who are able to survive the failure of prophecy with their faith intact. Much less research attention has been paid to those who decide to exit after confronting disillusionment. It is true that in many cases, faith remains when prophecy fails, and it is interesting to examine the ways in which believers confront failure while remaining loyal to their beliefs. Koestler struggled to remain a loyal Communist, but eventually he could not carry his faith anymore. In this chapter, therefore, I will seek to explore the circumstances in which Arthur Koestler found himself unable to maintain his faith.

Prophetic failure

Political messianism is a term that comes to define totalitarian ideologies in the twentieth century. Arthur Koestler described his attachment to communism in prophetic and messianic language, thus the description of secular religions fits him well. Although Communism is an atheist movement, many of its most fervent followers saw themselves as participants in a utopian social experiment that would lead to messianic times. However, people who are engaged in prophetic beliefs may fall into a crisis of faith when their prophecies fail to materialize. A similar case happened to Koestler.

The subject of prophetic failure is critical to our understanding of the development of any messianic faith. The most quoted study in this field is *When Prophecy Fails: A Social and Psychological Study of a Modern Group That Predicted the Destruction of the World*,[8] which examined the small UFO cult led by "Marion Keech" (an alias) that believed in an imminent apocalypse and later developed a cognitive mechanism to explain why this event did not occur. Festinger's team reached two main conclusions. First, beliefs that are clearly falsified will be held even more intensely after falsification; and second, the group will increase its active proselytization efforts after prophetic failure. The team used the term "cognitive dissonance" to refer to the distress caused when two contradictory ideas, or cognitions, are held simultaneously. In the case of a messianic or millennial individual or group, cognitive dissonance is said to occur when a fervently held belief appears to be contradicted by empirical evidence. The cognitive dissonance theory argues that those involved will be strongly motivated to resolve the tension between the contradictory ideas.

According to this theory, the process proceeds as follows. The emerging gap between expectation and experience generates cognitive tension. This dissonance creates discomfort in the believer, thus creating pressure to reduce this discomfort. Individuals must then either change their beliefs, opinions, or behavior, secure new information that mitigates the dissonance, or forget or belittle the importance of the information that produced the internal contradiction. In order to succeed in this, the believer must receive support from either his psychological or his social environment. Without such support, the chances are that the effort to moderate the dissonance will prove unsuccessful.[9]

The cognitive dissonance theory became very dominant; Ralph W. Hood, a specialist in the psychology of religion, suggests that over 1,000 follow-up studies in university laboratories confirmed the theory.[10] However, the study of prophetic movements has developed considerably since Festinger et al. published their book, and today there is a more comprehensive and multidimensional understanding of the topic.

Social psychologist Joseph Zygmunt, in his study of Jehovah's Witnesses, a movement that has gone through six unmaterialized end dates, came to conclude that through closer readings of the Bible the movement was able to argue after each disconfirmation that a fulfillment in fact occurred, albeit in a spiritual, not a physical sense.[11] Religious historian J. Gordon Melton added that since the millennial groups do not acknowledge empirical disconfirmation in the way an outsider might, for them prophecy seldom fails.[12] Religious scholar Jon Stone argued that while prophets offer nonempirical evidence that their prophecies have in fact been fulfilled, they do it in a way that renews faith in their message.[13]

Lorne Dawson's model,[14] which is based on his own work in the sociology of religion together with accumulated insights from Zygmunt, Melton, and Stone,[15] addresses three survival methods: intensified *proselytization*, various *rationalizations*, and acts of *reaffirmation*. Whereas Festinger and his team argued that proselytization is a key component for the survival of the movement, many case studies published after *When Prophecy Fails* have shown that proselytization actually rarely occurs.[16]

Rationalization is the key tool for dealing with failure, and this may be mani-fested in several ways. The spiritualization of prophecy is a major form of ration-alization, while another approach is to argue that the prophecy was a test of faith, and that God is putting the believers through miseries in order to examine their strength. A third form of rationalization is to blame failure on human errors such as misinterpretation, or to blame others for misunderstanding or interfering with the fulfillment of prophecy. Reaffirmation takes the form of inward-focused work to increase social solidarity through special educational activities, celebrations, and rituals.[17]

What factors lead to the demise of a prophetic faith? The term used to describe a retreat from faith is "deconversion," which is identified as a loss or deprivation of religious faith. This process entails intellectual doubt, moral criticism, emo-tional suffering, and disaffiliation from the community. Deconversion may take the form of a sudden dramatic reversal, but it can also be manifested through a protracted or even inconclusive process of doubt and uncertainty.[18]

The remainder of this chapter will focus on Arthur Koestler's deconversion, and on how and why he decided to change his beliefs.

The new star of Bethlehem had risen in the east

Arthur Koestler was born in Budapest in 1905, the only child of middle-class Jew-ish parents. The outbreak of the First World War led to the collapse of his father's business and the family moved to Vienna, where Koestler spent his adolescence. As a child he developed an interest in science and political thought. In 1922 he enrolled at the Vienna Polytechnical Institute, where his political consciousness was fully awakened in the Zionist movement among Jewish students. Koestler never graduated from Vienna Polytechnic. Instead, under the influence of Zion-ism, he traveled to Palestine in 1926. He lived for a short time in Kvuzat Hephzi-bah, a small kibbutz in Jezreel Valley (his biographer Michael Scammel states that this experience lasted only ten days[19]), but he soon moved to Haifa, a port city on the Mediterranean coast. During his Zionist period, Koestler was an admirer of Ze'ev (Vladimir) Jabotinsky, the leader of the right-wing Revisionist Party, and he was active in the party and its propaganda mechanisms. Historian Luis Gordon said: "One of the most significant influences of his life and work was Vladimir Jabotinsky. . . . Jabotinsky and the quest for a Jewish state haunted Koestler – sometimes even subconsciously."[20] His attraction to right-wing Zionist politics may explain why his kibbutz experience failed, since kibbutz ideology leaned strongly toward Communism. Koestler tried his hand at various professions, but in 1927 he joined the prestigious Ullstein chain of German newspapers as a Mid-dle East correspondent. Ullstein was the largest newspaper chain in Germany at that time, and by the age of 22 Koestler had become a member of the aristocracy of European journalism. He covered the Middle East for two years, but in 1930 he chose to move to Germany. His own appraisal was that he had lost interest in Zionism mainly due to his failure to overcome the language barrier and master modern Hebrew. As a writer, he concluded he had reached a dead end.[21] In his lifetime, Koestler had developed an ambivalent attitude toward Zionism. On the one hand, he saw it as a safe refuge for persecuted Jews; on the other hand, this solution was not good enough for him (I will discuss it in more detail below).[22]

Working as a journalist in Germany, Koestler covered the Graf Zeppelin Arctic expedition of 1931. Later in the same year he was appointed the foreign editor of *B.Z. am Mittag*, a large circulation newspaper in Germany.

In December 1931, Koestler decided to join the Communist Party. German society was in turmoil at the time. The Weimar Republic was entering its death throes, and many Germans believed the regime would fall either to Communism or to Nazism. As a Jew, Koestler did not have the option to join the Nazi Party. Theoretically, he could have joined the Social Democratic Party of Germany, which was one of the largest and strongest in Europe. However, once he had abandoned Zionism, he chose to join the Communist ranks. His attraction to Zionism and later to Communism reveals his preference for utopian and revolutionary ideologies. In his first autobiographical work, in a contribution to the collection *The God That Failed*, Koestler argued that his attraction to Communism was a mystical experience that could not be described in logical terms:

> [S]omething had clicked in my brain which shook me like a mental explosion. To say that one had "seen the light" is a poor description of the mental rapture which only the convert knows. . . . The new light seems to pour from all directions across the skull; the whole universe falls into pattern like the stray piece of a jigsaw puzzle assembled by magic at one stroke. There is now an answer to every question, doubts and conflicts are a matter of the tortured past – a past already remote, when one had lived in dismal ignorance in the tasteless, colorless world of those who *don't know*.[23]

In this argument we can see an echo of William James' explanation of sudden conversion, like an act of magic.[24] Koestler was indeed converted, and he employed religious language to describe his attachment to the party. According to his own testimony, he was living in a disintegrating society thirsting for faith. He described his commitment as a true faith: "uncompromising, radical, purist; hence the true traditionalist is always a revolutionary zealot in conflict with pharisaical society."[25] In this quote we see that he confess he was radicalized, and he compared himself to the Second Temple zealots who led the Jewish Revolt against Rome. He likens the messianic revolution of the zealots to the messianic revolt that would lead to a classless Communist society, as promised by Karl Marx and Friedrich Engels, and he anticipates that this society would imminently be revealed in Germany. He notes that he was both enthusiastic about the emerging utopia and repelled by Nazism, and that both emotions led him to join the Communist Party.[26]

Koestler mentions on several occasions that, as a young boy, he developed a strong dislike of the rich because of the impoverishment of his own family. He also notes that a turning point in his political conscience came when he learned that during the Great Depression of the 1930s, wheat was burned, fruit was artificially spoiled, and pigs were drowned in order "to keep prices up and enable fat capitalists to chant to the sound of harps" while Europe's masses starved. "Every page of Marx, and even more of Engels, brought a new revelation, and an intellectual delight which I had only experienced once before, at my first contact with Freud."[27]

Koestler was ripe to be converted, as were thousands of other members of the intelligentsia and middle classes of his generation. He joined the party in 1931: "The new star of Bethlehem had risen in the East . . . the Promised Land."[28] This quote likens Communism to messianism, and implies that a new Jesus had been born. It is interesting to note that Koestler, a self-identifying Jew, used Christian imagery to describe his feelings, as he would do later on several occasions. His first published novel, *The Gladiator* (1939), is set in ancient Rome, and in the manuscript he discussed the different sects of Second Temple Judaism, such as the Pharisees and Essenes. Koester mentioned that he spent much time studying the ancient world by way of preparation for writing this novel, and accordingly, he must have been thoroughly familiar with the rise and the fall of the second Jewish Commonwealth. I would suggest that his choice of a Christian metaphor was no coincidence. Just as the Christian ethics of mercy and compassion, embodied in Jesus' Sermon on the Mount, evolved into the aggression of the holy war of the Crusades, so would be the case with the new messiah, the fresh start that was beginning in Eastern Europe. The Communist message of salvation through compassion and equality evolved into a monstrous state. This, I would argue, forms the background for his comparison of Communism with Christianity.

In a different source from this period not included in his autobiography, Koestler described his attraction to Communism in messianic language. In a speech quoted by Daniel Aaron, Koestler described Communism as a direct and logical development of the humanistic tradition: "A new fresh branch on the tree of Europe's progress through Renaissance and Reformation, through French Revolution and the Liberalism of the nineteenth century, toward the Socialist millennium." In this quote from the 1930s he saw a direct and deterministic path from the Judeo-Christian tradition to the Socialist "millennium," a term that identifies the End Days. In order to reach this paradise, he concluded, one should fight social injustice in a revolutionary way.[29] This quote supports the conclusion that during this period, he regarded Communism as a messianic religion.

In 1931, after discovering his new messianic faith, he berated himself as "a shame and a phony," paying lip service to the revolution while at the same time living the life of a bourgeois careerist. He was impatient to move from journalism to the barricades of the Revolution – which, 12 months before Hitler's rise to power, still seemed a literal and imminent possibility. "In short, my joining the ranks of the Communist Party was as much an act of faith as it was an expression of the yearning 'to become myself, and nothing else besides.'"[30] He applied for membership of the party on December 31, 1931.

Dialectic jargon

During his period as a member of the Communist Party, Koestler devoted himself to Soviet propaganda and eventually became one of the party's leading propagandists in Europe. Becoming a master of Soviet propaganda required that he devote himself to an intensive learning of jargon, vocabulary, and rhetoric. In his autobiography, Koestler devoted lengthy passages to the new language he had acquired. An analysis of these linguistic changes can help us understand the mind of the convert and, more particularly, the ways in which the cognitive dissonance may come into play in the mind of the believer confronted with messy reality.

Koestler remarked that for the converts, the party became like God:

> You and I can make a mistake. Not the Party. The Party, comrade, is more than you and I [*sic*] and a thousand others like you and I [*sic*]. The Party is the embodiment of the revolutionary idea in history. . . . History knows her way. She makes no mistakes.[31]

Having true faith in the party requires absolute commitment; no doubt should be expressed. This is absolute dualism: either you are with the sons of light or you are against them.

According to Koestler's testimony, jargonized thinking overtook him and emptied all of his original and creative thoughts. All of his feelings, his attitudes to art, literature, and human relations, became reconditioned and molded to the required pattern. In his autobiography, Koestler described how his vocabulary, grammar, and syntax gradually changed. He learned to avoid any original form of expression: "Language, and with it thought, underwent a process of dehydration, and crystallized in the ready-made schemata of Marxist jargon." He referred to this as the mental world of a "closed system."[32]

This linguistic jargon also demanded multiple quotes from Vladimir Lenin and Marx, and a regular technique of wordplay on the basis of their quotes. Also there was an intensive use of dialectics, in order to deconstruct reality and to mold it into desired analysis. Here is an example:

> It was, for instance, easy to prove scientifically that everybody who disagree with the Party-line was an agent of Fascism because (a) by disagreeing with the line he was endangering the unity of the Party (b) by endangering the unity of the Party he improves the chances of a Fascist victory; hence (c) **Objectively**, he acts as an agent of Fascism even if **subjectively** he had his kidneys smashed in a Fascist concentration camp.[33]

Koestler showed that once he had assimilated the jargon technique, he was no longer disturbed by facts; they automatically took on the proper color and fell into the proper place.

> Both morally and logically the Party was infallible. . . . Opponents of the Party, from straight reactionaries to Social Fascists, were products of their environment; their ideas reflected the distortions of bourgeois society; Renegades from the Party were lost souls, fallen out of grace; to argue with them, even to listen to them, meant trafficking with the Powers of Evil.[34]

More importantly still, a fundamental rule of Communist discipline was that once the party has decided to adopt a certain line regarding a given problem, all criticism of that decision becomes deviationist sabotage. Therefore, discussions always showed a complete unanimity of opinion. "We groped painfully in our minds not only to find justifications for the line laid down, but also find traces of former thoughts which would prove to ourselves that we had always held the required opinion."[35]

Koestler offers examples of the dualistic dialectics of the attitude of the Communist Party toward other potential allies in the German society. He argued that the propaganda machine had reconditioned the brains of the party member, so that they would have to accept any absurd line of action ordered from above, and to regard it as their innermost wish and conviction. According to this new idea there was no such thing as a lesser evil – this was a philosophical, strategical, and tactical fallacy; "a Trotskyite, diversionist, liquidatorial and counter-revolutionary conception . . . we had always been convinced that it was an invention of the devil."[36] This is a dogmatic thinking that does not see shades of gray and does not recognize potential supporters. It is the expression of dualism; either you are with the party or against it.

Koestler later argued that this approach had a disastrous outcome. As German society prepared for civil war, the Communist party refused to cooperate with the liberals and the socialists. Their greatest enemy would not be the Nazis but the Trotskyists.[37] At the time, however, Koestler was unable to see the absurdity of the Communist actions. He was blinded by his messianic faith, which blotted out reality and constructed an imaginary world above it. This inability can be explained in terms of the mechanism of cognitive dissonance: when reality does not fit theory, a cognitive mechanism pushes true believers into even greater commitment to their beliefs. "As long as I remained a true believer, my faith had paralyzing effect on my creative faculties, such as they are." According to him, the Marxist doctrine is a drug, like arsenic or strychnine, which in small doses have a stimulating, in large ones paralyzing, effect on the creative system.[38]

The trip to the Soviet Union (1932)

After his Communist identity was revealed to his employers, Koestler was asked to leave his job with Ullstein. Free of any other commitments, he willingly and wholeheartedly threw himself into the cause of revolution. As his financial means were decreasing daily, he decided that his main goal was to visit the Soviet Union. Two of his close friends, Alex and Eva Weissberg, had made the trip to the Soviet Union and established themselves there, and he decided to join them (the fate of this couple would later play a major role in his deconversion). He was eager to see the land of the Soviet miracle. He signed a contract to write articles that would be syndicated to some 20 German and European newspapers and published in book form as *Russia through Bourgeois Eyes*. Gosizdat, the Soviet State Publishing House, was willing to support his proposal. His expedition into Soviet lands took him into remote areas, including the republics of Central Asia.

In 1932, Koestler was granted a visa to the Soviet Union to write a book featuring a bourgeois reporter who is gradually converted by seeing the results of Socialist Reconstruction during the Five Year Plan. He stayed in the Soviet Union for more than a year, spending half this time traveling and the other half in Kharkov and Moscow, writing the book. For part of the latter period he lived in the home of Alex and Eva Weissberg. During the same period, the Nazis took control of Germany.

Koestler truly confessed, "I could wholeheartedly confirm that Soviet Russia was the writer's paradise and that nowhere else in the world was the creative artist better paid or held in higher esteem."[39] Nevertheless, the sights he witnessed did not fit his expectations. As the theory of cognitive dissonance suggests, he needed extra measures to strengthen his commitment to the theory.

By way of example, Koestler noticed that the people he interviewed were afraid to speak with him or merely repeated slogans, yet he interpreted this in a positive light as a sign of revolutionary discipline.[40] He saw countless beggars and hungry people, but was told that they were opponents of collectivization or merely lazy, and he accepted these explanations without criticism.

> I had learned that facts had to be appreciated not on their face value, not in a static, but in a dynamic way. Living standards were low, but under the Czarist regime they had been even lower. The working classes in the capitalist countries were better off than in the Soviet Union, but it was a static comparison: for here the level was steadily rising, there steadily falling.
>
> The necessary lie, the necessary slander; the necessary intimidation of the masses to preserve them form shortsighted errors; the necessary liquidation of oppositional groups and hostile classes; the necessary sacrifice of a whole generation in the interest of the next – it may all sound monstrous and yet it was easy to accept while rolling along the single track of faith.[41]

Koestler's cognitive dissonance, according to his own testimony, lay in the way he interpreted the sights he saw. Communist dogma, elastic jargon, and collective thinking allowed him to ignore reality and to offer explanations that supported the Communist myth. Thus he could proclaim his support for Communism and his hopes for its expansion, despite the fact that the Soviet example was clearly failing. He no longer believed in Communism because of the Russian example but in spite of it. "And a faith that is held 'in spite of' is always more resilient and less open to disillusion than one that is based on a 'because.'" His belief in the Bolshevik prophecy was strengthened not because it had proven correct, but because it showed clear signs of failure.

> In Germany, in Austria or France, the revolution will take an entirely different form. . . . "we shall know better." . . . it was this conviction that "we shall know better" that kept my faith alive. . . . It had become a rather wishful, rather esoteric faith, but all the more elastic.[42]

Paris (1934)

Koestler worked on his book for a year while spending time in Kharkov and Moscow, but the party eventually rejected the manuscript for publication on the grounds that it displayed bourgeois and individualistic tendencies.[43] Devastated, he looked for other ways to help the revolutionary cause.

In 1934, the Communist International (the Comintern) decided to establish the Popular Front for Peace and against Fascism, and Koestler moved to its headquarters in Paris under the leadership of Willi Münzenberg, a leading propagandist for the Communist Party. Koestler ran the anti-Fascist archive, working hard in propaganda. The exhausting work was like a drug for him, keeping his hopes and self-esteem alive following the rejection of his novel.

It was during this period that Koestler wrote his novel *The Gladiator*. The plot revolves around Spartacus, the leader of the slave revolt in Rome in the first century BC. The revolt was crushed and Spartacus was crucified.[44] In his autobiography, Koestler explains that Spartacus chooses as his mentor and guide a member of the Judaic sect of the Essenes, the only sizable civilized community at the time that practiced primitive Communism, preaching "what is mine is thine, and what is thine is mine." In short, what Spartacus needed most after his initial victories was a program and credo that could hold the mob together; and the philosophy most likely to appeal to the largest number of dispossessed seemed to be the one that a century later found a more sublime expression in Jesus' Sermon on the Mount – a philosophy that Spartacus, the slave messiah, had failed to implement.[45]

Koestler makes here a comparison between two different types of messiahs: the Jewish military leader, such as Bar Kochva, leader of the Jewish revolt against Rome in 132–135 BC, or the zealots as mentioned above, and Jesus – the spiritual leader who offers a message of nonviolence and hatred of private property in his Sermon on the Mount (Matthew 5–7). In the novel, Koestler associates Spartacus with the Essenes and with the message of Jesus that they failed to accept, and his historical comparison hints that just as the ancient revolt failed due to the overuse of power and manipulation, so the modern revolt will fail if it takes the same path. Koestler does not view Christianity as the proper path for salvation, however. For him, history was repeating the tragedy of the early Church – the spiritual spring tide that had carried the pure and humble toward the millennium and had left them stranded in the grip of debased papacy: the messianic faith at the beginning of the Crusades and their terrible end.[46] In the novel, Koestler raised several clear rhetorical questions about his own time. Given that the majority of the inhabitants of Rome were slaves, why did they not join the revolt? By analogy, why was the attraction of Nazism stronger than that of Communism? Also, was something going wrong with the Communist revolution? Was it losing its social compass? Needless to say, the party once again rejected Koestler's novel. Later, in 1939, after his deconversion from the belief system of Communism, he translated the novel to English and was able to get it published.

As we can see, by this point Koestler was already beginning to develop a certain critique of the party and to raise uncomfortable questions. This cognitive dissonance had to be resolved, and the way Koestler chose to do this was to join the Socialist enclave in Paris, which was an intensive pressure group. For him, the Socialist enclave in Paris had become his family, his nest, his spiritual home. "Inside it, one might quarrel, grumble, feel happy or unhappy; but to leave the nest . . . has become unthinkable."[47]

Koestler lived among a like-minded group of people, and all of his social interactions were with them. At that point, he was in a state of despair following the party's rejection of his second book. It was one of the most depressing periods in his life: "depressing from several points of view: poverty, failure as a writer, isolation within the Party."[48]

At that point, he had doubts about the path of the party, and he was dejected and in despair. Why, then, did he not do anything possible to free himself of this misery? The answer lies in the fear of excommunication: "But the basic cause for our paralysis lay deeper: it was the true believer's insurmountable horror of excommunication." At that point, many followers of Communist dogma sensed that something was going terribly wrong, but loyalty was demanded.[49] Here we see again the effects of cognitive dissonance on the mind of the true believer, where even if he is aware that reality does not fit the theory, his loyalty to his faith forces him to try to adjust from within. Hard work and peer pressure were the tools to overcome the crisis.

> The only dialectally correct attitude was to remain inside, shut your mouth tight, swallow your bile and wait for the day when, after the defeat of the enemy and the victory of World Revolution, Russia and the Comintern were ready to become democratic institutions. . . . Until that day you had to play the game – confirm and deny, denounce and recant, eat your words and lick your vomit; it was the price you had to pay for being allowed to continue feeling useful, and thus keep your perverted self-respect.[50]

Dialogue with death

On July 18, 1936, General Franco staged his coup d'état. As the civil war erupted in Spain, the Communist Party wanted to send Koestler to the war zone to spy under the guise of journalistic work. He managed to persuade the London-based *Weekly News and Chronicle* to send him to report from the field in Spain. In Seville, Franco's headquarters, he was recognized and denounced as a Communist, but he was able to escape. Six months later he returned to Spain to cover the war, but he was again captured in Malaga, tried and convicted, and sentenced to death. He spent four months in prison, during most of which time he was convinced that he was about to be executed. He was freed as part of a prisoner exchange following a campaign for his release.[51]

While in prison, and as noted sure that he was awaiting his execution, Koestler underwent a further transformation. The knowledge that prisoners were routinely tortured and executed, and that his turn might come at any time, caused him to enter into a state of spiritual shock. He found himself wondering whether Communism was a value worth dying for, and on the subconscious level, at least, the answer was no. By this stage he was already critical of the party and disillusioned by its hostile response to his novels. Moreover, inside a prison cell the peer pressure of the Communist enclave was losing its effect.

Koestler tells us that one day in prison, a guard by the name of Don Ramon asked him how a man of his stature and education had turned "Red." Koestler responded:

> "But I no longer am a rojo." I had spoken the truth but with the intension of telling a lie. Inwardly, I no longer was a Communist, but the break was neither conscious nor definite: and my intentions in uttering the phrase was, of course, that Don Ramon should report it. The shame of this episode has hunted me for years. . . . I kept telling myself that after all it was merely a matter of a phrase blurted out when I was caught unawares, and it was redeemed by the fact that I refused to sign the statement in favor of Franco.[52]

Koestler identified that moment as his breaking point. It began at the level of the unconscious, but would take him several years to say it publicly.[53] What caused this transformation?

> The experiences responsible for this change were fear, pity and a third one, more difficult to describe. Fear, not of death, but of torture and humiliation and the more unpleasant forms of dying. . . . Pity for the little Andalusian and Catalan peasants whom I heard crying and calling for their madres when they were led out at night to face firing squad; and finally, a condition of mind usually referred to in terms borrowed from the vocabulary of **mysticism**, which would present itself at unexpected moments and induce a state of inner peace which I have known neither before nor since . . . a type of a mystical experience.[54]

In *Darkness at Noon*, Koestler tells how Nicholas Salmanovitch Robashov, the protagonist of the novel, undergoes a mystical experience after he is sentenced to death. Here is a short sample of a much longer description: "One's personality dissolves as a grain of salt in the sea; but at the same time the infinite sea seemed to be contained in the grain of salt. The grain could no longer be localized in time and space."[55] One can assume that these accounts are based on Koestler's own mystical feelings in his prison cell.[56] The philosopher Yuval Jobani has noticed that among secular Hebrew writers of the twentieth century, a "religious model" has developed where secular substitutes for religion were established without entirely excluding the religious impulse. This model offers secular substitutes that are founded on the transferal of the religious state of mind from strictly religious objects to secular ideals and objects. Koestler's mysticism can fit into this model (I will expend more on this model in Chapter 5 on Haim Cohn).[57]

Koestler had undergone a mystical experience when he entered the Communist faith, and he had a mystical experience as he left it. He was a spiritual seeker, with multiple transforming experiences – later in his life, he would even become a follower of the occult. He was open to transformation and change and willing to constantly challenge himself. During the course of his life, he evolved from a Zionist to a Communist, re-emerged as an anti-Communist, and finally settled as a New Ager. His open-minded and self-critical approach, even while he was embedded in closed systems, is the key to his deconversion.

Denouncing the Soviet Union

Several factors led Koestler to renounce the Communist Party. He was unwilling to play the acrobatic game of denouncing those whom he had supported in the past. In particular, he refused to speak out against his own family and friends, including Alex and Eva Weissberg.

Following his release from prison, Koestler moved back to Paris, authoring a sex encyclopedia in order to support himself. While touring in Communist reading clubs, he was asked for his opinion about POUM, the Partido Obrero Unificado Marxista ("Workers Party of Marxist Unification"). POUM was a small leftist splinter group with Trotskyite leanings. Its leader, Andrés Nin, was a leading member of the Comintern but had sided with Trotsky against Stalin. During the Spanish Civil War, Nin and several other POUM leaders were removed from prison by an unidentified group of people and shot without trial. Among the Communists, POUM was treated as a cardinal enemy.

When asked for his opinion, Koestler was so exhausted from attempting to adhere to the mandated dialectic arguments that he simply said what he actually thought:

> I said that I disagreed with the policy of the POUM for a number of reasons which I would be glad to explain, but that in my opinion Andrés Nin and his comrades had been acting in good faith, and to call them traitors was both stupid and desecration of their death.

Every time the question cropped up, he gave the same answer.[58] The party did not respond to his remarks, perhaps because of the fame he had enjoyed in prison. For Koestler, however, this act of courage in standing against the official party line was the product of the inner change that had begun in his prison cell.

A couple of months later the Moscow show trials began. Nikolay Bukharin, general secretary of the Comintern's executive committee, whom Lenin had called "the darling of the Party," confessed treason. Koestler was well aware of the absurdity of the trials. In the novel *Darkness at Noon*, he later explored the twisted logic of the Communist show trials and confessions.

> To phatom the depths of absurdity reached in this trial one should bear in mind that it made the Purge and the preceding trials appear as the work of a

poisoner and degenerate; that all the traitors had being appointed to their key positions in the Soviet State by the wise and vigilant Stalin; and that the Communist International was, during the first fifteen years of its existence, headed by agents of the German and British Intelligence services.[59]

Koestler describes the party meetings of his Writer's Caucus. They struggled to explain why the leaders of the Revolution were vanishing without a trace day by day, and they all sat "earnestly discussing how to write the truth without writing the truth."[60] From this quote we learn that the cognitive dissonance of the show trials in Moscow was overcome by not telling the truth, emphasizing some facts that were more convenient while hiding others.

Another incident at that time was a false accusation against two members of the party in Paris. The couple known as Judy and Hans (Koestler used pseudonyms) were wrongly accused of being Gestapo spies. Hans appealed to the party, demanding that the Central Committee investigate his case. Koestler testified that Hans and Judy were boycotted by all their friends; Hans was by that time half-crazed, and Judy was on the verge of a breakdown. Koestler wrote a letter to the Central Committee protesting the public denunciation of two comrades without giving them a hearing and stating his conviction that they were innocent.

He subsequently learned that during the Russian mass purges, his brother-in-law and two of his closest friends had been arrested. All three were members of the German Communist Party.[61] Shortly thereafter, Eva Weissberg suddenly arrived in London. She had been expelled from Russia after 18 months in Lubyanka Prison. She was accused of inserting concealed swastika patterns into her designs for mass-produced teacups and of plotting to assassinate Stalin at the next party congress. She was freed thanks to her Austrian citizenship and the pleas of the Austrian consul. Koestler heard from Weissberg firsthand reports of the Soviet secret police's (GPU) methods for obtaining confessions.[62]

As his two close friends Alex and Eva Weissberg were denounced as Gestapo agents, and their photographs were printed in the party press accompanied by warnings not to associate with them, Koestler could no longer stand silent. He admitted that he had heard of such cases before, but he had shrugged them off and continued. But now that those involved were his friends, he took their side. When the case became personal, he could not allow them to be sacrificed on the party's altar.

The accusations against Alex Weissberg came from his colleagues in the Ukrainian Institute of Physics and Technology in Kharkov, where he worked as a scientist. Koestler was personally acquainted with most of Alex's colleagues in the Institute – a circle of scientists who used to come to the Weissbergs' flat after dinner to play cards or relax over a cup of tea. He met them while he was working on his first novel. Five years later, they all testified that Alex Weissberg was a Gestapo spy who tried to incite them to sabotage and assassination.

They were neither cowards nor evil men; they had to testify as they were ordered. At a later stage of the Purge, they were all arrested in their turn and signed confessions accusing each other and themselves of the same fantastic crimes.[63]

Still, however, although the shock was unbearable, at that point Koestler was unable to break his bond with the party. He was loyal to the point of the absurd.

> The logical course would have been simply to resign from the Party. But this idea didn't occur to me for quite a while. . . . One may cease being a practicing Catholic, but one does not send a letter of resignation to the Church.[64]

During the spring of 1938, Koestler gave another talk in Paris. He was once again asked to denounce POUM, but he refused.

> I had no intention of attacking the Party while the Spanish war was still being fought, and the idea of attacking Russia in public still carried the horror of blasphemy. On the other hand, I felt the need to define where I stood, and not to remain a passive accomplice of my friend's executioners.

He decided to end his speech with three sentences that marked a conscious break with the party:

> No movement, party or person can claim the privilege of infallibility. It is as foolish to appease the enemy, as it is to persecute the friend who pursues the same end as you by a different road. In the long run, a harmful truth is better than a useful lie.[65]

After delivering the speech, friends from the party ignored him. He was excommunicated. After a few days sitting alone in anticipation, he decided to take the initiative and resign from the party.

> I worked on my letter of resignation all night. . . . I still did not have the courage to go more than half the way. It was a farewell to the German C.P., the Comintern, and the Stalin regime. But it ended with a declaration of loyalty to the Soviet Union. I stated my opposition to the system, to the cancerous growth of the bureaucracy, the terror and suppression of civil liberties. But I professed my belief that the foundations of the Workers' and Peasants' State has remained solid and unshaken, that the nationalization of the means of production was a guaranty of her eventual return to the road of Socialism; and that, in spite of everything, the Soviet Union still represents "our last and only hope on a planet in rapid decay."[66]

The biographer Michael Scammell found the original letter of resignation, whose main complaint was the party's moral degeneration. According to Koestler, as quoted in the letter, the show trials were an expression of the sickness of the party that had to execute its supporters. He also attacked the policy of viewing any criticism of the party as disloyalty or even treason. He regarded the witch hunt and the hunt for spies as obsessive. However, he concluded his letter with a declaration of support to the Soviet Union: "For its *politics* we must defend the Soviet Union at all costs. But for its *theory*, it is an object of study, and study without criticism is unthinkable."[67]

His response, as we can see, was a partial exit, but at that time he was unable to break the bond completely, and accordingly his exit was narrated as an act of loyalty to the greater idea. In his letter, Koestler emphasized that he remained a Communist – indeed, he was the true believer, whereas the party had gone astray. Even as he resigned from the party, he remained a loyal follower of Socialism.

According to his testimony, he clung to this belief for another year and a half until the Hitler-Stalin pact destroyed this last shred of the torn illusion. The final breaking point came when he saw the swastika, the Nazi totem, hoisted above Moscow Airport in honor of the arrival of Nazi Foreign Minister Joachim von Ribbentrop, as part of the Molotov-Ribbentrop Pact, the treaty of non-aggression between Germany and the Soviet Union, and the Red Army band broke into the "Horst Wessel Lied," the anthem of the Nazi Party. "That was the end; from there onwards I no longer cared whether Hitler's allies called me a counter-revolutionary."[68]

The death of Koestler's faith was gradual and slow. He fought his cognitive dissonance, trying to avoid and reinterpret reality so that it would not confront his beliefs, but ultimately he could no longer remain silent. "The belief that the Soviet regime, in spite of its admittedly repulsive traits, is nevertheless the only basically progressive country and a great social experiment of our times, is a particularly elastic and comforting one."[69]

Political change

The political conclusion Koestler reached following his affair with Communism centered on the need to make compromises. A political utopia may be appealing, but messianic beliefs are dangerous. He was tempted to shift his allegiance from Lenin to Mahatma Gandhi and to adopt the cause of pacifism, but he concluded that this was merely another shortcut, a toppling over from one extreme to the other. "Perhaps the solution lay in the new form of synthesis between saint and revolutionary, between the active and the contemplative life."[70]

Faced with the residual support for Communism among the elite, even after the exposure of the Communist crimes, Koestler's explanation is consistent with the assumption behind the cognitive dissonance theory that people will seek to avoid evidence that disproves their beliefs. Thus, he explains, the utopian dream of Marxism is too good to be awakened, and the dreamer will take every possible measure to obscure and ignore life beyond the dream.[71]

Nothing henceforth can disturb the convert's inner peace and serenity – except the occasional fear of losing faith again, losing thereby what alone makes life worth living, and falling back into the outer darkness, where there is wailing and gnashing of teeth. This may explain how Communists, with eyes to see and brains to think with, can still act in subjective bona fides (a person's honesty and sincerity of intention), anno Domini (AD) 1949.[72]

When it comes to the need to confront aggressive powers, however, Koestler's conclusions are forthright:

> The lesson of the thirties: that an aggressive, expensive power with messianic beliefs in its own mission will expand as long as a power vacuum exists; that improvement of social conditions, however desirable in itself, is no deterrent and no protection against attack; that the price of survival is the sacrifice of a distressingly large part of the national income over distressingly long period; and that appeasement, however seductive and plausible its argument sounds, is no substitute for military strength but an invitation for war.[73]

Koestler compares his seven years in the service of the Communist Party to the seven years Jacob had to work for Laban, only to realize he had slept with ugly Leah rather than her sister Rachel (in the book of Genesis). "One would imagine that he never recovered from the shock of having slept with an illusion."[74]

Arthur Koestler's Jewish identity

Koestler discussed his Jewish identity and his approach to Zionism in several books. As mentioned, he found his first political identity in Zionism and he joined the Yishuv (Jewish settlement in the Land of Israel) in 1926, as a follower of the right-wing leader Ze'ev Jabotinsky. Scholar Bernard Avishai claims that Koestler never abandoned this ideology, thus his latter comments on the Jewish race have to be understood compared to this background, although the connection is indirect.[75] Koestler explained the failure of his Zionist experiment in terms of his inability to master the Hebrew language; he understood that he could not pursue a career as a writer in a language he could not articulate, and thus for personal reasons he decided to move to Germany.[76]

However, during 1946–1948, Koestler returned to Palestine as a journalist, and he published two books on the Zionist experience. In his autobiography, Koestler said that when he left Palestine in 1929 he believed that the Jewish problem would be solved by the Communist revolution, just like other national problems, such as that of the Black community in America. After he left Communism, he "came back" to Zionism, but not full circle. He had lower expectations now, and did not see Zionism as the full answer to the Jewish question. He reached the conclusion that Zionism can provide a safe haven for persecuted Jews, since only in Palestine can they find refuge from ghettos, concentration camps, and crematoriums. With no other alternatives, this is their only solution, and in that regard, "I am still a Zionist." Having said that, he still thought that Palestine, "this small and bitter country," did not embody messianic promise or any important message for the human race. He saw his roots in Europe: "if Europe went down, survival became pointless, and I would rather go down with her than take refuge in a country which no longer meant anything but refuge."[77] He acknowledged the need for the Jewish State to serve as a refuge for persecuted Jews, but it did not meet the heights of the European civilization he felt part of.

The main question for him was the legitimacy of Jewish life in Diaspora following the establishment of the Jewish State. In this respect he created a clear dichotomy. According to his analysis, the messianic expectation of Jewish tradition, reflected in the blessing "next year in built Jerusalem" from the Passover Haggadah, had been fulfilled with the establishment of the State of Israel in 1948. Now that the state existed, one could not recite this blessing without being a hypocrite. Every Jew who lives in the Diaspora must decide whether to be the citizen of the Jewish nation or to renounce his Judaism and become a citizen of another nation. In this respect, Koestler adapted out-of-date models of loyalty applied by assimilated Jews during the nineteenth century in Europe who were accused of having double loyalties to the Jewish and German (or French) nations. According to Koestler, the establishment of the State of Israel only strengthened this tension:

> The Jewish religion is not merely a system of faith and worship, but implies membership of a definite race and potential nation. . . . To be a good Jew one must profess to belong to a chosen race, which was promised Canaan, suffered various exile and will return one day to its true home. The "Englishman of Jewish faith" is a contradiction in terms. His subjective conviction creates the objective fact that he is not an English Jew, but a Jew living in England.[78]

The practical conclusion of this analysis is an obligation to break the circle. Koestler presented a moral dilemma: if Jews in the Diaspora wish to maintain their unique identity, they must renounce their racial presumption and national exclusivity and adhere solely to the moral principles of Judaism. However, he was uninspired by this option, since he rejected the idea of reformed Judaism. According to his understanding, the religion is one body of rituals and beliefs that one is not permitted to change. As a result, he presented his argument as a zero-sum game.

Koestler chose cosmopolitanism. In this context he was happy that the State of Israel had been established, since it allowed him, and people like him, to move beyond their commitment to Jewish solidarity, now that there was someone else who would take care of the Jews:

> These conclusions, reached by one who has been a supporter of the Zionist movement for a quarter century, while his cultural allegiance belonged to Western Europe, are mainly addressed to the many others in a similar situation. They have done what they could to secure haven for the homeless in the teeth of prejudice, violence and political treachery. Now that the State of Israel is firmly established, they are at least free to do what they could not do before: to wish it good luck and go their own way, with an occasional

friendly glance back and helpful gesture. But, nevertheless, to go their own way, with the nation whose life and culture they share, without reservations or split loyalties.[79]

In his book *The Thirteenth Tribe* (1976), Koestler returned to Jewish identity and radicalized his arguments. In this book, he argues that the Ashkenazi Jews, the majority of the Jewish people, are actually descendants of the Khazar tribe, who converted to Judaism during the eighth century and settled along the Danube River. Thus, the majority of Jews are not descendants of those exiled from the Land of Israel after the destruction of the Second Temple (AD 70) but are members of a Turkmen tribe from Central Asia. Since the Khazars and the Magyars are related tribes, and since the Hungarian people see themselves as the heirs of the Magyars, he concludes that Ashkenazi Jews, in their racial essence, belong to Europe and not the Land of Israel, the focus of their religious yearnings. The idea that Ashkenazi Jews are decedents of the Khazars has roots in the nineteenth century, however Koestler was inspired to write his book by the work of Israeli historian Abraham Polak.[80]

This book received much criticism and was perceived as an artificial attempt by Koestler to solve his personal Jewish dilemma by developing a weak formula that would allow him to claim authentic Hungarian roots.[81] It is indeed strange to observe centuries of Jewish civilization in Europe through purely racial and genetic lenses, and observers have identified this book as another attempt to obscure his Jewish roots.[82] Koestler's theory was refuted by many scholars, however it received new life with Shlomo Sand's *Who Invented the Jewish People?* (2010). Sand, a self-defined Communist even after the collapse of the Soviet Union, used the Khazar theory in order to delegitimize Israel's raison d'être while defining himself as a post-Zionist or non-Zionist.

In his book, Koestler repeated the dichotomy that every Jew must choose between immigrating to Israel or assimilating into European cultures. He emphasized that there is no contradiction here, since the Jewish right to the State of Israel is built on the decisions of the United Nations and international law, so no one can take it away from Jews without committing genocide.[83]

Koestler defined the tragedy of Judaism as fencing itself within itself. Judaism brought the world the idea of monotheism, but kept this for itself, based on a fictitious illusion, since most of the Jews are descendants of a Turkmen tribe. The purpose of his book, Koestler concluded, was to shatter the illusions regarding the uniqueness of the Jewish race.

To conclude, Arthur Koestler agreed with the Zionist idea of the negation of exile, but in a convoluted manner he expected Jewish identity in the Diaspora to disappear, mainly as a result of the growing numbers of interfaith marriages. He supported Zionism, but his last book dealt this support a strong blow, since according to his new understanding, Zionism is based on a lie. The racial nature of Koestler's later arguments is particularly puzzling when presented by a Jewish author after the Holocaust.

Discussion

Scholars who studied the biography of Arthur Koestler described him as an adventurer constantly seeking intellectual and emotional thrills. Anne Applebaum commented that Koestler was "fascinated by every philosophical fad, serious and unserious, political and apolitical, of his era."[84] Michael Scammell suggested that "part of his fascination with propaganda methods was that he identified with them and was probably aware of it."[85] Ben Jay Redman argued that Koestler's deconversion from Communism was itself an act of faith: "He has longed, and still longs, for faith; but he has been unable to repeat his act of 'intellectual self-castration.'"[86]

These explanations can certainly enrich our understanding of Koestler's personality. As research into narrative inquiry has shown, an analyst should be open-minded to multiple ways of analyzing the narrative.[87] In this chapter, I suggested another way of understanding Koestler's path out of the Communist party.

Koestler published his autobiography several years before the publication of *When Prophecy Fails*, so he could not have been influenced by it, although we know that he was an amateur student of psychology, and particularly the teachings of Sigmund Freud (his mother was one of Freud's patients). Our analysis of his narrative has shown that he perceived his association with Communism through the metaphors of religion, and his case therefore resembles the cognitive dissonance of a prophetic believer. Cognitive dissonance occurs due to a gap between expectation and experience that must be addressed. To a believer, it is hard to see the fault of his faith, and this tension pushes to action.

Following Dawson's model, which includes intensified proselytization, various rationalizations, and acts of reaffirmation, we see that Koestler's case fits all three survival models in order to reduce the cognitive tension. Proselytizing to Communism through propaganda was Koestler's main act of service to the party. As mentioned, he was one of the party's main propaganda agents in Europe. Drawing people into the party during the same period when he began to question its actions may be understood as an act of easing tension.

When it comes to rationalization, Koestler admits that this was his main technique for repelling haunting questions. One of his rationalizations was to argue that Communism is worthy despite the Soviet experience. Accordingly, he could continue to advocate for revolution in Germany and France. "The theory that the Purges, the slave-camps, the disfranchisement of the people, were merely surface phenomena and temporary expedients on Russia's road to Socialism, is a typical last ditch rationalization of this kind."[88] Thus, even after he resigned from the party, he rationalized his exit as an act of loyalty to his faith, while blaming a third party for sabotage. Linguistic acrobatics, jargon, and dialectical thinking allowed him to repel doubts while narrating them as bourgeois – and therefore illegitimate – distortions.

Life in the Communist enclave in Paris allowed Koestler to block what he considered to be blasphemy. The experience of the enclave fits Festinger's thesis that social cohesion helps one to confront cognitive tension. Living in the like-minded enclave can also create the dualistic mindset whereby all those inside the enclave are like the sons of light, while all others have fallen from grace, and their despicable ideas should not even be considered.

Koestler's main act of reaffirmation to his beliefs in order to confront the cognitive dissonance took the form of volunteering to spy on the Franco regime. He embarked on a dangerous mission that almost cost him his life in order to manifest his loyalty to the party in the most unequivocal way. He did so during a period he described as the most depressing of his life, after two novels he wrote were rejected by the party's censorship apparatus. One also can understand his decision to travel to Spain as a manifestation of his adventurous nature and as an opportunity to distance himself from the environment he was living in at the time. Michael Scammell writes: "The secrecy of the assignment appealed to Koestler's imagination."[89]

Koestler's way out of faith is also worth examining. According to his testimony, he made his first confession that he was no longer a Communist in his prison cell in Spain. At that point, he had already been held in solitary confinement for four months. Thus we can conclude that his disconnection from the peer pressure and collective thinking of the enclave allowed him to think independently. By this point his doubts were already influencing his thoughts, and there was no one there to correct him.

It is important to recognize the personal aspect of his case. Koestler was sentenced to death, and the fear of death profoundly shocked him. Furthermore, following his release, the party's attacks on his close friends and the harsh treatment they endured in Soviet prisons, even though he knew they were loyal party members, were too much for him to bear. He admits that he saw other people undergoing similar experiences, but when he was personally acquainted with those involved, he could no longer remain silent. Therefore, one can conclude that personal traumas played an important role in his decision to rebel against the party.

In his early days, Koestler supported utopian ideologies, and this can explain his early attraction to Zionism. His disillusionment pushed him to the alternative Communist utopia. The need to compromise, the logical conclusion he drew after his second disillusionment, also led him to moderate his attitude toward Zionism. However, this compromise in itself bothered him, and eventually he authored a book to dispute it. The fact that he saw Jewish identity in the Diaspora as an internal contradiction reveals another unresolved cognitive tension. One can explain *The Thirteenth Tribe* as an attempt to resolve the tension between his particularistic identity (Jewish) and universalistic identity (European). In his latter days, he was able to release himself from another cognitive dissonance that wounded his soul, and he claimed his identity as a member of Europe's body with no need for apologetics.

Koestler had an unusual personality. He had the ability to examine himself throughout his life and to make drastic changes accordingly. He emigrated to Palestine as a young man, without even graduating from college, but after three years changed his mind and moved to Germany. He had a good journalistic job that he enjoyed, but he gave it up in order to examine the Soviet miracle. His ability to remain open to change and self-criticism ultimately allowed him also to deconvert from Communism. Koestler was a "serial converter," and communism was only one of his conversions.

The case of Arthur Koestler has shown us that cognitive dissonance is a very powerful psychological force. It has a paralyzing effect on people. In order to overcome it, an individual needs to have the rare personality trait of being capable of seeing his or her own flaws. As in the case of Koestler, the personal blows must be strong or even traumatic, and peer pressure must be reduced in order to allow a change of heart. This case can serve as a lesson for treating social flaws in our contemporary society.

Notes

1 Sections from Chapter 1 are reprinted with the permission of Springer Nature. Originally published as "The 'Deconversion' of Arthur Koestler – A Study in Cognitive Dissonance," *Contemporary Jewry* 38 (1) (2018): 127–149.
2 John V. Fleming, *The Anti-Communist Manifestos: Four Books That Shaped the Cold War*, New York: W.W. Norton, 2009, 21–98; Martine Poulain, "A Cold War Best-Seller: The Reaction to Arthur Koestler's 'Darkness at Noon' in France from 1945 to 1950," *Libraries & Culture* 36 (1) (2001): 172–184; Roger Berkowitz, "Approaching Infinity: Dignity in Arthur Koestler's *Darkness at Noon*," *Philosophy and Literature* 33 (2) (2009): 296–314; Jonathan P. Eburne, "Antihumanism and Terror: Surrealism, Theory, and the Postwar Left," *Yale French Studies* 109 (2006): 39–51; Ioan Davies, "The Return of Virtue: Orwell and the Political Dilemmas of Central European Intellectuals," *International Journal of Politics, Culture, and Society* 3 (1) (1989): 107–129.
3 Anne Applebaum, "Yesterday's Man," *New York Review of Books*, January 11, 2010, www.anneapplebaum.com/2010/01/11/yesterdays-man/ (viewed on November 17, 2016).
4 Ben Redman, "Radical's Progress," *College English* 13 (3) (1951): 131–136.
5 Michael Scammell, *Koestler*, New York: Random House, 2009, xix.
6 On the biography of Koestler, see David Cesarani, *Arthur Koestler: The Homeless Mind*, New York: Free Press, 1999 and Scammell, *Koestler*.
7 Donald Spence, "Narrative Smoothing and Clinical Wisdom," in: *Narrative Psychology*, edited by Theodore Sarbin, New York: Praeger Special Studies, 1986, 211–232.
8 Leon Festinger, Henry W. Reicken, and Stanley Schachter, *When Prophecy Fails: A Social and Psychological Study of a Modern Group That Predicted the Destruction of the World*, Minneapolis: University of Minnesota Press, 1956; see also Jon R. Stone, ed., *Expecting Armageddon: Essential Readings in Failed Prophecy*, London: Routledge, 2000.
9 Festinger, Reicken and Schachter, *When Prophecy Fails*, 3–32.
10 Ralph W. Hood, "Where Prophecy Lives: Psychological and Sociological Studies of Cognitive Dissonance," in: *How Prophecy Lives*, edited by Diana Tumminia and William Statos Jr., Leiden: Brill, 2011, 21–40.
11 Joseph F. Zygmunt, "Prophetic Failure and Chiliastic Identity: The Case of the Jehovah's Witnesses," *American Journal of Sociology* 75 (6) (1970): 926–948.
12 Gordon Melton, "Spiritualization and Reaffirmation: What Really Happens When Prophecy Fails," *American Studies* 26 (2) (1985): 17–29.
13 Jon R. Stone, "Introduction," in: *Expecting Armageddon: Essential Readings in Failed Prophecy*, edited by Stone, New York: Routledge, 2000, 1–30.
14 Lorne Dawson, "Clearing the Underbush: Moving Beyond Festinger to a New Paradigm for the Study of Failed Prophecy," in: *How Prophecy Lives*, edited by Diana Tumminia and William Statos Jr., Leiden: Brill, 2011, 69–98.

15 Jon R. Stone, "Prophecy and Dissonance: A Reassessment of Research Testing the Festinger Theory," *Nova Religio* 12 (4) (2009): 72–90.
16 There are many exceptions to this rule, such as early Christians, the followers of Sabbetai Zvi, Jehovah's Witnesses, and Lubavitch Hasidim. See Dawson, "Clearing the Underbush," 73.
17 Ibid.
18 John Barbour, *Versions of Deconversion: Autobiography and the Loss of Faith*, Charlottesville: University Press of Virginia, 1994, 1–4.
19 Scammell, *Koestler*, 48–49.
20 Louis A. Gordon, "Arthur Koestler and His Ties to Zionism and Jabotinsky," *Studies in Zionism* 12 (2) (1991): 168 (149–168).
21 Scammell, *Koestler*, 64–65.
22 Bernard Avishai, "Koestler and the Zionist Revolution," *Salmagundi* 87 (1990): 234–259; Malachi Haim HaCohen, " 'The Strange Fact That the State of Israel Exists': The Cold War Liberals Between Cosmopolitanism and Nationalism," *Jewish Social Studies* 15 (2) (2009): 37–81. See also Arthur Koestler, *Promise and Fulfilment Palestine 1917–1949*, New York: Macmillan, 1949.
23 Arthur Koestler, "Arthur Koestler," in: *The God That Failed*, edited by Richard Crossman, New York: Harper Colophon Books, 1949, 23.
24 William James, *The Variety of Religious Experience*, New York: Random House, 1909, 186–253.
25 Koestler, "Arthur Koestler," 16.
26 Ibid., 16–17.
27 Ibid., 20.
28 Ibid., 22.
29 Daniel Aaron, "A Decade of Convictions: The Appeal of Communism in the 1930's," *Massachusetts Review* 2 (4) (1961): 743.
30 Arthur Koestler, *Arrow in the Blue*, London: Vintage, 2005, 412–413.
31 Arthur Koestler, *The Invisible Writing*, London: Vintage, 2005, 31–32.
32 Ibid., 34.
33 Ibid.
34 Koestler, "Arthur Koestler," 34.
35 Ibid., 50.
36 Ibid., 44–45.
37 Ibid., 35.
38 Koestler, *The Invisible Writing*, 35.
39 Koestler, "Arthur Koestler," 57.
40 Ibid., 60.
41 Ibid., 61.
42 Koestler, *The Invisible Writing*, 189.
43 Ibid., 283–284.
44 Barry Baldwin, "Two Aspects of the Spartacus Slave Revolt," *Classical Journal* 62 (7) (1967): 289–294.
45 Koestler, *The Invisible Writing*, 325.
46 Ibid., 300.
47 Ibid., 287. For more on the communist enclave in Paris, see Maria Gough, "Paris, Capital of the Soviet Avant-Garde," *October* 101 (2002): 53–83.
48 Koestler, *The Invisible Writing*, 299.
49 Ibid., 300–301.
50 Ibid.
51 On Koestler's descriptions of the Spanish Civil War, see Peter N. Carroll, "The Spanish Civil War in the 21st Century: From Guernica to Human Rights," *Antioch Review* 70 (4) (2012): 641–656.

52 Koestler, *The Invisible Writing*, 438–439.
53 Ibid., 436.
54 Koestler, "Arthur Koestler," 67–68.
55 Arthur Koestler, *Darkness at Noon*, New York: Scribner, 1968, 260–262.
56 It is interesting to compare Koestler's narrative of conversion to that of the famous Russian novelist Feodor Dostoevsky, which also happened while he was incarnated in a labor camp in Siberia between 1850 and 1854. It is possible that Koestler's narrative was influenced by Dostoevsky's. I want to thank the anonymous reader of this manuscript for drawing my attention to this comparison.
57 Yuval Jobani, "The Lure of Heresy: A Philosophical Typology of Hebrew Secularism in the First Half of the Twentieth Century," *Journal of Jewish Thought and Philosophy* 24 (2016), 95–121; Yuval Jobani, "Three Basic Models of Secular Jewish Culture," *Israel Studies* 13 (3) (2008): 160–169.
58 Koestler, *The Invisible Writing*, 467.
59 Ibid., 469.
60 Ibid., 471.
61 Koestler, "Arthur Koestler," 69.
62 Koestler, *The Invisible Writing*, 470.
63 Ibid., 194–195.
64 Ibid., 470.
65 Ibid., 472.
66 Ibid., 474–475.
67 Scammell, *Koestler*, 161–163.
68 Koestler, "Arthur Koestler," 74.
69 Koestler, *The Invisible Writing*, 474–475.
70 Ibid., 437.
71 The eminent philosopher, Karl Popper, in: *Conjectures and Refutations: The Growth of Scientific Knowledge*, edited by Popper, New York: Harper and Row, 1965, 33–39 described the Marxist ideology as non-science or pseudo-science, since in some of its earlier formulations (for example in Marx's analysis of the character of the "coming social revolution") its predictions were testable, and in fact falsified. "Yet instead of accepting the refutations the followers of Marx re-interpreted both the theory and the evidence in order to make them agree. In this way they rescued the theory from refutation; but they did so at the price of adopting a device which made it irrefutable. They thus gave a 'conventionalist twist' to the theory; and by this stratagem they destroyed its much advertised claim to scientific status." Popper's analysis is similar to that of Koestler.
72 Koestler, "Arthur Koestler," 23.
73 Koestler, *The Invisible Writing*, 231.
74 Ibid., 477.
75 Avishai, "Koestler and the Zionist Revolution," 234–259.
76 Koestler, *Arrow in the Blue*, 244.
77 Koestler, *The Invisible Writing*, 462–463.
78 Arthur Koestler, *Promise and Fulfilment: Palestine 1917–1949*, New York: Macmillan, 1949, 332.
79 Ibid.
80 Avraham Polak, *Khazaria: History of a Jewish Kingdom in Europe*, Tel Aviv: Mosad Bialik, 1951 (in Hebrew).
81 Avishai, "Koestler and the Zionist Revolution."
82 Robert Bloomstock, "Going Home: Arthur Koestler's Thirteenth Tribe," *Jewish Social Studies* 48 (2) (1986): 93–104.
83 Arthur Koestler, *The Thirteenth Tribe: The Khazar Empire and its Heritage*, New York: Random House, 1976.

84 Applebaum, "Yesterday's Man."
85 Michael Scammell, "Arthur Koestler in Civil War Spain," *AGNI* 54 (2001): 95.
86 Ben Radman, "Arthur Koestler: Radical's Progress," *College English* 13 (3) (1951): 136.
87 Spence, "Narrative Smoothing and Clinical Wisdom," 211–232.
88 Ibid., 474.
89 Scammell, "Arthur Koestler in Civil War Spain," 87.

2 "Is it good for the Jews?" The conversion of Norman Podhoretz, editor of *Commentary* magazine, from the New Left to neoconservativism

Jews in America tend to vote for the Democratic Party and to support liberal opinions. During the 1960s, a more radical version of liberalism developed in the United States. Often referred to as the New Left or "counterculture," this approach rejected conventional social norms, protested against racial segregation, and opposed the war in Vietnam. Norman Podhoretz identified with the New Left, and as the editor of *Commentary* magazine he was in a strong position to promote these ideas, to the point that he came to see himself as one of the intellectual leaders of this movement. Under Podhoretz's leadership, *Commentary* magazine gained credibility as a prominent journal of New York intellectual circles. Although *Commentary* was sponsored by the American Jewish Committee (AJC), Podhoretz enjoyed full editorial independence and the AJC had no say on the content of the journal, which often contradicted its own position. During the early part of his period as editor-in-chief, from 1960 to 1964, Podhoretz considered himself a radical liberal. However, from 1967 he began to undergo a profound change. His process of transformation into a conservative Republican took many years and included some major milestones. By the time he completed this transformation, he had come to see the New Left as un-American, illiberal, and dangerously anti-Semitic. This political transformation was accompanied by changes in his lifestyle, as he consciously strove to avoid cigarettes, alcohol, and lust. In an interview with his biographer, Thomas L. Jeffers, he declared that he underwent a spiritual awakening in the early spring of 1970.

During his first period as an editor, Podhoretz showed little interest in Jewish-related subjects, although the journal was sponsored by a Jewish organization. In the second period, the journal became Jewish-centered and regarded the security and success of the State of Israel as a key focus of Jewish identity and concern. Following his spiritual awakening, he came to assess every social debate in America according to the question, "Is it good for the Jews?" Under the new banner, Podhoretz positioned himself as a neoconservative, disillusioned by liberal politics. Accordingly, *Commentary* became a major intellectual force for the Republican Party. What caused him to change? What social, intellectual, and spiritual conditions facilitated this transformation? This chapter will attempt to answer these questions.

Podhoretz has written a very detailed narrative of aspects of his life in four books.[1] These works were published at different points in time when he held distinct political opinions, and accordingly combine to provide a fascinating illustration of the transformation in his views. In addition, he was the subject of two independent biographies: Thomas L. Jeffers wrote a comprehensive study with Podhoretz's support and collaboration,[2] while Nathan Abrams wrote a "negative" biography without his subject's involvement or support.[3] It is important to note, however, that Podhoretz gave interviews to Jeffers in which he discussed important aspects of his personal life that were not known to Abrams.

Although Podhoretz's first autobiography, *Making It* (1967), was written at a time when he still considered himself a liberal, it is already apparent that he was more than willing to express unpopular opinions and valued the role of the intellectual in criticizing orthodoxy. These works offer a detailed reasoning for his decision to change, and accordingly constitute an important source. However, Podhoretz did not disclose everything in his four books. His explanations presented logical and comprehensive intellectual views, but he declined to touch on irrational and personal factors. He hinted that his past friends thought that he had lost his mind, and it is possible that he was embarrassed to share with his readers his personal and spiritual awakening. Indeed, in his interview with Thomas Jeffers he mentioned that his children had asked him not to talk about it in public. We are fortunate that he was eventually willing to share these intimate experiences. I am thankful to Professor Jeffers for sharing these transcripts with me, with the permission of Norman Podhoretz.

In his autobiographies, Podhoretz frequently used terms such as "conversion" and "apostasy," although it might be argued that these were merely metaphors. However, after reading his full interviews, I am convinced that although Podhoretz sought to present himself as a man of logic and intellect, at his core he was a spiritual person who was profoundly connected to his Jewish background. As a young man, he tried to distance himself from his Jewishness, but at the age of 40 it returned and became a major aspect of his identity. In his later books he allowed himself to focus on Judaism, as illustrated in titles such as *The Prophets* (2002) and *Why Are Jews Liberals?* (2009).

In this chapter I will outline the path that led Norman Podhoretz to convert from a radical leftist position to that of a sworn neoconservative. I will pay attention to his childhood and early years, his education at elite universities, his decision to develop a journalistic rather than an academic career, the radicalization that accompanied his growing reputation as a critic, his appointment as editor-in-chief of *Commentary* at the age of 30, and his ultimate transformation into a neoconservative.

William James on conversion

William James' *The Varieties of Religious Experience* is a celebrated milestone in the philosophical and psychological study of religion. Podhoretz himself referred to this book in his interview with Professor Jeffers, and accordingly we may assume that it influenced his narrative to some extent. James' *Varieties* is now more than 100 years old, and several scholars have challenged various aspects of his argument. Nevertheless, James' descriptions of the inner feelings of people who decide to convert and the process they undergo are still highly illuminating. This is particularly important when we outline the events that shook Podhoretz in the early spring of 1970, which I refer to as his "conversion."

In his discussion on the origins of conversion, James begins with the assumption that happiness is the chief concern of human life. Some men, whom he describes as "healthy minded," are born with the inclination to happiness, and everything makes them happy – the flowers, the butterflies, and the green grass. These "once-born" people have a healthy consciousness; James mentions the poet Walt Whitman as an example of such a personality. The "once born" are blinded to the role of evil, James said, and when presented with opposing facts they tend to ignore them in an attempt to avoid being unhappy (an example of the cognitive dissonance I discussed in the previous chapter). Repentance by the "healthy-minded" Christian will allow him to get away from sin, "not groaning and writhing over its commission."[4] James argues that happiness is the ideal type of human existence and we are all trying to achieve it. The "once born" already have it in their personality.

A second type of personality is the "sick soul." James describes a radical pessimist who has a "pathological melancholy"[5] and has lost his appetite for all life's values. He offers the Russian novelist Leo Tolstoy as an illustration of this type. Tolstoy considered suicide, saw no meaning in life, and eventually chose to disengage from the ordinary pleasures of life.

According to James, the "divided self" is a person who is deeply melancholic yet seeks inner peace. The "sick soul" longs to be happy and to be reborn as a "healthy mind." This gap between the bad condition of the self and its need for healing is referred by James as "unification":

> It may come gradually, or it may occur abruptly; it may come through altered feelings, or through altered power of action; or it may come through new intellectual insights, or through experiences which we shall later have to designate as "mystical."[6]

The purpose of this unification is to make men happy. Religion is one of the ways to gain this gift, but it need not necessarily assume a religious form. Tolstoy needed two years to reach unification, James said. He realized that his problems were not with life per se, but with the life of the elite; he was living wrongly and he had to change, escape falsehood, and embrace truth. Tolstoy found the existence he was seeking in the simple life of peasants.

This process of overcoming sickness and moving to be "twice born" is referred to by James as "conversion." It occurs when a divided self who feels inferior and unhappy becomes unified, consciously superior, and happy.

To be converted means to gain grace and assurance. The process may be gradual or sudden. James argues that to be converted means that religious ideas that were previously peripheral in the consciousness now assume central place, and religion becomes the "habitual center of men's personal energy." Sick souls who suffer from depression, feelings of imperfection, anxiety, and sin may convert in order to feel happiness, hope, security, and resolve.

A candidate for conversion has two things in mind: "First, the present incompleteness or wrongness, the 'sin' which he is eager to escape from; and, second, the positive idea which he longs to compass."[7] In most cases, the "sin" takes the attention, so that conversion is a process of struggling away from sin rather of striving toward righteousness.

James distinguished between two types of conversion process: *volitional* and *self-surrender*. The volitional type usually takes the form of a gradual process that builds up piece by piece to form a new set of moral and spiritual habits. James explained that in this type there are critical points that move the process more rapidly. The self-surrender type requires the individual to abandon his own will. Resistance to change breaks, and a person embraces a new identity. Self-surrender is a vital turning point in religious life, and it occurs in a flash.

In the sudden self-surrender type, some may encounter a "vision" in which "a whole programme of future operations will appear dotted out at once, the rays shooting far ahead into definite directions of advance."[8] Most people will not have this experience but will move from one point to another in a long process. James probably drew on Sigmund Freud's analysis of the unconscious, arguing that in the margin of the conscious there is a "magnetic field" that guides our behavior and determines the next focus of our attention.[9] This magnetic field, the unconscious, can burst out to become the habitual center of men's personal energy. Past memories float beyond the margin, turning into the center of one's life. Thus, the "sudden conversion is connected with the possession of an active subliminal self."[10] Through this process, memories of childhood may become a compass for life, following a strong mystical vision. The role of the unconscious seems to me to be important in the case of Podhoretz, and I will discuss it below.

James concluded that conversion is a personality change: "the man is born anew."[11] The new man obtains a state of assurance. This process encompasses three features: first, the loss of all worries and a sense that all is ultimately well; second, a sense of perceiving previously unknown truths, so that the mysteries of life become lucid; third, assurance with the change that was made. All these combine to produce happiness.[12]

James acknowledged, albeit only in a brief aside, that a similar course of unification "can be intellectual in its process" in some cases, and not spiritual.[13]

Making it

Norman Podhoretz was born in the Brownsville section of Brooklyn in 1930. His father Julius immigrated to the United States in 1912, and his mother Helen (née Henyeh), in 1920. The parents were distant cousins. Norman had an older sister called Millie, and the family lived in a small apartment that they shared with assorted grandparents and uncles. The family's origin was in Galicia (then part of the Austro-Hungarian Empire). One of his grandparents, M'shitzik, who lived with them in the apartment, was a Hasid; Norman did not like him much and referred to him as "an angry Jew."[14] His father was a hard-working milkman who delivered milk to houses at night (even on the Sabbath), and made a small but steady income. In their small apartment, stuffed with family members, Norman had to share a bed with an uncle. The family was Orthodox but rarely attended synagogue. The father who was forced to work on the Sabbath considered himself as "a bad Jew."

Since two grandparents who lived in the home spoke only Yiddish, this was the language young Podhoretz grew up with. Thus, when Norman began to study at P.S. 28 at the age of five, his English was so weak and heavily accented that the school sent him to speech therapy. A heavy Yiddish accent, he later explained, was viewed as a stigma and an obstacle to the process of Americanization.[15]

The school had about one-third Jewish students, another third Italian, and one-third African-American.[16] In his article "My Negro Problem – and Ours," Podhoretz wrote about his experiences as a Jewish boy in an integrated school, where the ethnic and racial divides were very much alive, with much hostility and violence between the groups.[17]

As in many other Jewish families, Podhoretz's parents wanted their child to be a good student, go to college, and find his way out of the working class. His mother wanted him to be a lawyer or dentist. Podhoretz was an excellent student and caught the attention of his high school teacher, Harriet Haft (in his book he refers to her as "Mrs. K," possibly in homage to Kafka's "Mr. K" from his novel *The Castle*), who was determine to get him accepted to Harvard. She invested time, money, and effort to prepare him for the interview, even buying him new clothes for the occasion and teaching him good manners. He applied to Harvard, Columbia, and NYU. He was accepted to Harvard but without financial aid. Columbia did offer aid, so that's where he went. He became a commuter student, traveling 90 minutes each way to and from school.[18]

Alongside his studies at Columbia, he also enrolled for a degree program at the Jewish Theological Seminary (JTS), which was located just a few blocks away from Columbia. He decided, at his father's request, to gain a degree in Jewish Studies. Podhoretz himself attached little importance to this degree, which he pursued mainly in order to appease his parents and his Hasidic grandfather, who had wanted him to study at a yeshiva. One of his teachers at the JTS was Abraham Joshua Heschel (1907–1972), a famous rabbi and one of the great scholars of Hasidic Judaism. Heschel taught Podhoretz about the Hasidim joyfully worshipping God through song and dance, and asked the young student about the customs of his Hasidic grandfather. "I thought 'What'? I had never seen my grandfather *smile*, let alone sing or dance," said Podhoretz.[19] Podhoretz makes very few mentions of Hasidic Judaism in his long autobiographical narratives, and most of the references are dominated by the same negative tone seen in the above quote. Nevertheless, I believe that living in the same household with a Hasidic grandfather had a tremendous impact on him, albeit perhaps a subconscious one. The mystical experience Podhoretz encountered in the early spring of 1970, which I will discuss in detail below, and the impact it had on him, can be compared to Hasidic mysticism.

Podhoretz regarded the education at the JTS as parochial. He was determined to move up the social ladder and saw JTS as part of the world he wanted to leave behind. He was fascinated by the cosmopolitan allure of Columbia, which he experienced as a new found land. He decided to focus his academic interest on English literature. At first he wanted to become a poet, but later he changed his mind and decided to build a career as a literary critic. He became the protégé of Lionel Trilling, the first tenured Jewish faculty member in the English department.

Podhoretz argues that during his Columbia education he underwent a process of "conversion" into the culture of the middle class; he was studying how to become a "gentleman," a "WASP," and a "snob."[20] He argued that his education encouraged him to adopt the "Columbia code," which he argues is a paradox. On the one hand, this code establishes that wealth, power, and fame are desirable goals; on the other hand, as a student of literature, he developed the awareness that not everything that is "successful" necessarily means "good," and that "good" does not necessarily mean "successful." He also claimed that a young person who studies literature is effectively joining a political party within the American cultural order: "the party of opposition to the presumed values of the business world. A negative attitude toward success is a requirement of membership in this party." According to this code, hunger for worldly success was regarded as ignoble, ugly, and something to be ashamed of.[21]

After graduating from Columbia, Podhoretz's mentor Trilling helped him secure a Kellett Fellowship to study at Cambridge University in England. During his time abroad he became a student and devotee of F.R. Leavis (1895–1978), a renowned British literary critic, and he called himself a Leavisian.[22] After getting his degree, he had to make a decision regarding his future. He wanted to stay at Cambridge and study toward a PhD, but dropout rates were almost 50 percent. He applied to the PhD program at Harvard and was accepted. At the same time, he began to write reviews for intellectual journals and realized that he could survive as an intellectual without having an academic career. Accordingly, he returned to the United States determined to seek a career in literary criticism.

Editor-in-chief

Commentary magazine was established in 1945 by the AJC to promote conversation on Jewish-related affairs. Elliot Cohen, the first editor of the magazine, demanded full editorial independence and shifted the magazine toward mainly non-Jewish subjects. The journal was pro-American, and the editor wanted to appeal to the general audience. It had an anti-Stalinist line, and Podhoretz speculated that it was partly established in order to prove that not all Jews were Communists. The magazine's line was also non-Zionist.[23]

In 1953, with Trilling's recommendation, Cohen commissioned Podhoretz to write a review on Saul Bellow's new novel, *The Adventures of Augie March*. The book was highly praised by critics as an American classic,[24] but Podhoretz disagreed, harshly attacking the novel. Bellow was offended by the review, and Podhoretz's biographer Nathan Abrams speculated that the piece was a deliberate provocation in an attempt to be noticed by New York intellectual circles[25] – "the Family," as Podhoretz called the group of intellectuals he sought to join. His review sparked the anticipated reaction, and "the Family" duly admitted the young critic into its ranks, although some of them did not like his attacks on the novel.

"The Family" was a group of New York intellectuals, mostly Jews, who, according to Podhoretz, were avant-garde in their artistic views and revolutionary Marxists in their politics. The *Partisan Review* was their main organ; established by the Communist Party in the 1930s, it had later supported Trotsky against Stalin. The members of "the Family," Podhoretz explained, were poets, novelists, critics, and scholars. In general terms, he argued, they disliked America and their interests centered on Europe. They were determined to protect themselves against "contaminating influences from the surrounding American world: from *kitsch*, from middlebrowism, from commercialism, from mass culture."[26] Their attitude toward Judaism was that this distinct identity should be dissolved within the socialist utopia, while they criticized Zionism as bourgeois nationalism.[27] Podhoretz identified two generations within the group, the first more alienated than the second, but both adopted the idea of the alienation of the intellectual who cannot find his home in his own country.[28]

In December 1953, Podhoretz was drafted to the army, returning to New York in 1955, where a spot had been reserved for him as a junior editor at *Commentary*. He eventually left the journal in order to become an independent freelance writer, but after Cohen committed suicide in 1959, he returned to *Commentary* as the editor-in-chief. He was just 30 years old when he entered the leading position in the magazine.[29]

As chief editor, Podhoretz was determined make changes and develop a unique line for the magazine. He shifted the editorial line strongly to the left, softening the journal's anti-Communist approach. *Commentary* under Cohen was influenced by Hannah Arendt's arguments in *The Origins of Totalitarianism* (1951), particularly the claim that Soviet propaganda dehumanizes people such that it is impossible to reverse from totalitarianism, and that the totalitarian state will change only in the direction of more perfect control. The magazine argued that only America stood in the way of the fanatical Soviet ambition to rule the world. Nikita Khrushchev, the leader of the Soviet Union after the death of Stalin, gave a secret speech in 1956 which later became public in which he denounced Stalin's crimes. Podhoretz saw in that speech a proof that Arendt's theory was wrong, and that there is no place for the hard anti-Communist line.[30]

At that time, Podhoretz saw himself as strongly alienated from his country of birth: "It meant simply the feeling that this is not *my* country; I was not really part of it." He felt like he was living in an intellectual ghetto, surrounded by a hostile environment.[31]

The magazine paid special attention to the emerging New Left, a movement that included radical political activism on campuses, the emergence of the militant wing of the civil rights movement, and the consolidation of the movement to end the Cold War. In the first three volumes under his editorship, he published large sections of Paul Goodman's *Growing Up Absurd*, which had previously been rejected by 19 publishers, but was forthcoming with Random House. The book criticized the social institutions of the 1950s and the control of major corporations, and it quickly became a sensation. Podhoretz refers to this manuscript as "the bible" of the counterculture. After publication, the book sold over 100,000 copies.

Commentary under Podhoretz provided space for anarchist, revisionist, progressive, and democratic socialist ideas that were critical of American society. Podhoretz allowed voices in the magazine who blamed the Cold War on America as much as on the Soviet Union. Podhoretz began to associate with the peace movement, and *Commentary* expressed a new belief in the possibility of doing something to reduce the danger of a nuclear war. Podhoretz published articles severely critical of American policy in Vietnam from as early as 1961, when this was still a non-issue among many intellectuals.[32]

Another important change was that Podhoretz wanted to break away from what he perceived to be Cohen's Jewish parochialism. *Commentary* was founded as a replacement of the *Menorah Journal*. Cohen was "less Jewish" certainly, but he was at times too parochially Jewish for Podhoretz's taste, who wanted to make the journal more widely appealing, not just for Jewish audience. Nathan Abrams explained: "It was a magazine run by intellectuals who happened to be Jewish, for other intellectuals and the 'common reader,' Jewish and non-Jewish alike." In keeping with this orientation, *Commentary*'s coverage of Israel declined.[33]

A turning point in Paradise Island

The magazine did well and by 1965 had some 60,000 subscribers – three times higher than when Podhoretz was appointed editor-in-chief. The journal even came close to making a profit. Podhoretz became a celebrity figure and was invited to banquets, parties, television programs, and even the White House.

Alongside the growing success of the magazine, Podhoretz tells us, he underwent his first turning point – one can even call it a mystical experience. In the book *Making It* (1967), he relates that in the fall of 1962 he was invited to a conference in a resort called Paradise Island in the Bahamas. Over the five days of the symposium, he experienced completely new feelings: he could drink without getting drunk, he could be awake all night long without getting tired: "My senses had never been so alert, my brain never so alive, my spirits never so high. I loved everyone, and everyone loved me. I did not blame them; I even loved myself."[34]

What caused these feelings of elation? In Paradise Island he came to realize that "this is what success looks like. . . . This is what it means to be rich." And he continues:

> To sleep in a huge bright room with a terrace overlooking an incredible translucent green sea, to stretch one's arms out idly by the side of the swimming

pool and have two white-coated servants vie for the privilege for depositing a Bloody Mary into one's hand.[35]

He suddenly realized that he was a famous man, the equal of anyone else at the symposium. Until that moment, he said, he was "thinking poor." All his life he had not expected money, fame, or power outside the tiny circle of those similarly inclined. But no more. Growing up in poverty, working hard for a modest salary, living according to the literary code that despises success and wealth, believing in loosely socialist dogma – all of these were challenged in his five days on Paradise Island. He came back a new man, convinced that people must demand in order to receive.

His awakening brought him to a revelation at the age of 35: it is better to be rich than poor; it is better to be a success than a failure; it is better to be famous than unknown; it is good to have power. He grew up in a culture in Brooklyn that was hungry for success, but when he got to college he realized that success was seen as rotten, and that the values of the literate elite were the opposite of American values. But the hunger for success is the "dirty little secret" of the educated elite, he said, and accordingly they are all hypocrites. Even those who oppose success long to be successful deep inside. In support of Podhoretz's descriptions, Jeffers quotes a letter written by Podhoretz's wife, Midge Decter,[36] in which she declares that her husband has undergone a "revolution in his spirit." Ever since Columbia he had felt "guilty toward his friends" due to his success, but now he made the simple discovery that he does what he does better than they do, therefore prizes and jobs properly came to him: "he earned that."[37]

Breaking ranks

Podhoretz could not commit himself fully to the radical version of the New Left. He felt it was important to avoid clichés and tasteless radicalization. For example, while it was more than reasonable to question whether the United States was completely innocent in the start of the Cold War, it was another thing entirely to argue that Stalin bore none of the blame. It was one thing to be critical of American society, institutions, and foreign policy, and another to be nihilistically dismissive of the democratic system as a total fake. He refused to be a mouthpiece for the argument that America is rotten, racist, imperialistic, and counterrevolutionary.[38] He also was skeptical of the promise of integration as a solution for racial issues of America.[39]

The *New York Review of Books* was established in 1964 by Podhoretz's good friend Jason Epstein. Podhoretz saw *Commentary* as roughly in the political center, whereas the *New York Review of Books* stood much more clearly to the left, hosting authors such as Noam Chomsky and, later, Edward Said, whom Podhoretz would never publish. He disagreed with the *New York Review of Books'* support for the student demonstrations in Berkeley (1964) and to the nature of their opposition to the Vietnam War (which he also opposed). The difference between the two magazines, for him, was that *Commentary* believed in American institutions and hoped to fix social problems from within, whereas the *New York Review* and the more radical line could find no good in these institutions and no good in America overall.

With this in mind, it is important to tell the story of how as an editor he rejected the Port Huron Statement of the winter of 1962. This statement was written by Tom Hayden, leader of Students for a Democratic Society (SDS). It later become a flagship document of the New Left. Podhoretz felt that the statement did not deserve publication in terms of its intellectual merits. It offered no fresh thinking; indeed,

> in addition to being morally smug and self-satisfied, this kind of thinking was inherently authoritarian. Hayden and his friends congratulated themselves over and over again on their commitment to freedom and democracy and their faith in the "people," among whom they said they wanted to live and work, but what they were actually saying was that *they* knew what was best not only for themselves but for everyone else as well.[40]

A few years later, during the campus riots of 1968, members of this group shouted down speakers with whom they disagreed "on the ground that only the 'truth' has a right to be heard," said Podhoretz. Later, some of its members even practiced forms of terrorism, with the establishment of the Weather Underground.[41]

In 1964 there were massive student demonstrations at UC Berkeley. The events drew the attention of many liberals toward this new movement, which suddenly did not seem to be so marginal. Why were these radicals demonstrating against the American education system and the sins of American society in general? This movement scared many who saw that the alienation and the rebelliousness were spreading from the poor and the dispossessed to the privileged and the future leaders of American society.

Podhoretz said that he felt guilty because he had helped build the intellectual foundation for this movement, with articles and books, thus paving the way for SDS and the Berkeley uprising. The translation of the ideas of the Port Huron Statement (which, we should recall, was first sent for publication in *Commentary*) terrified him:

> There was very little actual violence at Berkeley but there was a great deal of rhetorical violence in the speeches and manifestos. . . . The violence that was done was precisely to language and ideas, everything was simplified into slogans, fit for shouting and chanting.[42]

The intellectual violence he referred to included the blurring of the distinction between the poor black and the privileged students on campus; violence was applied in the analogy between the oppression of tyrannical states and the "oppression" of academic disciplines and the focus on courses and grades. Podhoretz saw the demonstrations as an expression of hatred for intellectual values. He criticized the *New York Review* for its loyalty to the demonstrators at the expense of intellectual integrity, a phenomenon he compared to the loyalty of old-school Communists to the party line in the 1930s: "Like the 'working class' in the thirties, the 'young' and the 'blacks' in the sixties could do no wrong, and to oppose them was to be accused of opposing the forces of political and social health." On Berkeley, Podhoretz argues, the *New York Review* was following "the party line," accepting the political propaganda of the rebels without question. By so doing, they were "betraying the values of the intellectual tradition in which [the *Review*] implicitly claimed a place."[43]

He emphasized that he and his colleagues at *Commentary* did not see themselves as becoming conservatives or moving to the right. They were merely taking a critical stand regarding the Berkeley uprising. They did not deny the grievances against the university, and neither did they dispute the need for changes there and in the American system of higher education generally. That would be the conservative and right-wing position. "What we did deny was that the situation had become so bad that nothing less than a revolution could possibly do any good."[44] Mark Gerson has identified *Commentary*'s criticism of the student's uprising in Berkeley and other places (including Podhoretz's own Columbia) as the turning point at which the writers of the journal evolved into a distinct political movement that would later be called "neoconservative." The neoconservatives felt that the New Left was attacking liberals and liberal ideas, and they were infuriated by the inability of most liberals to defend liberalism against this radical onslaught.[45]

As the New Left grew and expanded into additional areas, Podhoretz became increasingly alienated from its positions. Voices within this movement were by now endorsing the use of violence. As an example, Podhoretz noted that following bloody clashes in the black ghettos in 1967, the *New York Review* published a diagram on its front cover showing how to make a Molotov cocktail and denounced Martin Luther King Jr. for advocating nonviolence, retorting that morality begins "at the barrel of a gun."[46]

Podhoretz presents Noam Chomsky's article "The Responsibility of the Intellectuals," published in the *New York Review* in February 1967, as an example of the worst of this anti-American rhetoric. The article analyzes American behavior in Vietnam, vis-à-vis the opinion of several intellectuals, among them Irving Kristol, who by then already saw himself as a conservative and supported America's stay in Vietnam. Chomsky ends his article with the statement that if intellectuals will not stand up, America will end up with a "final solution." He quotes a Nazi soldier who was about to be hanged by the Russians and asked "What have I done [wrong]?" Chomsky warned that the intellectuals will be asking the same question if they fail to speak out.[47] Podhoretz responded that comparing America to the Nazis, as Chomsky did, was a rhetorical method designed to silence any other views, with devastating effects: "those who still disagreed . . . lapsed into prudent silence; those who continued speaking up in favor of American policy were isolated or even excommunicated by students and colleagues alike."[48]

I found myself more and more parting company with the Movement in general and *The New York Review* in particular. Not only did I reject the view that the United States was as evil in its way as Nazi Germany has been; I even objected to the idea it was evil in any degree. That there were many things wrong with the country I had been saying for a long time. But *evil*? Beyond redemption? In need of and deserving to be overthrown by force and violence? I could not believe that the condition of the blacks, let alone the young, justified any such apocalyptic verdict.[49]

As we have seen, Podhoretz was critical of the radicalism of the young as manifested in the riots at Berkeley, feeling that they had gone too far and that their anti-American sentiment was becoming a tool for silencing other opinions and even for condoning violence and terrorism. The gentle critic of fine arts found himself standing in front of a monster that was very different from the utopian vision he had once supported.

He viewed with alarm the growing trend to silence speakers on campuses, lamenting that booing and heckling of speakers whose views differed from the accepted radical line of the movement had become a common practice. He was horrified that such behavior was happening in universities ostensibly committed to free discussion and diversity of ideas.[50]

Another red flag was the growing support for the idea of affirmative action, including the admission of black students to universities by a quota system. He argued that the admission of unqualified persons in order to fill predetermined quotas, a system that was created in order to fight discrimination, was itself implicitly racist, since it assumed that blacks would never be able to compete with whites on equal footing. He believed that true liberals should treat individuals as individuals and not as members of a group. The quota system, on the other hand, would discriminate against Jews due to their low numbers in America – not to mention any "white" candidates with academic credentials that were stronger than those granted admission on "affirmative action" grounds.[51]

Podhoretz was also concerned by anti-Semitic tendencies in the New Left. He noted two milestones in the late 1960s: the 1967 Arab-Israeli War (Six Day War) and the New York City teachers' strike of 1968. The teachers' strike took place after the City of New York gave the African American community in Brownsville, Brooklyn, full control of one of its school districts as an experiment of improving the school by self-control. Most of the teachers in this particular school were Jews, and the principal decided to fire several of them and hire African American teachers instead. The decision led to a four-month strike and exacerbated racial tensions between blacks and Jews in New York.[52] For Podhoretz, the way in which this dispute was narrated by the *New York Review* and the Black Power movement was that "the legitimate demands of oppressed blacks were being blocked by a gang of racist Jews."[53] For him, the strike brought black anti-Semitism into widespread public view. Those who tolerated black anti-Semitism were tolerating anti-Semitism, seeking to explain and understand the phenomenon instead of condemning it. According to Podhoretz, the identification of Jews as white supremacists pointed to Jews as the main oppressors of American blacks: "Jewish landlords and Jewish storekeepers were, they said, exploiting them economically, while Jewish social workers and Jewish schoolteachers were oppressing them culturally."[54] Another anti-Semitic argument that worried Podhoretz was the charge that Jews were "overrepresented" in universities, in the professions, in business, and even in the literary world. He said that some saw the Jews as excessively rich and powerful, and accordingly sought to limit their numbers through a quota system that would both advance the blacks and curtail the Jews.[55]

Then there was the threat on Israel's borders in May 1967, in the events that led to the Six Day War; they evoked dormant feelings of Jewishness in Podhoretz. He experienced a profound sense of solidarity with Israel and, 20 years after the Holocaust, feared that anti-Semitism was still alive. Nathan Abrams states that the 1967 War converted Podhoretz to Zionism, and as a result Israel became a central cause for *Commentary* over the following years.[56]

While Podhoretz moved toward Zionism, the New Left was turning against it. Podhoretz argued that, by 1970, everyone recognized that the radical Left was hostile to Israel. Although he acknowledged that opposition to the State of Israel is not necessarily a form of anti-Semitism, he argued that the "anti-Zionism" of the New Left was becoming increasingly indistinguishable from anti-Semitism. After the Israeli victory of 1967, propaganda emanating from the Soviet Union and the Arab world portrayed the Israelis as new Nazis – a theme that was propagated by various elements within the New Left in America and Europe.[57] Another line of argument common among the New Left was to represent the Jews of Israel as "white imperialists living on stolen land and oppressing dark-skinned natives to whom it properly belongs."[58] Podhoretz feared that black anti-Semitism coupled with the New Left anti-Zionism would spark a fresh new wave of anti-Semitism in the United States.

Another red flag for him had a more personal background: the negative reaction to the publication of his memoirs *Making It* in 1967. In this book, he "exposed" the dirty secret, as he saw it, that all intellectuals seek power and influence. The book was not well received among the critics. Indeed, his desire for success was seen as the very problem afflicting and corrupting America. Against the background of the counterculture of the late 1960s, Podhoretz's open declaration that he sought success must indeed have sounded to his critics like an offensive statement. At that time, Podhoretz said, the new radicalism was riding so high that the prevailing mood refused to listen to anything but allegiance, praise, and flattery. As a result of his changing opinions on the New Left and the publication of his book, he was cut off from most of his left-wing friends and acquaintances, which also meant that he was detached from the most fashionable and influential circles of New York. Though initially hurt and bewildered, he came to feel good about breaking away from false positions. Since he was paying a personal price, no one could suggest that he was selling out.

By 1968, Podhoretz had already made the switch: the negative response of the New Left to Israel, the student revolts on campuses (including Columbia in 1968), the New York teachers' strike, and the cold reception to his book had all consolidated his position against the New Left. Nevertheless, he still considered himself a liberal who sought to fix the left from within.

Mystical experience

At this point, it is relevant to discuss some aspects of Podhoretz's lifestyle. He was a heavy drinker, and prided himself on a comment by his friend Pat Moynihan, who was the American ambassador to India and the United Nations and later a New York senator, to the effect that Podhoretz could drink an Irish man under the table. In his interview with Jeffers, he said that he started drinking because he was working almost 24 hours a day and he was unable to sleep; drinking helped him separate himself from work. He was also a heavy smoker. In his book *Ex-Friends*, he tells about various affairs he had, including participating in two orgies with his friend Norman Mailer (an American novelist, journalist, and playwright) and another woman.[59] Another aspect of his life was depression; in various interviews and articles he has claimed that he had suicidal impulses, especially during periods of writer's block.

"I ate, drank, slept *Commentary*. I'd lie in bed, having trouble falling asleep, making up tables of contents in my head," he said in his interview with Jeffers (all the quotes below are taken from that interview). In the summer of 1970, Podhoretz decided to take a long vacation after ten years of hard work in the magazine.

He planned to devote his vacation to writing a book on the 1930s. He signed a contract with Random House and received a large advance, equal to more than a year's salary, but shortly realized that he could not write on this subject. He suggested changing the book's focus to the 1960s, but Random House refused. He managed to convince Simon and Schuster to buy the subject from Random House and used the advance to purchase a property in Delaware County in upstate New York, close to his friend Pat Moynihan, where he sat to write his book.

He wrote a draft but his wife told him it was no good, and he attempted to rewrite the work. His heavy drinking was already beginning to affect his cognitive abilities and he became depressed. He was at Yaddo, the artists' community in Saratoga Springs, New York.

> One evening Kenneth Burke, the famous critic, a little guy, not at all what I'd imagined . . . gave me the evil eye (laughs), telling me in effect that my approach to this book would not work.[60]

Kenneth Burke was an American literary theorist who had a powerful impact on his field. Although Podhoretz laughed at his reference to "the evil eye," he returned to the incident later in the interview. In Jewish folklore the "evil eye" is a common metaphor; Rabbi Louis Jacobs defined it as the ability to bring about evil results by a malicious gaze. It is a belief that some human beings have the power of sending destructive rays, so to speak, in order to cause harm to those they envy or dislike.[61] References to the evil eye can be found in the Mishna, the Babylonian Talmud, and in the mystical book of the Zohar.

Practical Kabbalah is a branch of mystical Judaism concerned with the use of magic that synthesizes all the magical practices that developed in Judaism from the Talmudic period down through the Middle Ages.[62] Hasidic Judaism was established by a popular healer, the Baal Shem Tov, who used healing techniques drawn from practical Kabbalah and was highly influenced by mystical teachings and magic. His followers, and other Hasidic masters who continued him, used amulets, magic, and psychic abilities for healing, including for the purpose of granting protection from the evil eye.

Podhoretz tells us that the day after he got the "evil eye" from Kenneth Burke, he decided spontaneously to get into the car, leave Yaddo, and get to Delaware County.

> So the next day, in my cups, drunk but still able to keep going . . . I packed up my stuff and without even telling anyone I got into my car – it was snowing – and I drove along two-lane country roads for over a hundred miles: it was a miracle I made it, no snow tires, and I was drunk.

In his words, although he was drunk, driving on icy and snowy roads for hours, late at night, nothing happened to him – something he sees as a miracle. The reason why he went on this dangerous trip was because he had to escape the evil eye of Burke, as well as the evil eye of "of all the other wonderfully productive painters, composers, and writers at Yaddo." At that point, this is how he viewed things: he had writer's block, he was depressed and drunk, he thought that everyone was putting an evil eye on him, and he was under a spiritual and mental siege.

The next day there was a snowstorm. Over the course of the day, he kept thinking of a line from one of Donne's poems: "Blasted with sighs, surrounded by tears, hither I come to seek the spring." And this was the point at which his block was opened and he realized that he must restructure his book on the 1960's: a hundred pages on the blacks, a hundred on the young, and a hundred on the war in Vietnam. Here we see the first sign that he was starting to free himself from the influence of the evil eye.

He went to a nearby cabin to write, but after working for hours, he still felt his efforts were worthless: "I fell into another state of despair." What was wrong, why could he not write? In retrospect, he realized that it was because he was not honest with himself:

> I later realized what was wrong: I had not yet dropped the other shoe. I was still writing from the inside – still doing what I said those others [Howe and Kazin et al.] were doing, trying to hold on to my left-wing credentials. What I actually wanted to do, but wasn't aware of it, was to say goodbye to all that.

He saw himself as a liberal dedicated to fixing problems from within. Dropping the other shoe meant that he needed to get out of this mood, he had to change. "It needed a more decisive point of view: I needed to go the whole way." He needed to depart from the leftist camp.

At that moment, he said, he underwent "a serious religious experience, a revelation" – one that he said was along the lines of William James' *Varieties of Religious Experience*:

> I was walking along this little road, in front of my house, that went along through the fields and the farms, a little country lane. My house was situated up a slope, and as you faced it there was to the left a gully, a little rivulet as the snow was beginning to melt – it was a sunny day – in the afternoon, the sun still out. I would take a walk after working – up the lane and down again – very pretty – I was finished working and was carrying a martini with me. There I was, walking on this beautiful, chilly, early spring day and the snow was melting on the hill – on my hill – melting in rivulets, the sun hitting the snow. I was feeling very content, benign, the writing had gone well, the day was beautiful, I had an excellent drink, *and all of a sudden I had a vision.*
> (emphasis added)

He explains his vision:

> What I saw was not eternity or a great whatever of light: I saw physically, though it was obviously in my head, in the sky a kind of diagram that resembled a family tree. And it was instantly clear to me that this diagram contained the secret of life and existence and knowledge; that you start with this, and you follow to that, and it all had a logic of interconnectedness.

Podhoretz told Jeffers in the interview that this was the most important piece of information about him to describe in his biography, and indeed Jeffers wrote on the cover of the book that Podhoretz had a mystic clarification that changed his life.

In the mystical teachings of the Kabbalah, there is the diagram called *The Tree of Life*. This diagram, arranged in three pillars, presents a series of divine emanations of God's creation: the nature of revealed divinity, the human soul, and the spiritual path of ascent by man. In this way, Kabbalists developed the symbol into a full model of reality, using the tree to depict a map of Creation.[63] From his descriptions it seems that the diagram Podhoretz saw in his vision resembles the Kabbalistic *Tree of Life*. The *Tree of Life* is also a book written by Rabbi Haim Vital, and is considered an important source for Kabbalah and Hasidic Judaism.

It took him 30 seconds to see the secret of life and existence of knowledge, as he coined it, and what it meant was: "this was the only life, there was no after life. Man and woman created he them. From that union came life. That's it. You're born, and you'll die." Another thing he saw in that vision was that Judaism was true; Judaism of the Bible, not of the Talmud. He explains that he saw that there was only the life God gave you, and that God was law. Here he entered into polemics with Christianity, which proposes that God is love. Saint Paul offered an antinomian position that law will bring death, since a mortal cannot stop sinning. Unable to obey the law, people were compelled to turn to the love of a gracious

God – someone who would grant them eternal life in spite of their failings. Podhoretz responded to Saint Paul in the following terms:

> The diagram said Judaism was true in sense that God was law: not, as Christianity would have it, that God was love. . . . If Paul had put his questions to Judaism itself, the answer would be (a) that no one will deliver you from the body of this death, and (b) yes you can obey the law. I've placed it (said God) not in the heavens above: I've created you such that you can, if you will, follow my law. And my love doesn't consist of saying "Poor baby, it's okay that you can't obey." My love consists of enabling you to live in such a way as to have the fullest life possible on earth.

To sum up, the revelation he saw was that life leads to death; accordingly, one should live the fullest life without expecting any afterlife. In order to live in the fullest, one should obey God's laws from the Bible, not the rabbis. There is free choice; God is law; and His love consists of telling you what the law is about:

> That's it. What follows from this – having all the life there is to live – means to be fully aware at all times of the blessings of life. And the rabbis did indeed prescribe – in this they were very true to the spirit of the Bible – that you should say a blessing for practically everything: I mean, when you're on the toilet – everything. You're to be in a state of eternal gratitude, for everything that comes to you in life.

This law about the meaning of life applied to everything, Podhoretz emphasized. By placing yourself in a state of such exquisite conscious gratitude, you get not only all the life there is to live, you get almost too much.

> So you don't complain about not having enough. The law meant to discipline yourself to rise like a lion,[64] to live, to seize the day, make yourself aware of all the blessings around you. It required a world-view of self-acceptance, personal acceptance: that your limits should be embraced rather than resisted. Your limits are good not bad. They are actually liberating rather than restricting, if properly observed. This was the key to spiritual vitality.

He realized he had to change his lifestyle and his attitude toward life. From a gloomy, depressed, suicidal, alcoholic, he rose up happy and full of consciousness. In his descriptions we can see how James' analysis fits this case. Podhoretz was a "sick soul" who desired to be happy. His unification was a long process that ended up with a mystical experience whereby he acquired an understanding of the meaning of life. He was converted and, as a "twice born," he developed a new optimistic vision for life.

One of the immediate impacts this experience had on Podhoretz was that he abandoned his use of alcohol, convinced that it would eventually kill him. Another major aspect was that, after gaining this new knowledge, he began to heal others.

The descriptions he provided are strikingly similar to those of Hasidic Masters who use practical Kabbalah as a method of healing:

> I developed not the evil but a benevolent eye. I was really working at being aware of everything: I actually could see into people's souls. This sounds cuckoo, but over and over again, I was like a fortune-teller, I could talk to you, look at you, and tell what was bothering you and what you should do about it. Like a doctor. What was eerie was that I was always right. I couldn't do that now, by the way. I realized that that was what it must have meant to be a saint or a prophet: someone who never lost the capacity to see into people's souls.

Menachem-Mendel Schneerson, the Lubavitcher Rebbe, whom Podhoretz saw only once when he went to a Yom Kippur service with Mailer at the Chabad head-quarters in New York in 1963, was known to have similar characteristics of deep penetrating eyes and observations. Yitzhak Rabin, Israel's prime minister, said that "it was the eyes of the rabbi that impressed me, the blue, penetrating eyes that expressed wisdom, awareness and deep penetration."[65] Podhoretz offers a similar depiction of himself as a Hasidic saint (he also has deep blue eyes).

Podhoretz said that, during this period, he could help people because the diagram helped him see things in simple way. "That line at the top of the diagram [in my vision]: everything was simple, a sort of Occam's razor." He could cure people from headaches or cold:

> A cold, I decided, was a form of weeping and it was caused by self-pity. I had a whole rationale for this. Heart-attacks came from failures of courage. . . . Bad backs (I still believe this), Midge for a while had a bad back. What is a spine? The source of pride. And bad back is injury caused by excessive pride.[66]

The mystical enlightenment Podhoretz underwent in the early spring of 1970 can be compared to a Hasidic experience. He had a vision, he saw a diagram of the divine order, like the Kabbalistic *Tree of Life*. He accepted the truth of biblical Judaism, and he developed healing techniques. He was able to block the evil eye and develop a benevolent eye. The vision took place at the age of 40, not a coincidence, since according to traditional Jewish understanding, this is the age at which it is permissible to engage with Kabbalah.

In his long and detailed books, Podhoretz rarely describes any connection with Hasidic Judaism. When he does, it is always in a negative tone: his grandfather was "an angry Jew"; his teacher Heschel in the seminary spoke of a Hasidic Judaism in very different way from the reality of Hasidic life he had witnessed first-hand; and when he visited once the Chabad synagogue on Yom Kippur in 1963 he left before the service ended, feeling he had had enough.[67] Hence, I can only speculate that his mystical experience was shaped by the influence, even subliminal, of his grandfather who lived with him in the same small apartment during his childhood years. Podhoretz probably observed him as a young boy, and the memories of his grandfather's conducts and beliefs floated back at the age of 40, imbuing his life with new meaning. Podhoretz's descriptions fit well with James' accounts of sudden conversion, where past memories float beyond the subconscious, turning into the center of one's life.

The vision brought him to change his lifestyle; he stopped drinking and no longer had extramarital affairs. He also developed an understanding that politically he had to leave the radical left. His colleagues thought he had gone crazy: "What scared them was that I was like some sort of magician or fortune-teller. A kind of clairvoyant with therapeutic abilities." But the vision gave him a new point of view: he was a "twice born." Although he confessed that he was unable to genuinely apply his vision to his religious practice – like his father, he was "a bad Jew" – he was certainly able to apply it to his intellectual life.

Political change

Podhoretz was unable to write his book. He sold the farm and repaid the advance to his publisher. Eventually he would write *Breaking Ranks*, published in 1979, but the process of breaking ranks took him a long time; he became a committed republican only with the rise to power of Ronald Reagan in 1980.

Coming back from his vacation to *Commentary*, his co-workers saw in him a new man: "He reminded us of Moses coming out from Mount Sinai, but his commandments were not limited to ten."[68] Podhoretz came back with the decision to fight the New Left and countercultural radicalism in all its manifestations.

The issue that alienated him from the New Left was its tendency to antinomian nihilism: they despised the current social order and its laws. His revelation was that there is a divine law that governs all things. Accordingly, he was profoundly alarmed by a movement that sought to break all laws and social norms. He was particularly concerned at the violent repudiation of America by Americans, university students of the most prestigious institutions – its most privileged citizens, who had less reason than anyone else to feel disaffected. One of the manifestos of the counterculture was an essay titled "The Student as Nigger," published by Jeffery Farber in 1969.[69] Podhoretz called this essay "ridiculous."[70] Using Norman Cohn's magisterial *The Pursuit of the Millennium*, he compared the New Left to medieval movements that aspired to reach the End of Days but on their way turned to nihilism and apocalyptic violence. According to him, the counterculture had fallen onto a similar path: "a nihilism that expressed itself in the terrorism practiced by the Weather Underground,[71] in the ideology of 'revolutionary suicide' preached by the Black Panthers,[72] and in the spread of drug addiction among the affluent young."[73]

He referred to the movement as "secular messianism" because of the radicals' belief that America's flaws can be cured, reaching a "perfect world and painless life" through the action of the government. When the state responded and the trouble remained, a sense of oppression deepened. His alternative to the messianism of the radical Left was a skeptical attitude toward the power of any political program, including his own, to solve most of the problems of human condition. The belief that the government can solve any problem, he concluded, can lead to the "totalitarian temptation."[74]

Another conclusion Podhoretz reached was that he needed to identify his own needs and speak on their behalf. He confronted the intellectual community which pretended to speak out of superior political knowledge, and argued that the lesson of the 1960s was that the intellectuals as a class possess no such wisdom. He argued that the intellectuals on the radical left threatened to destroy the very university system in which many of them were employed, thus working against their own interests. The lesson he drew was that the general public, which was much more moderate on social issues than the intellectuals, actually possessed far more wisdom.

Despite the failure of the Vietnam War,[75] he still believed that the United States should continue to play an active role in defense of freedom around the world and should maintain a strong military capability.

> I'd come to the conclusion that, Vietnam aside (I thought we should get out), . . . America's role in the world was to block the spread, the possible victory, of Communism. My duty was to defend this country, to make it clear that we were not a force for evil but for good, both abroad and at home – and I would later amend that "good" to "great." And this all grows out of self-acceptance, and out of a judgment as to what was at stake.[76]

His support for a strong American presence in the international arena was also a reflection of his perception of Jewish interests. He believed that a strong American foreign policy could help Israel. He despised the authoritarianism of the Soviet Union, which he saw as an enemy of the State of Israel and the source of left-wing anti-Semitism. A strong American military would ensure support for Israel, he concluded.

Another aspect of his change concerned sexual norms, regarding which he adopted the conservative agenda. He became an advocate of marriage, opposed abortions, and under the banner of self-acceptance opposed "self-hatred" as manifested in radical feminism and the gay rights movement.[77]

As we have seen, the process of moving to the right took Podhoretz almost a decade. At first, he helped establish a social democratic movement inside the Democratic Party. But the nomination of George McGovern as the presidential candidate of the party in the elections of 1972 distanced him even further. McGovern was viewed as the candidate of the radical Left, and eventually lost in a resounding defeat.

> My becoming a neoconservative was not sudden – a point I keep making to no avail – it was a gradual process – certainly politically it was gradual, with this way-station with the social democrats. I made an effort to remain somewhere to the left of center. Those were the years when I wasted a lot of energy – I came to think of it as wasted energy – trying to insist that "we"

were the real liberals – I mean myself and a few friends who were going along with me. But I later decided it was silly: the label [liberal] had been kidnapped and it just caused confusion to try to explain.[78]

Between Koestler and Podhoretz

The cases of Arthur Koestler and Norman Podhoretz are strikingly similar. They were both radicalized as young men to the vision of Socialism; they both faced haunting questions about the path of the social revolution; they both disliked the authoritarian tendencies and self-righteousness of the radical left; and they were both repelled by the way in which the messianic vision of the radical left was moving. By way of a counter-reaction, both decided to move to the right.

Koestler and Podhoretz both had mystical experiences that they considered milestones in the reversal of their political path. Strikingly, both authors mentioned two experiences. In both cases, the two visions were separated by at least seven years. Neither included an image of God speaking to them, but both brought a clearer understanding of their political affiliation. In Podhoretz's case, the descriptions he provided resemble a Hasidic influence that can be explained by his contact with Hasidism as a child. Koestler's vision was more "science fiction" in style, reflecting his scientific education.

Podhoretz and Koestler had their visions at moments of crisis and despair. Koestler had a vision while expecting his execution; Podhoretz was considering suicide due to his inability to write. The connection between depression and change has been noted by William James, who himself suffered from depression.[79]

Both authors were able to release themselves from the pressure group of their social peers, the community of intellectuals who did not follow their path to the right. They both mentioned how hard it was to be excommunicated from the enclave of like-minded people. Both remained firm in the face of pressure to hide their true beliefs, while completely understanding that they would pay a heavy personal price for speaking out. Such behavior is certainly evidence of courage.

The two writers reached different conclusions regarding their Jewish identity. Koestler chose universalism: he wished to assimilate into European culture, disappear as a Jew, while showing indifference toward the state of Israel. Podhoretz went the opposite way, strengthening Jewish solidarity in America while showing strong support for Israel by making it the main pillar of his Jewish concern.

Both authors wrote their last books on Jewish identity, and in these books they justified their choices. Koestler turned to the story of the conversion of the Khazars in an attempt to justify his decision to assimilate into European culture, since he concluded that the Jews are descendants of a Turkmen tribe and not the heirs of ancient Judaism. Koestler's response to the dilemma of Jewish identity was to view Judaism as a religion but not a nation; however, those religious rituals that distinguish Judaism were no longer relevant for him.

Podhoretz devoted his last work to the question as to why Jews are liberals. He sought to explain that this choice works against their interests, and that Jews should clearly identify their true needs and vote accordingly. For him, the resolution of the dilemma of Jewish identity came in his call to defend and sustain Jewish interests as a nation, primarily by protecting Israel.

Arthur Koestler was a "homeless mind" and alienated man who chose to end his own life. By contrast, Norman Podhoretz has "made it" in America. The son of immigrant parents, he loved America, he was successful, and he wanted to protect his country; he loved his Jewish people and also sought to protect them. Since Koestler abandoned all the anchors of his identity, he might be viewed as a "sick soul"; Podhoretz was able to find meaning and thus become a "twice born."

Notes

1 Norman Podhoretz, *Making It*, New York: Harper Colophon, 1967; *Breaking Ranks: A Political Memoir*, New York: Harper and Row, 1979; *My Love Affair with America: The Cautionary Tale of a Cheerful Conservative*, New York: Free Press, 2000; *Why Are Jews Liberals?* New York: Doubleday, 2009.
2 Thomas L. Jeffers, *Norman Podhoretz: A Biography*, New York: Cambridge University Press, 2010.
3 Nathan Abrams, *Norman Podhoretz and Commentary Magazine: The Rise and Fall of the Neocons*, New York: Continuum, 2010.
4 William James, *The Varieties of Religious Experience*, New York: Modern Library, 1902, 126.
5 Ibid., 142.
6 Ibid., 172.
7 Ibid., 205.
8 Ibid., 227.
9 Ibid.
10 Ibid., 235.
11 Ibid., 236.
12 I quoted from chapters 5–10, on pages 77–253.
13 Ibid., 201.
14 Podhoretz, *My Love Affair with America*, 14.
15 Ibid., 40.
16 A long description of his childhood memories can be found in Podhoretz, *My Love Affair with America*, 1–61.
17 The article can be found in: Neil Jumonville, ed., *The New York Intellectuals Reader*, New York: Routledge, 2007, 327–340.
18 Podhoretz, *Making It*, 3–18.
19 Jeffers, *Norman Podhoretz and Commentary Magazine*, 14–15.
20 Podhoretz, *Making It*, 42.
21 Ibid., 53–55.
22 Ibid., 79.
23 Ibid., 134–135.
24 *Time* magazine listed it in its all-time 100 best novels (http://entertainment.time.com/2005/10/16/all-time-100-novels/slide/all/ (viewed on July 26, 2017).
25 Abrams, *Norman Podhoretz and Commentary Magazine,* 16.
26 Podhoretz, *Making It*, 118.
27 Hannah Ardent, one of the members of the Family, expressed similar opinions on Israel in her *Eichmann in Jerusalem* (1963).
28 Podhoretz, *Making It*, 121.
29 Jeffers, *Norman Podhoretz*, 47–64.
30 Podhoretz, *Making It*, 292–295.

31 Ibid., 314–315.
32 Abrams, *Norman Podhoretz and Commentary Magazine*, 31–32.
33 Podhoretz, *Breaking Ranks*, 34.
34 Ibid., 334.
35 Ibid.
36 In this chapter I do not give Midge Decter much space, but she is the most important figure in Podhoretz's adult life. According to Jeffers, the two books she published in the early '70s were very much in harmony with the "new" thinking Podhoretz was embracing (private correspondence with Jeffers).
37 Jeffers, *Norman Podhoretz*, 75.
38 Podhoretz, *Making It*, 317–319.
39 Podhoretz, *Breaking Ranks*, 169.
40 Ibid., 200.
41 Ibid., 201.
42 Ibid., 208–209.
43 Ibid., 212.
44 Ibid., 213.
45 Mark Gerson, *The Neoconservative Vision: From the Cold War to the Culture Wars*, Lanham, MD: Madison Books, 1996, 73–142.
46 Ibid., 217.
47 https://chomsky.info/19670223/ (viewed on July 26, 2017). An excellent review of the debates between the New York Review and Commentary can be found in Gerson, *The Neoconservative Vision*, 116–122.
48 Podhoretz, *Breaking Ranks*, 235.
49 Ibid., 219.
50 Ibid., 328.
51 Ibid., 301–302.
52 Wendell E. Pritchett, *Brownsville, Brooklyn: Blacks, Jews, and the Changing Face of the Ghetto*, Chicago: University of Chicago Press, 2003.
53 Podhoretz, *Why Are Jews Liberals?* 161–162.
54 Podhoretz, *Breaking Ranks*, 330.
55 Ibid., 332–335.
56 Abrams, *Norman Podhoretz and Commentary Magazine*, 71–75.
57 For more on left-wing anti-Semitism, see: Jeffery Herf, *Undeclared Wars with Israel: East Germany and the West German Far Left, 1967–1989*, New York: Cambridge University Press, 2016.
58 Podhoretz, *Breaking Ranks*, 320.
59 Norman Podhoretz, *Ex-Friends: Falling Out with Allen Ginsberg, Lionel and Diana Trilling, Lillian Hellman, Hannah Arendt, and Norman Mailer*, New York: Free Press, 200, 195–200.
60 Jeffers, interview with Podhoretz, July 15, 2004.
61 www.myjewishlearning.com/article/evil-eye-in-judaism/ (viewed on July 26, 2017).
62 Gershom Scholem, *Kabbalah*, Jerusalem: Keter Publishing House, 1974, 183.
63 Maureen Bloom, *Jewish Mysticism and Magic*, London: Routledge, 2007.
64 "To rise like a lion" is a metaphor used in opening chapters of Shulhan Arukh, the code of Jewish law, written by Rabbi Joseph Karo in 1565.
65 Sue Fishkoff, *The Rebbe's Army: Inside the World of Chabad-Lubavitch*, New York: Schocken Books, 2003, 69.
66 Jeffers, interview with Podhoretz, June 15, 2004.
67 Jeffers, *Norman Podhoretz*, 99.
68 Quoted in Abrams, *Norman Podhoretz and Commentary Magazine*, 93. The source is anonymous.
69 https://ry4an.org/readings/short/student/ (viewed on July 26, 2017).

70 Jeffers, interview with Podhoretz, July 15–16, 2004.
71 A terrorist organization established by students in Ann Arbor, Michigan, who planned to overthrow the US government, and targeted bombing government buildings in the 1970. Jeremy Varon, *Bringing the War Home: The Weather Underground, the Red Army Faction, and Revolutionary Violence in the Sixties and Seventies*. Berkeley: University of California Press, 2004.
72 Revolutionary suicide was the ideology of Black Power and black self-defense. "Revolutionary Suicide" was also the title of the autobiography of Huey Percy Newton, one of the founders of the Black Panthers.
73 Podhoretz, *Breaking Ranks*, 321.
74 Ibid.
75 Norman Podhoretz, *Why We Were in Vietnam?* New York: Simon and Schuster, 1982.
76 Jeffers, interview with Podhoretz, July 15–16, 2004.
77 Podhoretz, *Breaking Ranks*, 362–363.
78 Jeffers, interview with Podhoretz, July 15–16, 2004.
79 David Nikkel, "William James: The Mystical Experimentation of a Sick Soul," unpublished paper.

3 From anti-Zionist Orthodoxy to messianic Religious Zionist

The case of Yissachar Shlomo Teichtel[1]

Rabbi Yissachar Shlomo Teichtel (1885–1945), the chief justice of the rabbinical court (*av bet din*) and chief rabbi of Pishtian (Piešťany), a renowned spa city in Slovakia, embodies the tragic fate of European Jews prior to the Holocaust. Rabbi Teichtel was part of a radical ultra-Orthodox community that opposed Jewish emigration out of Europe during the interwar period. After Slovakia fell to the Nazis in 1942 he recognized his mistake, but it was already too late, and all he could do was write a book and hope for salvation. Originally, Rabbi Teichtel was influenced by radical Hungarian Orthodox ideology, which opposed any type of change in Jewish lifestyle, and accordingly was fiercely opposed to Zionism. During the last years of his life, before his premature death on the way to Auschwitz, he concluded that the path of Hungarian Orthodoxy was a complete disaster on the political and the spiritual level, which caused a heavy price. He targeted Rabbi Chaim Elazar Shapira, "the Munkacser Rebbe" (1871–1937), as the source of the mistake, and he authored a polemic book titled *Em HaBanim Semekhah* (A Happy Mother of Children) to show the fault of the Hasidic leadership.

The Munkacser Rebbe was one of the most influential leaders of radical ultra-Orthodoxy in the interwar period. He opposed any changes in the traditional Jewish lifestyle, including modern schooling and modern Jewish politics, and became one of the fiercest opponents of Zionism in the Orthodox world.[2] His resistance to change and his opposition to cooperation with Zionist activists, even on a tactical level, brought him into conflict with other Hasidic leaders, such as R. Avraham Mordechai Alter, the Gerrer Rebbe (Poland), one of the most important leaders of Hasidic Judaism prior to the Holocaust.[3] Yissachar Shlomo Teichtel was a follower of the Munkacser Rebbe and initially supported his anti-Zionist approach. However, he changed his position following the rise of the pro-Nazi state in Slovakia and its persecution of the Jews. In 1942 he began to write the book *Em HaBanim Semekhah*, in which he refuted his rebbe's position and offered a justification for Zionism. Since the 1980s, the book has been a central feature of the Religious Zionist curriculum in Israel.[4]

In this chapter, I will present Shapira's argument against Zionism, followed by Teichtel's journey from support to opposition, and show that the two apparently polarized opinions are rooted in the same assumption that the end times are drawing near, and that the Jews must prepare accordingly. In his book, Teichtel confronted his master Shapira regarding the operative conclusions as to how to prepare for the messianic time. I will situate the teachings of the two rabbis on a background of classical rabbinical texts concerning the messianic era. This background enables the analysis and comparison of the teachings of the two rabbis.

Messianism and Orthodoxy

Traditional Jewish sources reflect different perceptions of messianic redemption. Dov Schwartz usefully distinguishes between apocalyptic and naturalistic messianisms. Apocalyptic messianism is not only miraculous or supernatural, but refers to a profound and basic transformation in the cosmos, amounting to its very demolition and reconstruction. Divine providence plays a crucial role in a dazzling messianic sequence with strong mythological overtones. For naturalistic messianism the end of the world is a not requirement for redemption. According to this approach, hope should not be abandoned that this present world can be repaired. This approach lessens, and sometimes completely removes, direct divine intervention as a force in the process of redemption.

Some visions in the biblical, Talmudic, and Midrashic sources prophesied a day of vengeance and reprisal, and anticipated a totally transformed world for those who fear God (and, in most cases, only for the Jews among them). Popular perception anticipated a great and terrible Day of the Lord on which he would wreak vengeance on the gentiles for the suffering they had caused. Authorities of a more rational Judaism such as Maimonides and the Rashba struggled to counter the apocalyptic stream by softening the messianic rhetoric interpreting traditions to highlight universal and enlightened qualities. The world will continue to function normally, and the essence of redemption will lie in the establishment of a just authority and society – a future world that will devote its energy and resources to cultural development and to spiritual and intellectual productivity.[5] By contrast, the apocalyptic approach despaired of the redemptive potential in this world. Apocalyptic messianism is collective and public. In contradistinction to a naturalistic model, it makes less room for individual, intimate redemption.

Some of the explanations offered by Orthodox leaders for the enormous changes in the condition of the Jews in the modern times drew on analogies with the messianic age, and the difference between these two approaches is reflected in the teachings of the authorities discussed in this chapter. They agreed that modern reality should be interpreted as the realization of prophecies relating to the period preceding the coming of the messiah, but from there can be divided into two categories: optimists and pessimists.[6] Religious Zionist thinkers, tending to the optimistic, explained that the rise of Jewish nationalism represents the "first pangs of redemption," that is, the beginning of the messianic process. Based on natural messianism as described in Maimonides' writings, mundane actions by the non-religious Zionist pioneers reflect the first stages of redemption, which may be realized in full through the actions of mortals.[7] R. Yissachar Shlomo Teichtel thought this way, as did Neo-Orthodox leaders of Agudat Yisrael such as Yitzhak Breuer, who facilitated cooperation between the movement and Zionism.[8] On the other side were pessimists for whom the "pangs of messiah" – the spiritual decline of the present – were foreboding. Building on passages from the Babylonian Talmud describing the period of the *ikvata de-meshiha* (the footsteps of messiah) as marked by severe material and spiritual hardship,[9] men such as the Lithuanian R. Yisrael HaCohen of Radin, ordered his students to study the laws relating to the priests in the Temple in anticipation of imminent redemption. His disciple R. Elhanan Bonim Wasserman composed the influential book *Ikvata de-meshiha*, in which he interpreted the collapse of religious life as a sign of the approaching end time.[10] During the interwar period, the Chabad Hasidic movement developed a similarly acute messianism that would intensify still further after the war.[11] The Munkacser Hasidim adhered to the latter pessimistic school of thought, following its logic to an extreme conclusion.

Chaim Elazar Shapira – the Munkacser Rebbe

Chaim Elazar Shapira was born in Galicia on December 17, 1871, after his parents had attempted unsuccessfully to have children for many years. His family moved to Munkacs after his grandfather, Shlomo Shapira (1831–1893), was appointed the city's chief rabbi. At the turn of the twentieth century Chaim Elazar was appointed *av bet din* (chief justice of the rabbinical court), and following the death of his father, Zvi Hirsch (1850–1913), he assumed the role of spiritual leader of the Hasidic court in accordance with the customary hereditary transfer of rule there. Shapira, a prolific author who published dozens of books, was a tough and argumentative character. He died on May 12, 1937, at the age of 66.[12]

Although in his later years he became deeply entrenched in his battle against Zionism, Shapira did not leave us with a coherent anti-Zionist manifesto. I will outline his arguments from several sources, including his responsa *Minchat Elazar*, and the book *Tikun 'Olam*, which is a collection of letters by prominent rabbis against Agudat Yisrael.

Chaim Elazar Shapira's teachings sought to justify the Hasidic way of life, preserve the old traditions, and resist change. Thus Shapira fiercely attacked the Beis Yaakov schools of Agudat Yisrael, which provided a general and secular education for girls. He also opposed the inclusion of general core studies, such as math and foreign languages, in the curriculum for boys, and he harshly criticized Agudat Yisrael for permitting such studies in its schools.[13] Allan Nadler has shown that Shapira also opposed the use of scientific discoveries, such as modern medicine, and condemned those who chose to study architecture and engineering.[14]

Shapira's rejection of Zionism stemmed from the principle of political passivity. In his responsa *Minchat Elazar* (vol. 5, chapter 12), he analyzed Maimonides' approach, as discussed in his *Mishneh Torah* (Laws of Kings and Wars, chapters 11–12). Maimonides attributed national, political, and concrete goals to the King Messiah, and Religious Zionism found justification for its approach in Maimonides' naturalistic messianism.[15] However, Shapira interprets Maimonides in a completely contrary sense.

Maimonides devotes the last chapters of his Halakhic treatise, *Mishneh Torah*, to the subject of redemption. As a rationalist, Maimonides rejects apocalyptic and miraculous expectations of redemption, which he views instead as a gradual process dependent on the actions of the public. In his vision, the Halakhah will not be abolished in the messianic era: on the contrary, it will be realized in full. In *Mishneh Torah*, messianism is elaborated primarily in terms of the significance of a Halakhic society, rather than in the emergence of a supernatural society by means of a predetermined divine plan.[16]

While discussing Maimonides' description of the messiah's duties, Shapira argued that all the commandments that are associated with the construction of the Third Temple and the renewal of the monarchy are intended for the End Days and do not constitute commandments for the current generation. Thus, all the responsibilities of the messiah, such as the renewal of the monarchy, the reinstitution of the biblical laws, the conquest of the Land of Israel, and the reconstruction of the Third Temple, are the duties of a personal messiah who will come in the future. All of the above commandments "have nothing to do with Israel in this time." The King Messiah must implement these; they are not a collective duty incumbent on the nation.

Moreover, Shapira argues that some of the commandments cannot be fulfilled in a mundane way, but solely through miracles. He mentions the rebuilding of the Temple as one example of this. In the tradition, it was understood that the Third Temple will be built in heaven and will descend ready-made from the skies. This belief is based on Rashi's approach,[17] which argued that the Temple may be built instantaneously – even at night, and even on the Sabbath or a Holy Day. Accordingly, the construction of the Temple is perceived as a miraculous and supernatural event. Shapira claimed that since the Third Temple will descend from the skies, it cannot possibly be constructed by man, an opinion linked to the midrash: "The Temple of the future that we anticipate is constructed and equipped; it will appear and come from the skies, as it is written: 'The Temple of the Lord your hands will establish.'"[18]

The same approach was adopted regarding the renewal of the sacrifices. Shapira emphasized that Jews are not allowed to ascend the Temple Mount, since they do not have the ashes of the red heifer required to purify themselves for this purpose. Accordingly, he concluded, the sacrifices cannot be renewed without a miracle. Shapira also disputed the approach of R. Zvi Hirsch Kalischer (1795–1874), who in his *Drishat Tsion* proposed the reinstitution of the Passover sacrifice on the Temple Mount.[19] Shapira declared that this ritual, too, cannot be performed without the ashes of the red heifer. Finally, Shapira rejected Maimonides' idea that during the messiah's conquest of the Land of Israel, he will need to expel the seven nations that are living in it and to ban their property.[20]

To summarize Shapira's argument thus far: any collective emigration to the Land of Israel must have a messianic realization; he could not countenance any other options, such as secular and national action. The messianic fulfillment, according to the rabbi, can only be implemented in the future following the revelation of a personal messiah who will perform miracles. Accordingly, Zionist actions not intended for religious purposes are inappropriate.

Shapira has equally strong opinions about the pre-messianic Land of Israel, which he understands to intensify the qualities of human actions. Therefore, sins committed in the Land have greater weight than those committed elsewhere. "There is no similar judgment for a rebel in the kingdom inside the palace and outside of it," he writes in his response, implying that the divine punishment for Zionist pioneers who refused to observe the religious lifestyle inside the Land of Israel is far harsher than the punishment for those who rebel against God in the Diaspora. More than that, he says, the land is "a land that devours its inhabitants" (Numbers 13:32), a dangerous place that can kill people. Aviezer Ravitzky, scholar of rabbinic studies, described this approach as a "demonological conception of the Holy Land and of dark forces nesting within it and threatening its inhabitants."[21]

According to Shapira's understanding, the commandment to settle the Land applies only to those who seek to live in the Land in order to perform a religious duty. This was true of the Old Yishuv in Jerusalem, a long-standing community of observant Sephardi and Ashkenazi Jews who adhered to the traditional perception of settlement in the Land of Israel as a religious and spiritual value of importance to the entire Jewish people. They believed that Jewish settlement in the Land of Israel must fulfill a religious and spiritual function – prayer and Torah study – and accordingly, the Jewish Diaspora was urged to support such settlers.[22]

Shapira argued that following their exile, the Jews had lost their ownership of the Land of Israel, "until God would return us to our land with the messiah speedily in our days." Any type of emigration for the purpose of making a living or obtaining security impairs the belief in the messiah, he argued, because it usurps the duties of the messiah and transforms them into human action. This approach explains why Shapira regarded Zionism as an act of heresy.[23]

Another argument against emigration to the Land of Israel comes from the prohibition described in the Talmud's "three oaths" (*shalosh shavu'ot*). This belief has its origins in a passage in the Mishna Ketubot 111a:

> Why/What are these three oaths? One, that Israel should not storm the wall. Two, the Holy One adjured Israel not to rebel against the nations of the world. Three, the Holy One adjured the nations that they would not oppress Israel too much.

Traditional rabbinical exegesis interpreted these oaths as a prohibition against collective migration to the Land of Israel prior to the End Times. According to Aviezer Ravitzky, the Three Oaths are not a tactical device intended to protect the Jewish people and discourage rash action in exile; rather, they form a substantive manifestation of divine leadership and providence over the Jewish people.[24]

The oaths not to emigrate to the Land of Israel and not to rebel against the nations reflect an assumption that the nations oppose return. However, the Zionist movement gained the support of the nations with the Balfour Declaration (1917), which acknowledged the Jews' right to a national homeland in the Land of Israel. Shapira discussed the declaration and called it Ba'al Pe'or (playing on the similarity between this name and Balfour). The Bible mentions the Canaanite god Ba'al Pe'or as an example of the adoption of alien culture that leads to the abandonment of sexual prohibitions and to intermarriage. According to Itzhak Kraus, this approach should not be dismissed as mere semantics. It reflects Shapira's demonological view, which sees the success of Zionism as a proof of the rise of the evil powers that tempt Jews with false redemption.[25]

Shapira emphasized that even if all the Jews decided to move to Jerusalem, and all the nations supported them, the warnings of the three oaths still prohibited them from doing so. He explained:

> The end is unclear and maybe it is not the right time, only a temporary time of grace, and today or tomorrow they will sin again and we will have to be exiled for a second time, which will be even harder than the first time, thus [the oath] prohibits immigration until it [God] wills, heaven forbids, and until the time would come and all the land will be filled with knowledge . . . and we shouldn't trust the nations, even if they should agree [with us] right now in their schemes.[26]

It is not unreasonable to note the strange logic Shapira presents here: on the one hand, the Jews are not permitted to rebel against the will of the nations; on the other, they must do precisely that if the nations promote Jewish emigration to the Holy Land.

Shapira's opposition to Jewish emigration to the Land of Israel was also influenced by the secular character of the pioneers. Faithful to the approach of Hungarian Orthodoxy, Shapira urged his followers to disassociate themselves from anyone who deviated from his path, including secular Zionists, Religious Zionists, and Agudat Yisrael. He regarded these widely divergent groups as a single entity and called for a common action against them all. The faithful were not to maintain contact with them and must fight them with all their strength.[27]

It could be argued that Shapira failed to offer any relief for the hardship of his followers. He opposed any practical solution and failed to suggest any alternative during a period when Fascism was a rising force and the Jews faced increasing persecution. From Shapira's standpoint, however, he indeed presented a practical solution. He believed that the coming of the messiah was a tangible possibility in his own lifetime, and he believed that he could expedite this event.[28]

Shapira's immanent eschatological conservatism could not countenance religious deviation, opposed any modicum of moderation and compromise, and despised Zionism – only repentance could hasten the messiah.

Rabbi Yissachar Shlomo Teichtel

Rabbi Yissachar Shlomo Teichtel (1885–1945) was born in Hungary. He studied at the Pressburg Yeshiva, and later became the *av bet din* and chief rabbi of Pishtian in west Slovakia. The rabbi was a follower of the Munkacser Rebbe and shared his views on the importance of religious strictness and opposition to

Zionism. However, Teichtel argued that the role of a leader is to find solutions for the distress of his followers, even if this requires a measure of religious leniency.[29] In 1942, due to increasingly severe anti-Semitic persecution, Teichtel fled from Slovakia and arrived in Budapest as a refugee. He began writing his treatise *Em HaBanim Semekhah* (A Happy Mother of Children) while he was still in Slovakia, before the deportations to Auschwitz, and without understanding the full scale of the Nazi persecutions. The impact of his situation as a refugee left a mark on the subsequent development of the manuscript, which he only finished in 1943. In 1944 hearing a rumor that the deportations from Slovakia had ended, he decided to return, but was apprehended by the Nazis during his journey and died on the way to Auschwitz.[30] He wrote most of his book in an attic in Budapest, and as a result many of the sources he quoted were from memory alone. In the book he discussed the changing times and criticized Hungarian Orthodoxy for taking the wrong side on the question of supporting Zionism. Although he could not have foreseen the extermination of Hungarian Jewry, the book that was published just a year before the extermination included a powerful lamentation on the decision made by Orthodox leaders to instruct their followers to stay in Europe.[31] The rabbi confessed that he had once held the same views but stressed that he had now changed his mind.

In order to explain the transformation in Teichtel's position, we must first explain his original views. *Mishne Sachir* is a collection of Teichtel's sermons during his period of office as chief rabbi in Slovakia, summarizing his views on a variety of subjects prior to the Second World War.

In a sermon from 1923, the Rabbi spoke of the importance of studying the Torah with passion: "Let us all try to study our holy Torah in persistence and in effort . . . with little sleep and with little pleasure." The difficulty, said the Rabbi, was for the sake of bonding with God, a connection that he referred to as a "love connection" and as "forming a covenant."[32] This bond of love between God and the believer serves as a shield against the influences of the outside world. Young men would be firmly shielded only after the "acceptance of the yoke of the kingdom of heaven in complete." In these statements, the Rabbi approved of the segregationist tendencies of ultra-Orthodoxy.[33]

Teichtel used demonological language to label those who wished to study philosophy, which he descried as "filth, . . . crookedness, and lie."[34] He argued that those who are attracted to philosophy have bestial souls, just like gentiles. He said: "You should understand that one should not pay attention to this wicked wisdom."[35] He stood firmly against those who sought to educate their children in modern professions such as medicine and law rather than sending them to study Torah. He described this as an inverted world, where a father would be happy to see his son a doctor or a criminal (*Poshea*) (i.e. someone who deserted the religious way of life), but not a Torah sage. He concluded by declaring that it is better for a man to educate his sons "only in Torah and fear (of God) and not make them apostates so that they can rise to power."[36] The rabbi also opposed a change in the physical appearance by shaving the beards in order to look modern.[37] From these positions, we can see that Teichtel was not much different from the mainstream of radical ultra-Orthodoxy, because he supported segregation and opposed the assimilation and acculturation of Jews. He saw Torah study as a shield against integration.

Teichtel also attached great importance in this period to the sanctity of Torah sages and faith in their wisdom. In a sermon whose date is unknown (probably between 1921 and 1926), he addressed a ruling he heard from Yoel Teitelbaum, who was at that time the chief rabbi of Orshiva, that one should not accept financial support from the government. At first, he did not understand the logic behind this ruling, but eventually he agreed with it. The conclusion he reached was that one should not oppose the words of the famous Tzadikim, for the spirit of God speaks through their tongues.[38] The fortification of the Orthodox enclave included a component of sanctification of its leadership. Teichtel indeed expressed such ideas, though later he would change his opinion on the matter and eventually he would come out strongly against the Hungarian ultra-Orthodox leadership.

During the period prior to the Holocaust, Teichtel expressed opinions that supported the idea of faith in miraculous redemption and opposition to Zionism. Thus, for example, he argued that redemption could flourish suddenly when there is a lot of despair and no hope.[39] He also argued that even if Israel are not worthy of redemption, due to their low religious merits, God may still bring redemption suddenly.[40] The Rabbi declared that only trust in God could stop the deterioration of the physical conditions of the Jews, with its persecutions and hardships: "God has promised that He would bring us salvation, and we should only put our trust in God with truth and faith and believe in the prophecies of His prophets, and then we will receive salvations suddenly in our days Amen."[41] Salvation could only be achieved through trust in God in a miraculous way, and nothing else can expedite it. Over the years, he would retract this opinion.

Teichtel expressed his apocalyptical beliefs in the introduction to the essay *Tov Yigal* (1926), where he argued that the End Days are fast approaching. In the author's proofreading section, he said that in the days of the *Akavta DeMeshicha* (prior to the coming of the messiah) heresy will spread across the land and it will be hard not to fall into the trap of the sinners. He explained that prior to the coming of the messiah there would be the War of Gog and Magog, which he allegorized to a spiritual war "between the faithful and loyal against the emissaries of the *Sitra Achra* (the 'Other Side,' a term used to describe Satan) and his soldiers." The battle will be hard but God has promised victory: "Heaven will help the righteous to stand up and fight." According the Babylonian Talmud, the Son of David, the Messiah, will come in a generation that is either completely righteous or completely wicked (TB Sanhedrin, 98a); this is interpreted as implying that during the End Days there will be a strong dichotomy between the two poles. Winning the battle, Teichtel declared, is based on a heavenly selection between good and evil, where it will emerge that the wicked are the reincarnation of the Erev Rav. Thus Teichtel repeated the demonological terminology of radical ultra-Orthodoxy that viewed the secular as fake Jews. According to his argument, the abandonment of religion by the Jewish masses should paradoxically be a "great comfort," since this is the clearest indication that "the year of salvation and day of redemption is fast approaching."[42] The scholar Itzhak Hershkowitz argues that during this period, Teichtel indeed compared secular Jews to complete gentiles.[43]

The book *Tikun 'Olam*, edited by the students of the Munkacser Rebbe, included numerous expressions of opposition to Zionism and to Agudat Yisrael. Among other contributions, the work includes a brief letter of support from Teichtel. *Tikun 'Olam* was published in 1936, and the letter on Teichtel's behalf was written close to the time of publication. In his letter, Teichtel argues that the essential purity of Land of Israel is covered with impurity. He distinguished between the earthly and the heavenly Land of Israel, and argued that it is impossible to win the earthly Land without first purifying it. The only way to do this is to adhere to the religious way of life. Any attempt to gain the land without holiness (as a Zionist) would achieve nothing, since the land is "a land that devours its inhabitants." Only God can remove the shell of impurity, and this depends on repentance which will hasten the messiah.

According to his approach, the secular Zionist pioneers were unworthy of the land. He concluded that no human action or conduct will enhance the value of Zion and Jerusalem until "God send[s] from heaven a spirit of cleanness" – which is to say, by a miracle.[44] In his letter of support, Teichtel repeated a set of positions that accord closely with those held by Shapira.

Shmuel Weingarten, who was the Mizrahi's chief secretary in Czechoslovakia prior to the Second World War, and who personally knew Teichtel, testified that Teichtel belonged to Shapira's followers,

> and I knew that anyone who fell under the influence of the Admor of Munkacs was as if hypnotized by him, and no powerful persuasion in the world could release him from the "trance" that the Rebbe placed him in.[45]

Yet by 1942, the rabbi already changed his mind. In the introduction to *Em HaBanim Semekhah* he argued that the Zionist question had not been a major focus of his interest when he wrote against the movement. "I was busy teaching students and writing essays," he declared. He noted that in the Talmud, sages at times confess their mistakes. Accordingly, if a man believes that his views are correct, he should not refrain from presenting them, since "the truth is key."[46] In the appendix to the third chapter, written just before the publication of the book, he added that his earlier letter to *Tikun 'Olam* had been written "in time of peace and tranquility" when Jews did not face mortal threats.[47] Moreover, Teichtel argued, if Shapira were alive today,

> he would also have said that we should leave the lands of exile and move to the Land of Israel that the kings of land have offered us (the British Empire) and not wait for the call of the messiah.[48]

In his book, Teichtel presents several personal testimonies that allow us to look more deeply into his change of heart. In the year 5706 (1942), a ruling was issued by the authorities in Slovakia to kidnap all unmarried Jewish girls over the age of 16 and to transfer them to an unknown place. At the time he was writing, the fate of thousands of girls remained unknown.[49] Accordingly, he decided to call his book *A Happy Mother of Children* as an allegory of a Land happy to see her children return in peace from their wanderings.

Teichtel also described the confiscation of Jewish property:

> Every gentile who sees an item that belongs to a Jew is allowed to say "give it to me," and the Jew is forced to give it to him, and thus all the Jews were left naked and with nothing.[50]

He described the confiscations of lands and houses, deliberate starvations, and deportations to Auschwitz, which he defined as "a land of exile," since at that point he was unaware of the actual destiny of the deportees. He emphasized that all his descriptions were "like a drop in the sea of cruelty that they have done to us without a reason, only because we are the seed of Abraham, Isaac, and Jacob."[51] Teichtel's personal diary, which survived the Holocaust and was published by his son in 1994, includes additional testimonials regarding the persecution of Jews in Slovakia, some of a personal nature. One of the more horrifying passages recalls how he was captured by the police, taken to jail, and subjected to physical torture.[52]

In the second introduction to *Em HaBanim*, Teichtel wrote that the troubling times do not allow him to concentrate on Talmudic subjects, not least because all his students had been deported and he remained alone. Accordingly, he had decided to study the subject of the messiah, and had formed the definite conclusion that the End Times were about to begin. However, various obstructions were preventing the messiah from appearing, thus one purpose of his book was to explain the severity of the situation and to offer a correction.

In the rabbinic literature, the "footsteps of messiah" are described as a miserable period characterized by spiritual and material decline. Sanhedrin states that the messiah Son of David will come only in a generation that is either entirely guilty or entirely innocent (TB Sanhedrin 98a), implying that redemption could even come in a completely wicked generation. The same source also states: "in its time, I shall expedite," meaning is that if the Jews have merits justifying their redemption then redemption will come speedily; if not, redemption will still come, but only "in its [appointed] time."

Teichtel calculated the end, determining that his days were at the end of the sixth millennium, and thus the Jews had reached the predetermined date established by God for their redemption:

> We are living in the year 5703 (1943) of the sixth millennium, and we have certainly already reached the period of "in its time." . . . From the year 5500 (1700) the time of the messiah has begun, but according to all opinions we have already passed two-thirds of the sixth millennium, thus is already "in its time."

According to the messianic model based on TB Sanhedrin 98, the prevailing physical and spiritual condition prior to the coming of the messiah must be wretched. The rabbi curtly assessed that "there is no shortage of baseness in our days." Yet messiah had still not appeared, and accordingly his discussion attempted to ascertain what might be holding him back: "We need to investigate and to understand what is the matter that stalling him from us."[53]

In order to explain his point, the rabbi tells the story of a Hasid who did not want to get married. "Why should I marry?" asked the Hasid, and he received the answer: "In order to have children." The Hasid replied that he would go the Rebbe and give him a note, the traditional way for Hasidim to ask the Rebbe to pray on their behalf. The Hasid went to see his Rebbe who told him: "What should a man do in order to have children? He should marry a wife." Teichtel interprets his own story by emphasizing that prayer alone is not enough; actions are also required.

> If a man prays on something, it is not enough to pray alone, even if the prayer is with great devotion, until he would take action and do what he needs to do, and only then will heaven help him get what he wants.[54]

In this parable, Teichtel confronted the passive principle of Orthodoxy, which seeks to expedite redemption by prayers alone and opposes any political action of conquering and settling the Land of Israel, as we saw in Shapira's polemics, challenging the religious leadership of his generation, and particularly the Munkacser Rebbe. Teichtel argued that leaders must think of the common good – that the troubles facing the Jews of his generation were the result of bad leadership. "All the blows we endure in exile were intended to awaken us up to return to our holy land." He continued: "We need that the beginning of action would come from men and later God would support it."[55] This approach echoes the ideas of R. Zvi Hirsh Kalischer (1795–1874), who is considered one of the harbingers of Zionism. Kalischer proposed several stages for human-led redemption, including the ingathering of a small number of Jews in the Land of Israel with the permission of the nations and the reinstitution of the Passover sacrifice on the site of the Temple. These human actions would be complemented by God, according to the principle "mundane actions cause sublime actions."[56] Teichtel developed this approach and proposed that with the ingathering of exiles in the Land of Israel – with the permission of the British Empire and the support of the League of Nations – a Third Temple should be built on the Temple Mount by the Jews. Then would the messiah bring down a heavenly Temple from above, thereby completing the mundane action.[57]

Thus we see that Teichtel now supported immigration to the Land of Israel. Since there was no doubt the messianic time had come, the promises of redemption would soon be fulfilled. As I discussed above, rabbinic literature presents different models for messianic realization. Teichtel sought to abandon the miraculous and apocalyptical model accepted by Hungarian Orthodox rabbis, and to replace it with a naturalist model. He explained: "How redemption will appear, with a miracle or with nature, is all dependent upon our actions and behavior." Redemption may come suddenly and miraculously, or it may appear in the form of a long and gradual process:

> Our true sages have already shown us that unlike many of our people who imagine and desire that the messiah would appear to Israel suddenly like a flashing river or from darkness to great light immediately, [however] their rise will be little by little from one step to the other.[58]

He goes on:

> Our master and rabbi, the holy genius, author of *Minchat Elazar* of blessed memory from Munckacs . . . with all due respect, I must indicate that he viewed all things from a meritorious perspective based on his lofty standards. Yet, in truth, this last generation, due to many transgressions "is not worthy." Redemption is, therefore, destined to be disguised in the natural process.

He criticizes the Munkacser Rebbe for holding that redemption must come only by way of a miracle. Teichtel agrees that this is the proper situation when everyone repents and the entire nation is as righteous as the Rebbe. However, since the situation of the nation is not as desired, and it is therefore "not worthy," redemption still will come, but through a gradual process.[59] It is worth noting that Teichtel's criticism of Shapira's approach on this matter was only published after the latter's death.

Teichtel was aware of the prohibitions made by the sages against calculating the end. However, according to his understanding, it was now permitted to act to force the End: "It is permitted, and allowed, and timely of us to ask these questions as to how long the road should be."[60] In the introduction to the essay, he encourages his readers to take a vow to raise the glory of the Land of Israel and to commit to emigrate to the Land after the war. "We must vow to return to our Holy Land. We must try to reestablish its glory. Then too its merits will release us from our distress, quickly in our days, Amen."[61] Emigration will force God to fulfill all the vows, and exile will then end: the classic model of messianic activism.

Teichtel attacked the traditional expectation that the messiah will carry the Jews to their homeland on the "wings of an eagle" – "a despicable opinion and a desecration of God's name." To support his case he quoted Maimonides, who argued that Jews must not rely on a miracle.[62] Teichtel went on to argue that the expected miracle cannot appear to the Jews who are living in exile, since the "spirit of cleanness" that supposedly will allow Jews to repent is impossible during the state of exile.[63] This argument embodies the complete reversal of his earlier statement in *Tikun 'Olam*, when he argued that that impurity that covers the Land of Israel will not allow life that is unholy in it. He now argues that impurity covers gentile lands and that this prevents repentance. Thus Teichtel adopted the Religious Zionist argument that repentance will come at the end of the messianic process, not at its beginning.[64]

He further challenged the ultra-Orthodox argument that no good can come from the settling of the Land of Israel by Zionist pioneers who do not keep the Torah and the commandments, arguing that the pioneers' actions are an example of a commandment that comes through transgression. "Even if the builders of the land in our days are committing sins and deliberately defying the will of God and not keeping the commandments, still God welcomes their actions of building the land with love and great affection."[65] In contrast, the Munkacser Rebbe disassociated himself from the pioneers due to their secular ways, and as a result abandoned the idea of building the land through human effort. "For him, it is better to be in a state of 'sit and do nothing' rather than build [the land] with transgressors." Teichtel went on to emphasize that pure nationalism is insufficient, since the Jewish nation is distinguished by its commandments.[66] Nonetheless, Teichtel thought that if the Orthodox cooperated with the Zionists, they might be able to influence them from within so that the pioneers would work according to the spirit of the Torah. If the believers moved to the Holy Land in their masses, their influence would grow, and this would help keep the Land holy.[67] He concluded: "We need you and your actions but you should know that you need also Torah sages."[68]

One of the main debates in early twentieth-century Hasidic discourse concerned the proper approach toward Jews who had abandoned Torah. Most Hasidic rabbis, including the Gerrer and Alexander Rebbes, argued that such offenders continued to form part of the Jewish people despite their offenses. Accordingly, the sinners retain their Jewish essence and efforts should be made to bring them back to the fold.[69] Leaders of the radical ultra-Orthodox movement, among them the Munkacser Rebbe, refused to accept this lenient approach, condemning and even demonizing those who transgressed religious law.[70]

One of the arguments against Zionism articulated by the Munkacser Rebbe and repeated by Teichtel in his letter published in *Tikun 'Olam*, was that the Land of Israel is "a land that devours its inhabitants" and will vomit out Zionists sinners who desecrate the Sabbath. Teichtel later reversed himself: "One should not call the immigrants in our days ugly or wicked, heaven forbid, or condemn their actions, or speak against them with contempt, because they were privileged to build our land and to make it bloom."[71] Indeed Teichtel devoted much of his essay to a condemnation of the separatist tendencies of Hungarian Orthodoxy.[72] He attributed eschatological meaning to Israel's unity and claimed that outreach to nonbelievers has the potential to expedite the redemption: "You must love even the worst man in Israel to unite the hearts and to push away anything that brings divisions, for the salvation of Israel is dependent upon it in times of trouble." He attacked the ideology of hatred that is associated with Hungarian Orthodoxy:[73] "Don't be a stupid and foolish Hasid to speak ill of Israel and to bring divisions among the believers." And he continued with declarations of love:

Even though the wicked among Israel are traitors, heaven forbid, still they do not cease to be the children of God. . . . And thus it is a commandment to love them and to bring them closer with great affection, and thereby we will reach salvation.[74]

In his eyes, those who left the traditional lifestyle are considered a "baby in captivity" – a Halakhic term used to refer to Jews who, for reasons beyond their own control, did not study and therefore do not know how to follow Jewish religious law. Such persons are not held liable for their behavior. Since the nineteenth century this term has been used by Torah scholars to grapple with the Halakhic status of secular Jews.

The unity of Israel is a precondition for redemption and it can only be achieved by emigration to the Land of Israel and observance of the commandments, Teichtel concluded. He confronted those "who act with evilness and detestation to make us hate our precious land." He adopted a punishment and reward approach model, claiming that the opposition to Zionism causes bitter exiles whose end cannot be seen. He advocated the development of a counter-propaganda mechanism and even offered to study how this technique was applied in Soviet Russia.[75]

To conclude, Teichtel came to reject the overall approach of Hungarian Orthodoxy, which opposed Zionism and encouraged retreat and segregation, relying on the expectation of miraculous salvation. He adopted the naturalist messianic model typical of Religious Zionist thinkers, and argued that by following this model and by emigrating to the Land of Israel after the war, the Jewish nation could secure redemption.

Discussion

Shapira and Teichtel lived in the same period and in geographical proximity. They were both inspired by the rabbinical worldview of Hungarian Orthodoxy and both were strict rabbis, in accordance with the tradition of their region. Based on the severe deterioration in the condition of the Jews in Europe, and Talmudic analysis, each believed that messianic redemption was imminent. In trying to explain the delay in the coming of the messiah, Shapira blamed the modernizers, the Zionists, and even Agudat Yisrael, while Teichtel blamed the Hungarian Orthodox leadership, and especially the Munkacser Rebbe himself, for refusing to support naturalist redemption. It is important to note that neither blamed God. The furthest Shapira could bring himself was to suggest that God was indifferent to the miseries of the Jews, thus expressing mild protest without shaking his ideological foundation.[76]

Benjamin Brown interestingly noted that by the nineteenth century all the Hungarian rebbes had adopted a highly nomistic approach: Hasidic leaders defended the Halakhah and adopted the ultra-Orthodox approach. The most radical of these figures was Tzvi Elimelech of Dinow, Shapira's great-great-grandfather. However, among these rabbinical circles a doctrine of "holiness of sin" had also developed and Tzvi Elimelech was one of the advocates of this approach. He argued that actions undertaken for the sake of Heaven, even if they constituted a transgression, would nevertheless count as good deeds.[77]

Traditional rabbinical literature forbids actions intended to hasten the End Times. Based on the research on Chaim Elazar Shapira and Yissachar Shlomo Teichtel, it might be hypothesized that taking action to draw the redemption closer could be understood as a "holy sin." It is possible that their fervent belief in the imminence of redemption, combined with the deteriorating in the state of Jewish existence in Hungary combined with deep conviction that their own intentions were pure and sublime, pushed them to transgress this prohibition, and in these cases we find a continuation of Hasidic traditions that go beyond the limits of strict norms.

For both rabbis, the miseries of the Jews were proof of the messianic times. Applying a Deuteronomic model of reward and punishment, Shapira understood the troubles as divine punishment for the abandonment of the religious lifestyle. For Teichtel, current woes constituted a divine punishment for neglecting the commandment of settling the Land of Israel after God had opened up an opportunity to do so, after the Balfour declaration.

In the teachings of the Munkacser Rebbe we can identify a continuation of ideas that were advocated by other Orthodox leaders of that time prior to the Holocaust like Elhanan Bonim Wasserman (1875–1941), head of the Baranowitz Yeshivah, Yosef Yitzhak Schneerson, the sixth Chabad Rebbe, and his son-in-law Menachem Mendel Schneerson. These rabbis argued, each one with his own nuance, that the rise of Haskalah, Reform, and Zionism brought to a declaration of war on God, and as a result caused the divine punishment of the persecution of the Jews. They also believed that the miserable situation of the Jews indicate that the messianic times are fast approaching.[78]

After the Holocaust, Menachem Mendel Schneerson, who for the meanwhile turned to be the leader of the Chabad dynasty, found it difficult to repeat these arguments, and instead offered different explanations which argues that humans cannot fathom God's ways. Even more, he said that Jews should not give victory to Hitler by abandoning their religious way of life, thus he established a massive outreach operation to bring sinners to the fold of religion.[79] After the war, Menachem Mendel Schneerson adopted approaches which are closer in substance to these of Teichtel, who argues that every Jew has an inner spark, therefore there is a need to reach out even to sinners, including Zionists.[80] Chabad has developed an extensive network of emissaries who operate throughout the Jewish world to draw Jews closer to its version of Jewish heritage.

On the other hand, Shapira's successor as the head of the Hasidic radicals, R. Yoel Teitelbaum (1887–1979), the Satmar Rebbe, took the anti-Zionist approach into the extreme. The two leaders shared an antimodernist approach and a profound opposition to Zionism. They both negated any Jewish activism in the Land of Israel that was not devoted solely to Torah study. Like Shapira, Yoel Teitelbaum also believed that he was living through the days preceding the arrival of messiah and that his generation had reached such a nadir that the only rational conclusion was that the just Redeemer was about to appear. However, the differences between the two figures are striking. Teitelbaum based his anti-Zionist approach on the Talmudic legend of the three oaths and thus claimed that the Holocaust was a divine punishment for the sin of Zionism. He opposed any action to expedite the End, even on the spiritual plane. Shapira, by contrast, did not put much weight on the three oaths with his opposition to Zionism. Moreover, he devoted himself to a spiritual endeavor to expedite redemption and bring the End.[81]

Thus we see that the Holocaust and the establishment of the State of Israel caused a change among several Hasidic masters who survived the war, though not all of them. The underlying fault lines of disagreement remained.[82]

Notes

1 Sections from Chapter 3 are reprinted with the permission of the University of Pennsylvania Press. Originally published as "Messianic Expectations and Hungarian Orthodox Theology Before and During the Second World War – A Comparative Study," *Jewish Quarterly Review* 107 (4) (2017): 506–530.
2 Levi Cooper, *The Munkaczer Rebbe Chaim Elazar Shapira the Hassidic Ruler – Biography and Theology*, Ramat Gan: Ph.D. Dissertation, Bar Ilan University, 2011; Allan Nadler, "The War on Modernity of R. Hayyim Elazar Shapira of Munkacz," *Modern Judaism* 14 (3) (1994): 233–264; Aviezer Ravitzky, *Messianism, Zionism, and Religious Radicalism*, Chicago: University of Chicago Press 1993, 40–62; Motti Inbari, "Messianic Activism in the Works of Chaim Elazar Shapira, the Munkaczer Rebbe, Between Two World Wars," *Cathedra* 149 (2013): 77–104 (in Hebrew).
3 The book *Tikun 'Olam*, authored by the Munkacser Rebbe's student contains a confrontation with the Gerrer Rebbe over his compromising attitude toward Agudat Yisrael and its school system. Moshe Goldstein, *Tikun 'Olam*, Mukacevo: Druck H. Gutmann, 5696/1936 (in Hebrew).
4 Yitzhak Hershkowitz, *The Redemption Vision of Rabbi Yissachar Shlomo Teichtel, HY"D: Transitions in His Messianic Perception During the Holocaust*, Ramat Gan: Ph.D. Dissertation, Bar Ilan University, 2009 (in Hebrew); Rivka Schatz-Uffenheimer, "Confession on the Brink of the Crematoria," *Jerusalem Quarterly* 34 (1985): 126–141; Eliezer Schweid, "A Happy Mother of Children: The Theodicy of the Zionist God of Rabbi Yissachar Shlomo Teichtel" in: *Minkhah LeSarah – Studies in Jewish Philosophy and Kabbalah*, edited by Moshe Idel, Deborah Diment and Shalom Rosenberg, Jerusalem: Magness Press, 1994, 380–398 (in Hebrew); Pesach Schindler, "Tikkun as Response to Tragedy: Em HaBanim Smeha of Rabbi Yissakhar Shlomo Teichtal – Budapest, 1943," *Holocaust and Genocide Studies* 4 (4) (1989): 413–433; Yitzhak Hershkowitz, "Em HaBanim Semekhah: From Canonic Treatise to a Dialectic Completion," *Alei Sefer – Studies in Bibliography and the History of the Hebrew Book Printed or Digital* 22 (2011): 115–127 (in Hebrew).
5 Dov Schwartz, *The Messianic Idea in Israel*, Ramat Gan: Bar-Ilan University, 1997, 9–12 (in Hebrew).
6 Gershon Bacon, "Birth Pangs of the Messiah: The Reflections of Two Polish Rabbis on Their Era," in: *Studies in Contemporary Jewry* 7: *Jews and Messianism in the Modern Era: Metaphor and Meaning*, edited by Jonathan Frankel, New York: Oxford University Press, 1991, 86–99.
7 Dov Schwartz, *Religious Zionism: History and Ideology*, Boston: Academic Press, 2009; Dov Schwartz, *Faith at a Crossroads – A Theological Profile of Religious Zionism*, Leiden: Brill, 2002.
8 Yosef Fund, *Separation or Integration: Agudat Yisrael confronts Zionism and the State of Israel*, Jerusalem: Magness Press, 1999, 19–63 (in Hebrew).
9 For example, see Babylonian Talmud, Sanhedrin 97a.
10 Gershon Greenberg, "Foundations for Orthodox Jewish Theological Response to the Holocaust: 1936–1939," in: *Burning Memory: Times of Testing and Reckoning*, edited by Alice Eckardt, Oxford: Oxford University Press, 1993, 71–94.
11 Menachem Friedman, "Messiah and Messianism in Chabad – Lubavitch Hasidism," in: *War of Gog and Magog: Messianism and Apocalypse in Judaism – Past and Present*, edited by David Ariel – Joël [et al.], Tel Aviv: Yediot Achronot, 2001, 161–173 (In Hebrew).

12 Cooper, *The Munkaczer Rebbe Chaim Elazar Shapira the Hassidic Ruler*, 64–76.
13 Inbari, "Messianic Activism in the Works of Chaim Elazar Shapira," 93–97.
14 Nadler, "The War on Modernity of R. Hayyim Elazar Shapira of Munkacz."
15 Menachem Kellner, "'And the Crooked Shall Be Made Straight': Twisted Messianic Visions, and a Maimonidean Corrective," in: *Rethinking the Messianic Idea in Judaism*, edited by Michael Morgan and Steve Weitzman, Bloomington: Indiana University Press, 2014, 256–273.
16 David Hartman, *Leadership in Times of Distress: On the Maimonides' Letters*, Tel Aviv: Hakibbutz Hameuchad, 1985, 111–116 (in Hebrew).
17 Rashi's commentary on Sukkah Tractate 41a, and his commentary on Rosh Hashanah tractate 30a.
18 Midrash Tanchuma, Pekudei, chapter 18.
19 Jody E. Myers, *Seeking Zion: Modernity and Messianic Activism in the Writings of Tsevi Hirsch Kalischer*, Oxford: Littman Library of Jewish Civilization, 2003.
20 On the question of God's ban, see Susan Niditch, *War in the Hebrew Bible: A Study in the Ethics of Violence*, New York: Oxford University Press, 1993, 28–77.
21 Ravitzky, *Messianism, Zionism, and Religious Radicalism*, 42.
22 Menachem Friedman, *Society and Religion – Non-Zionist Orthodoxy in the Land of Israel, 1918–1936*, Jerusalem: Ben Zvi Institute, 5738–1978 (in Hebrew); Ravitzky, *Messianism, Zionism, and Religious Radicalism*, 40–78.
23 Nadler, "The War on Modernity of R. Hayyim Elazar Shapira of Munkacz."
24 Ravitzky, *Messianism, Zionism, and Religious Radicalism*, 63–70.
25 Itzhak Kraus, "The Theological Responses to the Balfour Declaration," *Bar Ilan* 28–29 (5761–2000): 81–104 (in Hebrew).
26 Goldstein, *Tikun 'Olam*, 4.
27 Chaim E. Shapira, *Minchat Elazar* 5, chapter 12; also Ravitzky, *Messianism, Zionism, and Religious Radicalism*, 48–51.
28 Inbari, "Messianic Activism in the Works of Chaim Elazar Shapira."
29 Itzhak Hershkovitz, "The Halakhah as a Tool for Policy Makers: The Freedom of Ruling and the Responsibility of the Ruler in the Teachings of Rabbi Yissachar Shlomo Teichtel," *Dinei Israel* 26–27 (5769–70/2009–10): 67–88 (in Hebrew).
30 Hershkovitz, *The Redemption Vision of Rabbi Yissachar Shlomo Teichtel, HY"D*, 1–4.
31 Although some Hasidic leaders ordered their followers not to leave Europe, they themselves escaped it, leaving their followers to deal with the Nazis by themselves. See Mendel Piekarz, *Ideological Trends of Hassidism in Poland During the Interwar Period and the Holocaust*, Jerusalem: Bialik Institute, 1997 (in Hebrew).
32 Issachar S. Teichtel, *Mishne Sachir*, Jerusalem: Machon Keren Re'em, 5769–2009, 12–14 (in Hebrew).
33 Ibid., 18–19.
34 Ibid., 19.
35 Ibid., 19–20.
36 Ibid., 128–129. The sermon is from 1922.
37 Ibid., 50–51.
38 Ibid., 80–83.
39 Ibid., 16–17.
40 Ibid., 17–18.
41 Ibid., 9.
42 Issachar S. Teichtel, *Tov Igal*, Slovakia: Druck von M. Ch. Horovitz, 1926, 5–8 (in Hebrew).
43 Hershkovitz, *The Redemption Vision of Rabbi Yissachar Shlomo Teichtel, HY"D*, 71–87.
44 Goldstein, *Tikun 'Olam*, 104–107.
45 Shmuel Weingarten, "Miyvan metzula liyerushalaim shel maala," *Or Hamizrach* 19 (1970): 235–245 (Hebrew).

46 Yissachar Shlomo Teichtel, *Em HaBanim Semekhah*, Budapest: Druck von Salamon Katzburg, 5703–1943, 17–18 (in Hebrew).
47 Ibid., 314.
48 Ibid., 95.
49 Ibid., 36.
50 Ibid., 40–41.
51 Ibid.
52 Yisachar Shlomo Teichtel, *Faith Tempered in Holocaust Furnace*, Vol. 1, Jerusalem: Unclear publisher, 1994, 147–154 (in Hebrew).
53 Teichtel, *Em HaBanim Semekhah*, 100–101.
54 Ibid., 103.
55 Ibid., 28–30.
56 Myers, *Seeking Zion.*
57 Teichtel, *Em HaBanim Semekhah*, 296–306.
58 Ibid., 89.
59 Ibid., 94–95.
60 Ibid., 136.
61 Ibid., 24.
62 Ibid., 173–176.
63 Teichtel, *Em HaBanim Semekhah*, 75.
64 Motti Inbari, *Messianic Religious Zionism Confronts Israeli Territorial Compromises*, New York: Cambridge University Press, 2012, 15–36.
65 Teichtel, *Em HaBanim Semekhah*, 55.
66 Ibid.
67 Ibid., 204.
68 Ibid., 57.
69 Piekarz, *Ideological Trends of Hassidism in Poland During the Interwar Period and the Holocaust*, 122–156.
70 Menachem Keren-Kratz, *Marmaros-Sziget: 'Extreme Orthodoxy' and Secular Jewish Culture at the Foothills of the Carpathian Mountains*, Jerusalem: Magness Press, 2013 (in Hebrew).
71 Teichtel, *Em HaBanim Semekhah*, 192–194. Although some of Teichtel's arguments sound similar to those of Rabbi Avraham Itzhak Kook, the first Zionist Chief Rabbi, one cannot find any reference to Kook's writings in this essay, and it is probably incorrect to associate any influence of Kook's teachings on Teichtel. Still, scholar Daniel Reiser claims that there is a strong resembles between *Em HaBanim Semekhah* and the messianic religious Zionist approach of Rabbi Kook. Daniel Reiser, "Aspects in the Thought of Rabbi Yisachar Shlomo Teichtal and a Study of New Documents," *Yad Vashem Studies* 43(2) (2015): 143–190.
72 Benjamin Brown, " 'As Swords to the Earth's Body': The Opposition for East European Rabbis to the Idea of Congregational Schism," in: *Yosef Daat*, edited by Yossi Goldstein, Beer Sheva: Ben Gurion University Press, 5770–2010, 215–244 (in Hebrew).
73 Refael Kadosh suggests that the main innovation of the Rabbi Yoel Teitelbaum, the Satmar Rebbe and the leader of radical ultra-Orthodoxy after the Second World War, was to confine the concept of Ahavat Yisrael to his immediate community; regarding all other Jews, an obligation was imposed to distance oneself from their wickedness. Accordingly, boundless love for one's own is mirrored by hatred for everyone else. Refael Kadosh, *Extremist Religious Philosophy: The Radical Religious Doctrines of the Satmar Rebbe*, Cape Town: Ph.D. Dissertation, 2011, 134–160 (in Hebrew).
74 Teichtel, *Em HaBanim Semekhah*, 72. For more on this approach, see Hershkowitz, *The Redemption Vision of Rabbi Yissachar Shlomo Teichtel, HY"D*, 201–205.
75 Teichtel, *Em HaBanim Semekhah*, 264–268.
76 Psychological research has demonstrated that presenting some minor anger toward God can be a sign of strong relationship. Julie J. Exline, Kalman J. Kaplan and Joshua

B. Grubbs, "Anger, Exit, and Assertion: Do People See Protest Toward God as Morally Acceptable?" *Psychology of Religion and Spirituality* 4 (4) (2012): 264–277; Richard Beck, "Communion and Complaint: Attachment, Object-Relations, and Triangular Love Perspectives on Relationship with God," *Journal of Psychology and Theology* 34 (1) (2006): 43–52; Yochanan Muffs, *Love & Joy: Law, Language and Religion in Ancient Israel*, New York: JTS, 1992, 9–48.

77 Benjamin Brown, "The Two Faces of Religious Radicalism: Orthodox Zealotry and 'Holy Sinning' in Nineteenth-Century Hasidism in Hungary and Galicia," *Journal of Religion* 93 (3) (2013): 341–374.

78 Gershon Greenberg, "Elhana Wasserman's Response to the Growing Catastrophe in Europe: The Role of Hagra and Hofets Hayim Upon His Thought," *Journal of Jewish Thought and Philosophy* 10 (2000): 171–204; Friedman, "Messiah."

79 Gershon Greenberg, "Menahem Mendel Schneersohn's Response to the Holocaust," *Modern Judaism* 34(1) (2014): 86–122.

80 Adam Ferziger shows how this Hasidic debate over how to treat sinners transferred into American Orthodoxy, with a confrontation between two Orthodox rabbis: Adam S. Ferziger, "Hungarian Separatist Orthodoxy and the Migration of Its Legacy to America: The Greenwald-Hirschenson Debate," *Jewish Quarterly Review* 105 (2) (2015): 250–283.

81 Motti Inbari, *Jewish Radical Ultra-Orthodoxy Confronts Modernity, Zionism and Women's Equality*, New York: Cambridge University Press, 2016.

82 For a detailed discussion of Hasidic thought after the Holocaust, see Gershon Greenberg, "Hasidic Thought and the Holocaust (1933–1947): Optimism and Activism," *Jewish History* 27 (2013): 353–375.

4 From spiritual conversion to ideological conversion

The quest of Ruth Ben-David

"Who are you, Ruth Ben-David?" This was the question famously posed by Isser Harel, head of the Mossad, after he was charged with the task of locating the missing child Yossele Schumacher, whose grandfather Nachman Straks refused to return him to his parents' guardianship. Ruth Ben-David was suspected of smuggling the child out of Israel. "Who are you, Ruth Ben-David?" is indeed a tough question to answer. Was she a righteous convert or an international trickster? A "despicable woman," as Yossi Schumacher later called her, or a modest and virtuous lady? A ruthless child snatcher, or someone who saved Jews from the Nazis? A pathological liar, or a woman devoted to truth and justice? The many faces of Ruth Ben-David and the almost schizophrenic contradictions revealed in her personality make it difficult to offer an unequivocal answer. In this chapter I will attempt to shed some light on Ben-David's biography and on the events in which she was involved.

Born in France in 1920, Madeleine Lucette Ferraille underwent several dramatic transitions over the course of her life. Born to an agnostic father and a Catholic mother, she embarked on a personal intellectual quest that led her to seek her own identity in Greek philosophy and among the Seventh-Day Adventists. Eventually, however, she was entranced by the morality of the Hebrew prophets and entered the world of Judaism, undergoing a Reform conversion in Paris in 1951. On her conversion she changed her name to Ruth Ben-David. She continued her journey through the Jewish world, affiliating first with Orthodox Zionist circles but eventually finding her place among the supporters of Neturei Karta in the Meah Shearim quarter of Jerusalem. She completed her transformation after marrying Amram Blau, the leader of the Haredi zealots in Jerusalem. Madeleine L. Ferraille had now become Ruth Blau, completing a journey that essentially included two acts of conversion: entry into the world of pro-Zionist Judaism through a Reform conversion ceremony and later conversion from a lifestyle blending religion and modernity to an anti-modern approach. This latter stage included an Orthodox conversion for the sake of formality but also constituted an ideological conversion.

These transitions, which had an essentially personal and spiritual character, were accompanied by profound personal disappointments and dramatic events. Ben-David's life may be divided into several stages: her childhood and youth;

marriage, childbirth, and divorce under the shadow of the Second World War; her business activities, whose ultimate failure led her to spend time in a French prison for tax evasion on a massive scale; her journey to Switzerland for the purpose of studies and ongoing spiritual inquiry; her return to Paris and her conversion, while living a double life based in France and Israel; the kidnapping of Yossele Schumacher and his transfer to Europe, ending with the exposure of the kidnapping by the Mossad; her return to Meah Shearim and her scandalous marriage to Amram Blau, head of the Neturei Karta movement and one of the leaders of the Haredi world.

Ben-David is described as an attractive woman, elegant and well-educated. She was wooed by many men, and after her conversion had serious relationships with three. To her disappointment, some of these men caused her harm, and she experienced separation from all three of her partners (albeit temporarily, in the case of Blau). Ben-David was a delicate woman, and her autobiography reveals the mental torment she suffered due to her relationships with men. Her descriptions of the people she met over the course of her life are almost always unflattering when men are involved. She dreamt of marriage and happiness and she willingly submitted herself to the authority of the men who persuaded her to kidnap a child from his parents in the name of a zealous ideology. But men also brought her disillusionment, betrayed her, caused her sorrow, and led to her downfall. Above all these men hovers the spirit of Ben-David's father, with whom she maintained an almost Oedipal relationship, and according to whose yardstick she judged every man who came into her life and established her position of love or hate in his regard.

In my previous book, I discussed at length the biography of Amram Blau, the leader of the anti-Zionist Neturei Karta movement, including the story of his marriage to Ruth Ben-David. Yet Ben-David's story deserves examination in its own right, given its fascinating twists and turns. I drew on a number of sources in writing this chapter. Ben-David authored two autobiographies. One was written in 1962 but was only published in 1993, in a draft version and in English. The draft was essentially abandoned, and only a handful of libraries in the United States hold copies of the publication. This autobiography, produced on a typewriter with handwritten corrections, includes frank and detailed descriptions of various stages in Ben-David's life, concluding with the Yossele Schumacher affair and her mental torment following the exposure of the kidnapping by the Mossad. Ben-David wrote this autobiography in order to justify her actions in the face of harsh criticism.[1] The work was shelved under pressure from Haredi circles who feared that some of the material in the book might damage their community. Amram Blau prevented his wife from publishing the book because it was written in French and translated to English, languages which he did not understand. The Blau Archive, located in Boston University, contains a detailed letter from the translator (whose name I was unable to decipher), who translated the manuscript from French to English, imploring Blau to permit the publication of the work. The translator described the contents of the autobiography in detailed and gave a guarantee of its propriety, but his pleadings were to no avail.[2] Moreover, in 1964 the Beit Din

Tzedek of HaEda HaHareidit ordered Ben-David not to give interviews to the secular press: "It is an embellishment of His honorable Torah not to meet with secular journalists for conversations or to convey news and opinions, [. . .] and not to send letters or articles to the above-mentioned newspapers whatsoever."[3] Faced with such uncompromising prohibitions, Ben-David had no choice but to reluctantly shelve the publication.

In 1979, however, after the death of her husband and after she was less subject to the influence of his followers, Ben-David published short and bowdlerized excerpts in Hebrew and French relating to her life as a Christian and focusing mainly on the story of Yossele Schumacher. The material also included descriptions of her later life as the happy wife of Amram Blau.[4] After her book was published in Hebrew, the former Mossad chief Isser Harel published his version of the events leading to the solution of the kidnapping. Harel responded both explicitly and implicitly to Ben-David's narrative, sometimes contradicting her claims. Harel's book is important in that it provides a counterpoint to Ben-David's description of the events. It also allows us to crack her code, since she used pseudonyms to refer to all those involved in the kidnapping.[5] After Ben-David's death, her only son, Uriel, agreed to give an interview for the *Jerusalem Post* in which he presented his perspective, sometimes contradicting his mother's version of events and offering an alternative narrative for several incidents over the course of her life.[6] My own investigations suggest that Uriel's account is more credible in several cases, particularly regarding the circumstances that led his mother to undertake her first conversion, under the influence of her pro-Zionist stance at that time. Another important source is an interview Ben-David gave to the journalist Noah Zevuluni from the *Davar* newspaper in 1993. The interview was never published in the newspaper, but Zevuluni's sons published it online after their father's death.[7]

An autobiography is a problematic historical source due to the distance from the events described and subjective bias. In our case, the problems are particularly severe, since I have managed to refute several claims made by Ben-David, thereby undermining the credibility of her version. As mentioned, she uses pseudonyms in some cases, further complicating the task of unraveling her narrative. The sources by Uriel and Isser Harel clarified the identity of some of those involved, and I was able to decipher other pseudonyms by myself. Ben-David's autobiography is particularly problematic with respect to her past in France, regarding which we have only Uriel's brief testimony to confirm or refute her claims. In several other cases, such as the Second World War and her period in a French jail, I was able to find sources in French archives that supported Ben-David's own version of events.

Ben-David was a woman of contradictions: a lapsed Catholic who became a Haredi Jew; a free-thinking and promiscuous French woman who closed herself off in an environment that oppresses women; a devoted mother to an only son who caused immeasurable suffering to other parents who also had a son; a businesswoman in search of spirituality; a beautiful young woman who married an elderly and sterile man; someone who ostensibly found her placed in the traditional world of Meah Shearim, yet rebelled against the limited role of the submissive wife, fought to get what she wanted, and ultimately became almost a leader in her own right. How can we explain all these twists and turns? Before delving into Ben-David's biography, it is important to examine the psychological dimensions of conversion.

The psychology of conversion

Conversion has conventionally been regarded as an intellectual process of transformation that resolves the individual's questions of identity.[8] However, the scholar Chana Ullman has found that conversion can better be understood in the context of the individual's emotional life. It occurs against a background of emotional upheaval and promises relief through a new attachment. Conversion can be understood as a search for psychological salvation.

Ullman, who interviewed some 40 converts in the Boston area during the 1980s as part of her doctoral dissertation, argues that for the population of converts tested in her research, the religious quest is best understood in the context of a search sparked by emotional distress. The converts she interviewed were more likely to report an unhappy and stressful childhood. In addition, a sizable majority of the converts in her study described the two-year period preceding their conversion as fraught with negative emotions, and many reported that their conversion offered relief from this turmoil. The conversion process was an experience of love and acceptance; after their conversion, converts tend to espouse their religious beliefs more rigidly than non-converts.[9] In support of Ullman's conclusions, Paloutzian, Richardson, and Rambo have said that available evidence seems to indicate that people with a particular personality trait mixture might seek conversion as a way of dealing with life issues, finding expression through religion.[10]

One of Ullman's most interesting findings is that conversion stories often include a complex father-child relationship, including instances of an absent, passive, or aggressive father. She found that such relations occurred in around half of all cases she studied. Ullman claims that the emphasis on this relationship in the conversion stories suggests that it played a vital role in the religious transformation. Whereas converts tend to hold bad memories of their fathers, they develop an infatuation with a powerful authority figure who serves as a leader and mentor. Ullman suggests possible ties between the lack of benevolent parental presence and the actual conversion process.

Additional findings include the importance of the attachment to a new group of peers, as converts become members of a new community, and the role that powerful group dynamics often play in religious conversion.

This process of transformation endows the convert with new powers. A wish to unite with a perfect, idealized object, a sense of being pawned in a struggle of giants and yet being chosen or called for a special mission, and the perception of personalized miracles – these themes also viewed in Ullman's research among converts. She refers to these feelings as "narcissistic." Finally, in about one-fourth of the case studies in Ullman's research expressed the reason for their conversion in existential quest, an interest in ideological and existential questions that reach beyond the circumstances of the individual's life.[11] Ullman briefly mentions Ruth Ben-David's biography as a source that meets many of her findings; I will expand on it even more.

These psychological traits can illuminate the biography of Ruth Ben-David, who reported that she experienced an unhappy childhood with a tyrannical father; a life turmoil that ended up in jail prior to conversion; attachment to men "greater than life" as part of her conversion process; kidnapping a child through a sense of mission; and a need to prove herself fit for the community.

Childhood

Madeleine Lucette Ferraille was an only child born in 1920 in Calais in northern France. Her family moved to Paris when she was three. She describes her father Octave, an electrician by vocation, as an egotistical and weak-willed man with a tendency to materialism. She also notes – not by way of a compliment – that his external appearance resembled that of Charlie Chaplin. Her relations with her father were always tense due to what she saw as his aggressive behavior toward her mother.[12] The father imposed what she described as a spartan education on Madeleine. By way of example of his rigid approach, she recalls that he performed surgery on her without anesthetic in order to remove a piece of rotten wood from her knee. Nevertheless, she thanks him for having trained her to endure pain from her earliest childhood.[13] I should note that Ben-David did not mention her father's name in her autobiography, and I was obliged to locate this detail in other sources.

Madeleine was very fond of her mother, Jeanne Catherine Isaert, whom she describes as tall, thin, and beautiful: "She looked like an angel." Her mother died at the age of 54, after much suffering due to her stubborn husband.[14] Madeleine describes her maternal grandmother in positive terms as a beautiful and loved woman. In descriptions of her family background written after her conversion, Ben-David claimed that she was descended from the Marranos (Jews forced to convert to Christianity in sixteenth-century Spain), but who sometimes maintained certain Jewish practices. She argued that there is a strong probability, indeed very likely, that her mother's ancestral line is that of crypto-Jews from Spain.[15] Ben-David mentions several family customs that suggest Marrano roots: her grandmother was in the custom of boiling meat in water; they refrained from eating pork; and her grandmother's first name was Maginez, which Ben-David claims is a Jewish name. Ben-David sought to replicate the dichotomous model of Jews and inquisitors from the history of the Jews of Spain in her parents' home. She depicts her beloved mother striving to maintain the remnants of Jewish heritage in the way she cooked food, to the displeasure of her virulently anti-religious father. In his interview with the Jerusalem Post, Uriel Davidson (he changed his last name from Ben-David to Davidson) discussed his mother's attempts to claim a secret Jewish identity. He states that he spent much time with his grandmother as a child and has no recollection of the process of "koshering" meat that his mother described.[16] Ben-David's status as a convert – a newcomer to the Jewish world – irked her over the course of her life and created numerous problems.

Accordingly, it is only natural that she attempted to credit herself with a Jewish background, however flimsy. We may interpret Ben-David's narrative regarding her relations with her parents in a similar context. Having assumed a secret Jewish origin inherited through her maternal family, this side was accordingly depicted in glowing terms, while her father was portrayed as a cold and egotistical Christian with a brutal hostility to religion. I would add that, in general, Madeleine/Ruth describe agnosticism and anti-religiosity in dark terms as a force against which she was forced to wage an active struggle. Despite her predominantly negative depiction of her father, she thanks him for having given her various qualities that would usually be considered negative, such as stubbornness, rigidity, and a fanatical devotion to her goals.[17]

She claims that her doubts about the Church began at an early age. She refused to believe in the story of Father Christmas bringing toys down the chimney for the children.[18] She also claims that she refused to kiss the foot of an idol in St. Peter's Church due to hygienic concerns. She explains that these apparently incidental stories from her early childhood had a profound influence on her, convincing her that she wanted to seek the truth. Since the Catholic Church attached relatively little weight to the Old Testament and did not encourage its study, Madeleine rebelled by showing an interest in the Hebrew Bible.[19]

Madeleine's schooling from 1932 through 1939 coincided with a fateful period in French history. She mentions that she read Hitler's book *Mein Kampf* during this period and that her best friend was a Socialist. She recalls that while she did not know any Jews personally, her father had business associations with a number of Jews. She claims that one of these acquaintances asked to marry her when she was 17, but she turned down the proposal. She explains that this particular Jew was a Communist, and that even at this early stage she had a strong dislike for Communism.[20]

On September 5, 1939, a few days after the outbreak of the Second World War, Madeleine married Henri Baud. Baud was drafted for service immediately and Madeleine, who was 19 at the time, moved with her mother to Tarbes in the Pyrenees region of southwest France; Baud was stationed close by. The couple's son Claude (who would later be renamed Uriel) was born on October 1, 1940. In 1941 Madeleine was accepted to study classics at Toulouse University. While she progressed in life and acquired an education, she did not feel the same was true of Henri.[21] Madeleine sensed that she was wasting her time with her husband and was bored by their life together; she suddenly recognized that the only thing about him she found appealing was his external appearance. Determined to search for a deeper connection, she divorced Baud in 1942.

According to the narrative in her autobiography, Madeleine joined the French Resistance during the war and even helped to rescue Jews. She explains that she protected Jews and sheltered them in her home. She recalls in her autobiography traveling 700 kilometers from Tarbes to Nice in order to collect information for Jews who were living in her home, while leaving her baby son in the care of her mother and undertaking a perilous mission that could have cost her life. She reinforces the commitment to courage embodied in her descriptions by noting that her despised father received an award for heroism after the Liberation for his service in the Resistance.[22] She claims that she had no hesitation acting to save Jews, but notes that her mother was concerned that she would be caught by the Gestapo.[23] Uriel, however, refutes these stories, and commented: "She did many dangerous things during the war, but saving Jews was not one of them."[24] Conversely, the researcher Shalom Goldman claims that Madeleine "served as a courier between Resistance groups and on many occasions guided refugees to safety."[25]

A number of features are already becoming apparent in terms of Ben-David's autobiography. First, she shows a tendency to embellish her past and to create associations with Jews that in all probability did not actually exist. This tendency will be reinforced as we continue our exploration. Second, her son Uriel was not inclined to be charitable and refuted her claims in several instances; I will discuss the complex relationship between Ruth and her son Uriel below. The descriptions portray Ben-David as a brave, independent, and unusual woman. In the midst of a war, and while raising a newborn baby, she did not hesitate to divorce her husband and work in the Resistance, endangering herself and those dear to her. She had a strong social conscience and was willing to pay a heavy personal price for her principles. At the same time, she was selfish and not inclined to be considerate to those around her. In fact, the descriptions suggest that in many ways she was the image of her hated father – cold, rigid, tough, but a fierce fighter for liberty. We will return to these qualities later, particularly in our discussion of the Yossele Schumacher affair.

In 1947, Madeleine was accepted to advanced studies at the Sorbonne in philosophy and classics, after completing a degree in classics at Toulouse University. She worked as a translator to finance her studies, and looked for someone to take on the responsibility of caring for her son, who was now seven years old. After spending a year in Paris, Madeleine moved to Geneva to continue her research, placing her son in a Catholic boarding school. During this period she became involved in the insurance business, and in 1948 she opened a business importing chemicals from Switzerland to France while continuing to sell insurance policies.

An important episode in her life, and one she describes in detail, began when a family in Geneva refused to purchase a policy from her, declaring that her insurance was no good for them, because the Messiah is coming soon.[26] Madeleine became a close friend of the couple, who were members of the Seventh-Day Adventist Church, a Protestant movement whose members believe that they are chosen by God for redemption. Over the course of the twentieth century, the Seventh-Day Adventists announced six times that the End of Days was imminent. The members of the church observe a number of Jewish customs, including observance of the Sabbath (hence their name). Madeleine comments that she indeed met the couple in the city of Calvin, but she was the daughter of a Catholic mother and her son was enrolled at the time in a Catholic educational institution. She describes the jolting effect of her discussions with the couple. She began to study their doctrines one after the other. "I read all kinds of books at night, apart from long discussions I sometimes had during the day." During the same period, she attended Catholic services together with relatives of her father who lived in Geneva.[27]

Her friends' declaration that the Messiah was about to arrive, and their attempts to win her over to the Seventh-Day Adventist Church, had a profound influence on Madeleine. She did not consider them extremists and happily joined in their Sabbath meals. In a comment that underscores some similarities between this movement and Judaism, she recalls that she found the Friday night meals pleasant and interesting, and she was able to discuss the Old Testament with them. "I had acquired a certain respect for their way of life and their zeal."[28] The draft describes in detail her affectionate response to the couple, but the relationship was omitted from the book she published in Hebrew. Her connection with the couple shows that she began her spiritual search within the confines of Christianity and only later found her way to Judaism.

In 1948 Ruth suffered a stroke of misfortune after her business failed. She was accused of fraud and obliged to pay a substantial fine. She had been living in Geneva illegally and was eventually forced to leave the city. It is possible that this coerced departure led to the disruption of her connection with her Adventist friends. She returned to Paris, removed Claude from the Catholic school he had been attending, and enrolled him at a school in the country under the watchful eye of one of her friends. She met with her son at the weekends while continuing to work on her doctorate in Paris, devoting much of her time to reading works in the history of religions.

During this period Madeleine was disappointed with the poor moral standards of society at large and sought comfort in religion. She describes her situation in the following terms:

> As time went on troubles mounted, living alone with no family other than my infant son, almost secluded from society in which I was disillusioned, the burdens which fate had assigned to me became even more unbearable. I looked and searched for a spiritual satisfaction.[29]

Madeleine was attracted to the compassion and unconditional love (including love for one's enemies) advocated by Christianity, particularly as manifested in Jesus' Sermon on the Mount (Matthew 5–7). However, she was unable to overlook the hostility of the New Testament toward those who refused to adopt faith in Christ. She quotes: "Woe to thee Chorazein, woe to thee Bethsaida . . . thou wilt be thrown into hell" (Luke 10:13).[30] She found little mercy, love, and tolerance in the Gospels, but by contrast felt this value system was better represented in the Prophets. The values she sought in this period led her to reconsider her own faith. The gulf between the lofty standards of faith in Christ and their human implementation, including the Inquisitions and the Crusades, led her to question the essence of Christianity. As noted, Madeleine was raised in an agnostic home; she quotes her father's fierce attacks against the Christian religion. While her father found the antithesis to Christianity in his anti-religious fervor, Madeleine turned to the morality of the Prophets:

> Perhaps that was why the genuine humanity of the Pentateuch and the Psalms had such appeal to me. . . . I read the word of G-d through Moses and the

prophets, that calls his children back to him, and grants his forgiveness to patient sinners; the promise to eternal life and peace to the world.[31]

In an effort to overcome her spiritual doubts, Madeleine went to speak with a Catholic priest called Father Vincent, with whom she still maintained friendly contact at the time the biography was written. She remarked that one of the books he gave her – Edouard Schure's *Les Grands Initiés* – impressed her considerably.[32] First published in France in 1889, this book describes the author's lifelong quest for spiritual truth. The book examines the lives and deeds of human beings of exceptional stature: Rama, Krishna, Hermes, Moses, Orpheus, Pythagoras, Plato, and Jesus. Of these figures, Madeleine was particularly impressed by the character of Pythagoras. Schure's interest in the Greek philosopher led her to explore the world of philosophy. In the biography that was published only in draft form, she devotes many pages to quotes from the writings of Pythagoras: "I was so impressed by the writing and ideas of Pythagoras that I started to seek for commentaries or reviews on this remarkable philosopher. . . . I felt that his writings spoke directly to me."[33]

A principle of Greek philosophy Madeleine found particularly impressive was the belief that man has the means of mastering his passions by subjecting them to the might of his free will. She found in Greek philosophy a refuge from a world enslaved to political doctrines that fostered despair and sacrificed individuals for the good of the nation, class, or race. As noted, Madeleine's intense interest in religion and philosophy came during a period of personal crisis, including her expulsion from Geneva and her conviction for financial offenses, and at a time when she had been living on her own for several months. It is important to bear in mind that she had something of a tendency to depression and was undoubtedly undergoing a profound personal crisis at this time. The absolute political ideologies such as Communism, Nazism, and nationalism that were playing a central role in Europe at the time utterly repelled Madeleine. She also remained unimpressed by Catholicism, expressing doubts about the place of eschatology and the idea of the physical Second Coming of Christ.

In the summer of 1951, she abandoned philosophy and decided to move to what she saw as the source. It was Judaism that answered to her sense of universalism, to her concept of unity, to her need for satisfying thought, and "above all, to an inner call which developed and grew even stronger."[34] In the Bible, she found the roots, people, and truth she had been seeking.

Madeleine wished to convert to Judaism, but was not acquainted with any Jews. In an attempt to find a solution, her attention began to focus on the State of Israel. She met two Israelis who were involved in research in the French National Library; she became friendly with them and they even taught her Hebrew. A year later, one of the two men, whom she names as Simon (possibly a pseudonym), proposed to her, but she declined the offer. She was eager to join the Jewish people, but her suitor in this instance lacked the religious sentiments she was seeking. In the spring of 1951, she decided to visit Israel and consider the marriage proposal in greater depth. She reports that Simon's family welcomed her warmly and affectionately. Simon was a fervent Zionist, but as noted was not religious. "I wanted to come and live among Jews, in order to worship God and serve Him – not to sing Hatikva, even though I was not unmoved when this Israeli anthem was sung."[35] This quote is revealing, showing that despite her proclaimed lack of interest in the national dimension of Judaism, she tersely admits to being moved by the Israeli national anthem. Her unpublished autobiography includes additional comments showing that she had a positive attitude toward Zionism during her early years as a convert.

Her month-long visit to Israel "passed like a dream." She reluctantly returned to France, but not before promising to return to Israel after she completed her conversion. A professor at the Hebrew University of Jerusalem put her in touch with Rabbi André Zaoui (1916–2009), a Reform rabbi based in Paris, and she visited him in March after returning from Israel.[36] Zaoui was one of the pillars of French Jewry in the postwar period, an active intellectual who authored a number of books. He also translated Maimonides' letters into French.[37]

On page 79 of Ben-David's unpublished autobiography, a number of sentences were deleted by pen. Deciphering these lines reveals a significant detail: when Madeleine met with Zaoui and explained that she was interested in converting, she stated that her motivation was her desire to marry an Israeli man. In fact, she reached this decision at an earlier stage, though she postponed its implementation. Thus, while she indeed showed an interest in Judaism, her decision to convert indeed seems to have come after she met a man she considered suitable. In the Orthodox Jewish world, such a motivation is unacceptable – a "true convert" is by definition someone who chooses Judaism for pure motives, and not on the basis of any mundane self-interest, such as marriage.[38]

Madeleine underwent a Reform conversion, including the partial observance of the ritual commandments, such as the prohibition against eating pork and the partial avoidance of labor on the Sabbath. She claims that her conversion became a historic event in the history of the Reform Jewish community in France in the postwar era. However, in my interview with Zaoui's widow, she claimed that there were in fact a considerable number of converts to Judaism in this period, in a reaction to the Holocaust.[39] My attempts to clarify this point with the community itself did not enable me to reach a clear conclusion regarding these opposing assessments. The community stated that its conversion archives were destroyed after the building was flooded.[40]

While she was still undergoing the conversion process, Madeleine informed Simon that she did not intend to marry him. Thus her decision to complete the conversion she had begun indeed reflects pure motives, and indeed it is possible that she chose not to marry her suitor in order to prevent any blemish on her intentions in this regard. She reports that her friends and family were less than enthusiastic about her decision to convert, and in particular opposed the inclusion of her son in this process. Meanwhile, she gradually reached the conclusion that Reform Judaism was not spiritually satisfying for her.[41] Although she declared with hindsight that she opposed the approach of Reform Judaism from a principled standpoint, she was extremely positive in her comments about Rabbi Zaoui, who converted her and brought her into the world of Judaism. Reform Judaism was her entrance gate, and at the time when she went to pray in the Reform synagogue in Paris, she was unfamiliar with the different streams in Judaism and had never even heard of Neturei Karta. She completed her personal transformation by changing her name to Ruth Ben-David – a name suggested by Zaoui. The biblical Ruth was, of course, a convert herself, and accordingly this is a particularly popular name among female converts. According to the Bible, Ruth was the grandmother of King David – a further factor behind her choice of this name.

In May 1952, she left the Reform synagogue and entered the Mizrachi movement – the bastion of Orthodox Zionism. She became involved in the circles around the Consistoire, the umbrella organization of French Jewry, where she met Jean Poliatschek, a Modern Orthodox rabbi, in an encounter that would eventually bring her much heartache. As we have noted, Ruth was an attractive woman, and many men were captivated by her charms. Like others, Rabbi Poliatschek fell in love with her and wanted to marry her. She describes how the entire Jewish community stood firm in its opposition to the relationship, led by young single Jewish women and their mothers who hoped to provide the rabbi with an alternative match. The rabbi's insistence on marrying Ruth divided the community; Ruth faced accusations that her conversion had been insincere, and that she had converted in order to marry Poliatschek. After this claim was proved to be inaccurate, it was alleged that she converted in order to marry Simon. When this argument was also shown to be incorrect, criticism focused on her Reform conversion. Decades of animosity between the two movements have shown beyond all doubt that Orthodox Judaism does not accept Reform conversions.[42] The struggle over Ben-David's good name lasted for several months, as she fought for her right to marry a Jew, and even a rabbi. Ben-David identified two possible solutions to the challenges she faced. First, she would have to undergo a second conversion, this time of an Orthodox character. Second, the couple would need to marry outside France. These two decisions proved to be fateful to the future course of her life. Over a decade later, she would be forced to confront a similar situation within the world of Haredi Judaism when she sought to marry Amram Blau despite the united opposition of the Haredi community.

Rabbi Poliatschek introduced Ruth to Abraham Elijah Maizes, a strict Haredi rabbi who had managed to flee the oppressive regime in the Soviet Union and reach France. She recalls that Maizes took an interest in her plight and led her to understand that her ordeal arose from Heaven's will.[43] The rabbi convinced her that her problems were the result of predestination, and her acceptance of this belief represents a retreat from her earlier adherence to the principle of free will. She now accepted that she was doomed to suffer in the complicated situation in which she had become embroiled – a situation that was exacerbated by further developments on the financial front.

During this period, Ruth was a successful businesswoman active in importing merchandise to France. Her business partner was a Jewish man called Leon Swergold. In December 1952, Ruth was arrested by the French customs authorities on suspicion of tax evasion in the sum of 39 million francs (about $1.5 million at the

2015 rate[44]). She was convicted and states that she spent two months in jail. In her autobiography, Ruth claims that her business partner deceived her and was responsible for the massive tax evasion. Uriel claimed that Swergold fled first to Israel and later to the United States after the French authorities requested his extradition.[45] This claim is problematic, since Israel and France only signed an extradition agreement in 1958.[46] I found evidence at the court in New York of a commercial suit filed against Swergold and his brother Maurice, who were the directors of a company called Corta Corporation. In 1952 Swergold was fined approximately $20,000 for failing to pay his debts.[47] These findings suggest that while Ruth was penalized severely, spending time in prison, her business partner received a relatively lenient fine from the court. As will be recalled, this was the second time that Ruth had been apprehended for tax evasion. In the first incident she was fined, and only after the second offense was she sentenced to prison. Ruth claims that during her time in prison she suffered from the anti-Semitic attitudes of the warders. She claimed that her health deteriorated due to the poor quality of the food and her limited diet, due to the laws of kashrut; in general, her condition was poor during this period.

After her release from prison she continued the conversion process, this time through an Orthodox rabbi. At the same time, her fiancé left his position in France, and together they emigrated to Israel, planning to marry. Ruth intended to return to France after the wedding in order to sell her businesses and property and in order to close her debt with the tax authorities, which was estimated at some 30 million francs.

A date was set for the wedding and Ruth rented an apartment in Jerusalem. She planned to place her son in a school on Kvutzat Yavne, a Religious-Zionist kibbutz. However, it appears that her fiancé had many reservations about the match, and accordingly Ruth decided to cancel the wedding and return to France. Her son Uriel adhered to the original plan and emigrated to Israel. In her autobiography Ruth describes the groom who abandoned her before the wedding in extremely unflattering terms, as a weak man with a tortured soul.[48]

Returning to France after the failure of her engagement, Ruth found a new spiritual mentor in the form of Rabbi Leon Ashkenazi (1922–1996), spending every Sabbath and festival in his Beit Midrash. Ashkenazi was one of the leading figures involved in the rebuilding of French Jewry after the Holocaust, and he adhered to an educational approach based on a combination of Orthodox Jewish principles and a modern lifestyle. Following the Six Day War of 1967, Ashkenazi became identified with Merkaz HaRav and Rabbi Zvi Yehuda Kook – the core of Israeli Orthodox Zionism. Rabbi Ashkenazi became principal of the Orsay School in 1951, while Professor André Neher served as president.[49]

In 1954 Ruth visited Israel for the third time. However, she explains that by this visit the charm of Orthodox Zionism had begun to fade. She found herself unable to share the Zionist enthusiasm that dominated the Jewish world of the time.

> Their hearts overfilled with joy seeing a State of their own, with soldiers, sailors and airmen, officers and generals, ambassadors and that goes to make a state. The Jewish people, especially after the most terrible episode in their

history – the Hitler epoch – with its indescribable and untold horror, embrace the sight of marching armies of their own with tanks on the ground, airplanes in the sky, and ships in the seas, as something which could not be less than their ultimate goal. . . .

I, by virtue of my past, could not look upon all that with much excitement and emotion. Military parades with uniformed participants could not evoke in me elevation of the spirit. . . . The height of its military prowess did not keep me from leaving the French People, and how could I think that in much smaller measure such prowess should now constitute my hopes. . . .

I have left all my past, all my natural bonds, all the human attachment to family and friends. I have forsaken my land and my people, and crushed the gates of Judaism, for height reasons, for the longing of my soul to be included in the eternity and the holiness of the Jewish people; to participate in their sorrow and to share their hopes for eternal glory.[50]

This quote provides several insights into Ruth's character. She could understand why so many Jews were attracted to Zionism as a response to genuine distress, and she accepted that for those born Jews, Jewish sovereignty could be seen as the height of their aspiration. But for herself, as a convert, manifestations of nationalism held no particular interest: her motivation in joining the Jewish people had been spiritual and not national. As a native of the French people, she could have confined herself to French nationhood, which she claims is far more impressive, with larger military parades.

It is interesting here to turn to Ruth's son Uriel, who paints a very different picture:

He [Uriel] believes that the establishment of the State of Israel made a great impression on her. She visited Israel for the first time in 1949 and came away fired with Zionist fervor. She became a member of French WIZO, and paid dues from 1950 to 1953.[51]

Uriel's testimony appears to be credible. Ruth indeed visited Israel in 1951 (Uriel appears to have made a mistake regarding the year), against the background of her intention of marrying a secular Israeli. Her own remarks as quoted above support the conclusion that she could understand the appeal of Zionism. The Orthodox circles in which she moved at this time; Kvutzat Yavne, the kibbutz identified with Hapoel Hamizrachi where her son lived; and her friendship with Rabbi Leon Ashkenazi and circles close to the Consistoire all confirm her affiliation in this period with Modern Orthodoxy and Orthodox Zionism. Ruth was clearly a supporter of the Zionist enterprise at this point, made donations to its institutions on a regular basis, and was moved on hearing its anthem. However, she was disturbed by the fact that the Zionism of the time was essentially a secular movement detached from the observance of the commandments. At this stage, she admits, she did not yet understand what she found lacking in this religious experience, but she sensed that Zionism as a national movement could not meet her spiritual needs. As we have seen, her own narrative highlighted her suspicions regarding nationalism in general, and all the more so Jewish nationalism:

> I came to Judaism because of the impression that Judaism made on me. . . . What moved me was Jewish teaching – the teaching of the Torah. During the past six years I have learned a lot of these teachings. . . . At the time of my conversion Zionism was at the height of its popularity. . . . Six year ago, when I was last in Israel, I was, at times, carried away by general enthusiasm. . . . During the last six year, in which I became closer to the real Jewish religious concepts, I have moved still further away from my non-Jewish past and, together with that, from Zionism in which I could not see more than the provision of a non-Jewish concept for the Jewish people.[52]

Ruth increasingly identified with the paradigm of the Haredi world, according to which Zionism is a secular-nationalist movement that lacks any religious sentiment, and indeed is sometimes hostile to such sentiment. She came to see the desire of Reform Judaism or Orthodox Zionism, through which she had entered the world of Judaism, to strike a balance between the modern world and the Jewish religion, as a distasteful compromise that she was no longer willing to support. Moreover, in this period ultra-Orthodoxy was not resolutely anti-Zionist, and the Agudat Yisrael movement, which represented the Haredi community, actively cooperated with the Zionist enterprise.[53] In ideological terms, Ruth was attracted to the most extreme Haredi circles, led by Neturei Karta, who opposed and fought against Zionism. We can discern here a process of increasing extremism fueled by a desire for spiritual perfection. The Reform synagogue or the Consistoire contained modernity and saw no contradiction between a modern lifestyle and Judaism. For Ruth, by contrast, her disconnection from Catholicism also implied the abandonment of the modern way of life and its values, including the value of nationalism. She found the archetype of absolute Judaism and absolute truth in the character of Rabbi Maizes, whom as we saw above she had already met in France. This explains the important role Maizes played in shaping the religious practices Ruth later adopted. As Ullman has shown, the process of conversion often entails an attachment to a charismatic figure. Maizes provided Ruth with a role model and a source of imitation.[54]

Ruth again returned from Israel to France, moving her son from Kvutzat Yavne to Rabbi Ashkenazi's yeshiva. However, the yeshiva later closed due to financial difficulties. In 1956, on Maizes' advice, she enrolled Uriel at Yeshivat Chachmei Tzarfat, a stricter Haredi yeshiva in Aix-les-Bains. Uriel found it difficult to settle in his new surroundings, although the yeshiva combined religious and secular studies, but the connection with the institution was to prove critical for Ruth. Her abandonment of Zionism and her affiliation with ultra-Orthodoxy were closely related to the bond she developed with this institution:

> I felt during the Sabbaths I spent in Aix-les-Bains that spiritually, after many years, after many peregrinations and misfortunes, I have reached port. . . . I

found in this environment brotherhood, equality and peace of mind, complete observance of the mitzvoth and endeavor to help others to understand and draw ever nearer to true Jewishness.[55]

In the Haredi lifestyle, Ruth found a balm for the psychological difficulties and personal disappointments she had experienced during this period. As we have seen, this was a critical junction in her life, after she spent months in prison and following the failure of her engagement. She was required to modify her dress on entering the yeshiva and to adopt to the code of modesty of Haredi Judaism. She was captivated by the insular and isolationist character of this world and joined its struggle against modernity.[56]

Yet here, too, Ruth failed to find the respite she sought. After rumors spread that she was a convert, and it was even alleged that she had attempted to woo Rabbi Yitzhak Haikin, the rabbi of the institution, she was forced to leave the yeshiva. Nevertheless, she continued to be attracted to the Haredi lifestyle. Her conclusion was that she should live in the Haredi enclave in Jerusalem, close to Rabbi Maizes.[57] She left France in March 1960; her son had already left the yeshiva a year before, and was already living in Jerusalem under the supervision of Rabbi Maizes.

The Yossele Schumacher affair

Ruth depicts Rabbi Abraham Eliyahu Maizes (1901–1961) as the epitome of the modern martyr. Maizes grew up in the town of Slutsk in Belarus, was impoverished both physically and spiritually, and suffered appalling persecution at the hands of the Communist authorities and their Jewish supporters in the Yevsektzia. The rabbi was willing to give up his life in order to maintain traditional Jewish life, and he indeed paid a heavy price. He was harassed, tortured, and interrogated, and eventually sentenced to seven years' exile in Siberia. After returning from exile, he managed to leave the Soviet Union and reach France, teaching at a yeshiva in Bailly, near Paris, that had absorbed many refugees and Holocaust survivors. In 1953 he emigrated to Israel, joining and later heading the Torah VeYirah Yeshiva, which was affiliated to the anti-Zionist Neturei Karta movement. Ruth claims that Maizes agreed to serve as head of the yeshiva since he considered Zionism to be no less evil than Communism, and he was determined to continue his war against atheism. She was inspired by the fiery rabbi: "Maizes was of very high intelligence and with deep penetrating eyes."[58]

After arriving in Israel, Ruth bought an apartment in the Bayit VaGan neighborhood of Jerusalem, which at the time was a bastion of the Orthodox Zionist community. She found work as an interpreter. One day, Rabbi Maizes asked her to come to him urgently. In their meeting, the rabbi asked her to take a young boy called Yossele Schumacher outside the borders of Israel.

At the time this meeting took place, Schumacher had already been kidnapped for several months. The seven-year-old boy (born in 1952) was the son of Alter and Ida Schumacher. Alter, who was born in Poland, married Ida (née Straks), whose father Nachman was a member of the Breslov Hasidic sect who had been raised and educated in Uman, Ukraine. Nachman Straks' biography is striking similar to that of Rabbi Maizes. He also maintained a traditional Jewish identity under the Communist regime; he, too, was sent to Siberia to perform forced labor, losing his sight in one eye and losing several toes to the freezing cold. Like Maizes, Nachman Straks was a rigid man who struggled against Communist anti-religious coercion and managed to leave the Soviet Union after paying a heavy personal price. Straks and Maizes, two strong and long-suffering men who had survived the torture chambers of Siberian prisons, threw themselves into the efforts to "save" the young child. For Ruth, Straks was also a "martyr."[59]

After his daughter married a resident of Poland, the Straks family managed to secure a Soviet emigration visa in 1957. The grandfather Nachman and his wife Miriam settled among the Breslov Hasidim in Meah Shearim in Jerusalem. Their son Shalom, Ida's brother, was affiliated with the Chabad Hasidim and studied in the movement's institutions in Lod. Ida and Alter, however, did not maintain a Haredi lifestyle. Because of their economic difficulties and their uncertainty as to where they would establish their home, the parents decided that their two children – Yossele and Zena – should temporarily remain under the responsibility of the grandfather and brother, who gave them a Haredi education. The daughter Zena was sent to live in a Chabad residential school, while Yossele received a traditional religious education in a "Cheder" in Meah Shearim. It should be noted that in Soviet culture it was relatively common for grandparents to raise the children while their parents went out to work. The family met together at the parents' home in Jerusalem every Sabbath.

After some time, the parents Ida and Alter signed a contract to purchase a small apartment in a housing project in Holon and asked to take the children back into their care. The daughter Zena was taken out of the Chabad institutions and returned to her mother, while the parents enrolled Yossele at a state-religious school in Holon. The grandfather disapproved of the decision to remove the boy from his responsibility and decided not to return him to his parents. He asked his son for assistance, and Shalom smuggled the boy out of Meah Shearim, hiding him in Rishon Lezion, Safed, and Moshav Komemiyut in the Negev.[60] The parents turned to the court, which ordered the grandfather to return the boy to his parents. However, the grandfather claimed that had no information as to the child's whereabouts. In the meantime, the brother, Shalom Straks, had fled Israel and settled in the Chabad community in London. The court ordered that the grandfather be held in prison until he provided information leading to the boy's return, and issued an extradition request for the brother. The police undertook 270 raids in Haredi strongholds in an effort to locate Yossele, but without success. As the police began to close in on the location where Yossele was being held and to undertake arrests in Moshav Komemiyut, those involved in the kidnapping decided that the boy must be smuggled out of Israel.

As noted above, Maizes had considerable power over Ruth, who strongly admired the charismatic rabbi. He asked her to help in the affair, claiming that the father Alter was an ardent Communist who was disillusioned with life in Israel and planned to return to the Soviet Union together with his children. There they would inevitably abandon their religious Jewish lifestyle. Neturei Karta justified the kidnapping according to the traditional maxim that "the preservation of a human soul overrides the Sabbath" – by extension, in order to save the boy's spiritual soul it is permissible to kidnap him and ensure he receives an Orthodox education.[61] In an interview with the journalist Tom Segev in 2014, Yossi Schumacher stated that his kidnappers justified their actions to him by claiming that his father was planning to turn him into a Christian.[62] As a child raised in Haredi institutions, Yossele was horrified at this intention, and accordingly cooperated with his kidnappers. In her book, Ruth quotes the boy as saying "they don't want me to be a proper Jew."[63] Ruth herself was equally appalled at the father's ostensible intention to return a pure Jewish soul to the Soviet Union and detach him from Judaism.

The claim that the father was an ardent Communist who planned to return to the Soviet Union was completely groundless. Isser Harel disproved this version in his book on the Schumacher affair.[64] From any objective perspective, the story raises serious problems. If Alter Schumacher was so firm in his Communist beliefs, why did he leave the Soviet Union? If he was fiercely anti-religious, why did he marry the daughter of a Breslov Hasid and enroll his children in religious and even Haredi institutions? If he was planning to return to the Soviet Union, why did he purchase a house in Israel? The parents chose a state-religious (i.e., Orthodox Zionist) school for their son. It seems unlikely that a Communist planning to return to the Soviet Union would make such an educational decision.

The person responsible for hiding Yossele in Israel was Aryeh Schechter, who served as the personal aide of Rabbi Yaakov Yisrael Kanievsky (1899–1985, commonly known as "the Steipler"). Kanievsky was one of the leaders of the Haredi public in Bnei Brak and was well-known for his criticism of Agudat Yisrael.[65] Maizes put Ruth in touch with Schechter, who introduced her to Yossele. Thus it emerges that Kanievsky, one of the leaders of the Haredi community, was involved in the kidnapping affair, at least in its early stages. Ruth justified her willingness to get involved in the kidnapping as follows:

> I drew my courage from the aim of my mission, from the sincerity and authority of Rav Maizes, from the fact that I was rescuing a child from Atheism, Communism and the misguided ways into which his parents were bent on leading him.[66]

The supporters of the kidnapping in the Haredi world managed to obtain a declaration of support for the action from Rabbi Tsvi Pesach Frank (1873–1960), the chief rabbi of Jerusalem, shortly before his death. They presented the rabbi with a distorted version of events, again claiming that the father was planning to return to the Soviet Union together with his son. Frank released a letter supporting the grandfather's actions in concealing Yossele, and declared that "Mr. Starks is duty bound to prevent his grandson from leaving the Land of Israel for such a place where apostasy is carried out on Jews."[67]

The kidnapping and concealment of Yossele Schumacher reverberated around Israel and the Jewish world. The Knesset held three debates on the subject, and several members of the Knesset accused the Haredi public in general of supporting the action and hiding the boy.[68] The government also discussed the affair on several occasions. David Ben-Gurion accused the Orthodox Zionist rabbis of remaining silent on the subject, alluding to Rabbi Frank's support for the kidnapping.[69]

Member of Knesset Shlomo Lorentz from Agudat Yisrael attempted to mediate in order to secure the return of the child to his parents, in return for which the parents would undertake to appoint a guardian to ensure that the child received an Orthodox education, but the kidnappers rejected the proposal.[70]

Ruth returned to Geneva and forged her passport to change her son's name from Claude to Claudine. She replaced the child's picture with a photograph of Yossele disguised as a girl. She returned to Israel with the forged passport, sailing from Marseille on a ship carrying Jewish immigrants from Morocco. During the journey, which took several days, she met a family with a large number of children, one of whom was a ten-year-old girl called Claudine. Ruth became friendly with Claudine and even invited her to sleep with her in her berth on the ship. When the vessel docked in Haifa, Ruth managed to trick the immigration authorities, presenting Claudine as the "daughter" who appeared in her passport. She interpreted this coincidental meeting as divine providence and as evidence of the justice of her actions.[71] After arriving in Israel she disguised Yossele as a girl and managed to take him out of Israel as her "daughter" Claudine, taking a flight from Tel Aviv to Italy on June 21, 1960.

As part of her justifications for her actions, Ruth portrayed the cruel Communist father and the apathetic mother Ida, who left her son in her parents' charge due to her lack of interest in his well-being.[72] I found these descriptions fascinating. Ruth herself barely raised her own son. When he was still a baby, she left him in her mother's care while she studied at university. Later she always found institutions, friends, or relatives to look after him while she devoted herself to her studies, business, and spiritual searches. It is not unreasonable to hypothesize that her descriptions of Yossele's parents reflected her feelings regarding her own family: in Yossele's father she may have seen the image of her own agnostic father, while she cast herself in the character of the boy's mother, distant and uninvolved.

Ruth offered a whole series of additional justifications for her actions. She claimed that the affair was not a kidnapping but an outbreak of antagonism and propaganda against Orthodox Judaism: "The mother and father knew that Yossele was well and safe."[73] She emphasized that the action served a religious purpose. Ruth internalized the propaganda of Neturei Karta and labeled Agudat Yisrael "double agents"[74] due to their attempts to find a compromise in the affair. Moreover, she claimed that Yossele himself was grateful that he had been kidnapped: "His face was filled with happiness and his eyes reflected an immense gratitude."[75] She claimed that the kidnapping enjoyed widespread support, including the approval of Rabbi Pesach Frank, a Zionist rabbi. She also referred to the Youth Aliyah organization, which brought tens of thousands of young Jews from the Arab countries to Israel. The youths came to Israel before their parents and underwent a process of socialization in the country, particularly in the kibbutzim. The religious public was critical of the program, since most of the youths abandoned their religious lifestyle, sometimes under coercion. Ruth argued that the Zionists were kidnapping thousands of children from the Orient and leading them to spiritual annihilation, while she merely sought to save one child from such annihilation. Accordingly, she should be regarded not as kidnapping Yossele but as saving him, while the Zionist establishment – which portrayed itself as the boy's savior – was the true kidnapper.[76]

Ruth's rigid character and her absolute devotion to the task of kidnapping the boy, rejecting any counter-arguments, were enhanced by the moral support she received from Neturei Karta. This strengthened her conviction that her course of action was just.

Ruth quickly proceeded from Rome to Lucerne, Switzerland, placing Yossele in a yeshiva under the responsibility of Rabbi Moshe Soloveitchik (1914–1995), who was a friend of Rabbi Kanievsky, and of the Satmar Rebbe Yoel Teitelbaum. Teitelbaum was the leader of the anti-Zionist faction within the Haredi world. He spent nine months in Switzerland in 1944 after he was able to leave Hungary on the "Kastner Train," thereby avoiding the annihilation that befell Hungarian Jewry. Soloveitchik hosted Teitelbaum in his yeshiva in Switzerland, and the two men continued to cooperate on various issues over subsequent years.[77]

Soloveitchik agreed to admit "Claudine" to the yeshiva. Yossele resumed his identity as a boy, under the pseudonym Menachem Levi. Ruth left him at the yeshiva and traveled to London to meet with Yerachmiel Domb, a successful businessman and supporter of Neturei Karta, who offered her logistical support and raised funds for her. Isser Harel claimed that the committee that was ostensibly formed to raise funds for the legal defense of Nachman and Shalom Straks actually collected money to pay for the concealment of Yossele Schumacher.[78]

From London, Ruth returned to Israel to consult with Rabbi Kanievsky. She reports that the rabbi suggested that the boy undergo plastic surgery on his face in order to prevent his identification. In a gesture that was very important to her, the rabbi handed her a letter of support that she could show to Orthodox rabbis in the Diaspora in order to secure their assistance in concealing the boy. Kanievsky did not come from the maverick circles of Satmar or Neturei Karta, but represented the mainstream of the Haredi establishment at the time. He was one of the heads of Yeshivat Poniwiecz, the flagship institution of the Haredi world. His support for the kidnapping, and his suggestion to alter Yossele's appearance by plastic surgery, illustrate the strong support for the action among the Haredi public.[79] Neturei Karta was embroiled in protracted struggles with the State of Israel at the time regarding the character of the Sabbath in Jerusalem, and the broader Haredi public generally supported these struggles, which includes numerous demonstrations. The kidnapping of Yossele Schumacher constituted a further plank in the series of clashes between the Haredi and secular publics at the time.

During his time in Israel, Ruth's son Uriel joined the military. Six years of studies in Haredi and even anti-Zionist yeshivas had not led the young man to join the Haredi camp. On the contrary, Uriel argued that there was no contradiction between the state and religion, and that the Jewish people could be a nation like any other. Ruth's response is surprising: "I was happy and proud to see all this."[80] She certainly disagreed with his nationalist approach, but she was nevertheless proud that her brave son was to become an Israeli soldier.

After a year in Lucerne, Ruth decided to move Yossele to France for safety's sake. Again disguising him as "Claudine," she took him to the yeshiva in Aix-les-Bains, and then returned to Israel in order to prepare for her permanent move to the country. She found work as a French teacher. Thus we see that, with the exception of brief contact during Yossele's transfers from one place to the next, Ruth left him under the full responsibility of foster families – a similar course of action to that she had adopted with regard to her own son.

Rabbi Maizes died in 1961. His role in managing the Yossele affair for Neturei Karta was assumed by Rabbi Aharon Katzenelbogen, Amram Blau's partner in the leadership of the movement. On Katzenelbogen's advice Ruth returned to France. She subsequently traveled to Morocco in an attempt to find a place for Yossele among followers of Chabad in Casablanca. As noted above, the child's uncle Shalom Straks, a follower of Chabad, had been involved in the early stages of the kidnapping. Given the highly centralized nature of a Hasidic sect, it is impossible that the movement's leader Rabbi Menachem-Mendel Schneerson (the "Lubavitcher Rebbe") was unaware of this involvement. After Yossele was transferred into the care of Neturei Karta, Schneerson decided not to continue to cooperate with the operation. Accordingly, Ruth met with a cool response when she visited the Chabad followers in Morocco and they refused to join her plan. In her book, Ruth is sharply critical of the Lubavitcher Rebbe for his refusal to help and for instructing his followers to ignore her pleas for help. However, it should be emphasized that despite desperate requests from Agudat Yisrael, the Lubavitcher Rebbe does not seem to have helped in the efforts to locate the child. His position was that no assistance should be offered to the kidnappers, but at the same time the boy must not be handed over to the authorities.[81] This approach echoes the Halachic principle of *din moser* (the Law of the Informer): according to Jewish religious law, a Jew must not inform to the authorities on another Jew, and any disputes must be resolved within the Jewish community.[82] Thus, in general, the Haredi world did not support the kidnapping and attempted to find a compromise that would allow the affair to be resolved in a dignified manner, while ensuring that all those involved would be pardoned. However, the Haredi circles did not cooperate with the investigation of provide vital details needed to locate the child, despite the fact that this information was known to a number of figures involved in the affair, including the Lubavitcher Rebbe and Rabbi Kanievsky.[83] The principle of Haredi solidarity evidently required them not to reveal information about the child's whereabouts or about those involved in the kidnapping.

As the authorities began to close in, Ruth traveled to New York to meet with Rabbi Yoel Teitelbaum, the Satmar Rebbe. In her autobiography, Ruth is very careful not to incriminate Teitelbaum or to implicate him in the kidnapping. Accordingly, she does not describe any meetings with him on this subject. Though she criticizes American Haredi leaders, including Rabbi Aharon Kotler and the

Lubavitcher Rebbe, for failing to help her, she has nothing but praise for Teitelbaum. Reading between the lines, it is clear that he helped her in connection with the Yossele affair. Teitelbaum informed the press that he was not involved in the kidnapping: "I was unaware of Yossele's whereabouts from the day he disappeared in Israel and until he was found, on Saturday evening in New York."[84] An interesting testimony regarding a meeting that is not mentioned in Ruth's book, but which nevertheless took place, is provided by Isser Harel. Mossad agents who had penetrated the Haredi community in Antwerp heard an anecdotal rumor that helped them focus their investigations on Ruth. A woman in the community told a Mossad agent that when she visited the Satmar Rebbe in New York, she had been forced to wait for three hours after he entered into an unscheduled meeting. She was amazed to see Ruth leaving the Rebbe's office after such a protracted consultation.[85] In her book, Ruth relates that she became very friendly with the Rebbe's wife, Alte-Feige, whom she visited on a daily basis over a period of five months.[86] She put Ruth in touch with the Gertner family, who subsequently hid Yossele in New York. Alte-Feige was a very powerful figure within the Satmar movement; it is impossible that Ruth had a close relationship with her without her husband knowing anything about the Yossele affair. Ruth claims, somewhat implausibly, that while she did meet the Rebbe,[87] their conversation revolved solely around her financial troubles and she did not share with him the secret of the kidnapping. A list of all those involved in the affair, in their real names, appears in the archived draft. This list includes Rabbi Maizes, Katzenelbogen, and Domb, well as Alte-Feige Teitelbaum. Are we really to believe that Yoel Teitelbaum alone was left out of the picture?

A newspaper article that appeared in February 1961 caused Ruth great anxiety. The article claimed that the Israeli government had announced that it knew that Yossele was in France and was in the charge of a French citizen who had recently visited New York. Ruth realized that she must again move the boy to a new hiding place. By this point, the entire Haredi world was opposed to the kidnapping. Agudat Yisrael was working to find a compromise, and even Chabad was unwilling to help conceal the boy. Ruth was obliged to turn elsewhere. The idea of taking Yossele to Morocco was abandoned, since the boy spoke only Yiddish, and would accordingly stand out like a sore thumb. The only option left was to turn to the Satmar Hasidic movement in the United States. Alte-Feige put Ruth in touch with the Gertner family in Williamsburg, New York. The family was not part of the Satmar community, but belonged to an affiliated sect known as the Malochim. The family was probably chosen in order to implicate Satmar in the kidnapping. Since it was clear that those looking for Yossele would examine the possibility that he was being held among the Satmar community in New York, Ruth searched for alternative institutions where he might be concealed. However, all those she turned to rejected her request. Rabbi Aharon Kolter, one of the leaders of Haredi Judaism in the United States, refused even to meet her.[88] Rabbi Kanievsky changed his opinion on the affair and sent his assistant Aryeh Schechter to locate Ruth and persuade her to return the boy.

After moving Yossele to New York, Ruth returned to France in order to defend herself in a criminal prosecution. She attempted to sell a house she owned in the Loire Valley in order to pay her debts to the customs authorities, and at this point the Mossad agents managed to apprehend her. This is the juncture to explain Isser Harel's role in the Yossele affair. Israeli Prime Minister David Ben-Gurion decided to charge the Mossad with finding the boy after the affair evolved from a family quarrel to a national quarrel between secular and Orthodox Jews. It was fairly obvious that the boy was no longer in Israel and the police were lost for ideas. Harel sent agents to all the right places: Chabad in Morocco, the yeshiva in Aix-les-Bains, and the Jewish community in Antwerp. Harel concentrated his efforts on cracking the cell around Yerachmiel Domb in London, and to this end tapped his telephone. During a telephone conversation between Ruth and Domb, Domb carelessly mentioned Yossele by name. This enabled Harel to connect the dots, and his next goal was to seize Ruth and bring her in for interrogation. Harel decided to handle the interrogation personally and moved his office to France.

After Ruth placed her home on the market, Mossad agents arrived in the guise of potential buyers. The negotiations between the two sides led Ruth to catch a ride with the "purchasers" in order to meet their attorney and close the deal. She got in the car and the agents took her to a rented house. As soon as she entered the door, she became a hostage. After an interrogation lasting almost two weeks, Ruth finally admitted her actions and revealed the location where the boy was being held. Both Ruth herself and Harel agreed that she showed considerable resilience in the face of her interrogators and consistently refused to offer any information. Both versions concur that she was eventually broken by testimony given by her own son Uriel, in which he incriminated his mother. Uriel agreed to cooperate with the Mossad in return for complete immunity for all those involved in the affair. Harel recalled:

> I told her that Uriel, who was in Israel at the center of the developments, had formed that conclusion that the Yossele affair must be resolved immediately and without delay, since the situation entailed grave dangers for all those involved.[89]

As will be recalled, Ruth had already spent time in a French prison – a period of her life she describes as one of profound humiliation. She could easily have been sentenced to many years for kidnapping Schumacher, and all those involved in the affair in Israel and elsewhere might also face lengthy imprisonment. The affair directly implicated prominent figures, such as Domb, Alte-Feige Teitelbaum, Kanievsky, and Katzenelbogen, not to mention her own son Uriel. The general pardon Ruth sought enabled all those involved to escape potentially harsh penalization.

While Ruth outwardly maintained her steadfast position, the exposure of the plot and the handing over of Yossele to the Mossad dealt her a heavy blow:

> I was being betrayed to the Shin Beth by those Religious circles that should have been helping me, that I was surrounded by enemies from all sides and that Shin Beth knew quite a lot – nearly all my engagement in the Yossele

affair.[90] . . . In such circumstances any attempt to win a conclusive achievement of arresting this process is doomed to failure. The attempt itself is valuable and lasting. The protest, judged by its strength, has its influence, if only to the extent that the truth be not completely extinguished.[91]

This quote illustrates Ruth's disappointment at what she saw as the treachery of the Haredi world in the Yossele affair. She adopted the rhetoric of Neturei Karta and Satmar, arguing that protest has an intrinsic value. Thus, even if the kidnapping was ultimately a failure, it was still a demonstration of brazen opposition to the Israeli and Haredi establishment – a separate value that can be gauged in its own right.

Ruth mentioned her concern that her son had given his testimony under torture.[92] The truth is that Uriel gave his testimony willingly due to his desire to end the affair. Although he had close ties to circles close to Neturei Karta, including Rabbis Maizes and Katzenelbogen, Uriel himself was a Zionist and had served in the military. When Ruth's interrogator informed her that Uriel had given testimony against her, she proclaimed, "No, no, no, he is no longer my son."[93] Uriel confirms that she indeed rejected him for a while, but adds that he was able to placate her and repair their relationship.[94]

After Ruth revealed Yossele's whereabouts, the Mossad contacted the FBI, which sent agents to locate the boy. His mother Ida and sister Zena were sent to New York, where the boy was reunited with his family. The kidnapping came to an end on June 30, 1962. Isser Harel adds that Yossele suffered from anxiety and met daily with a psychologist over a period of two and half years.[95]

Discussion

It is difficult to come to terms with the contradictions in Ruth Ben-David's personality. On the one hand, she was a delicate and curious woman, knowledgeable in general affairs and in the history of philosophy and religion; yet she was strangely attracted to a small and extreme religious group that sees the entire surrounding world as a threat and wages an uncompromising struggle to avoid the modern world. How did the basic curiosity that led her to Judaism draw her into the Haredi enclave in Jerusalem?

I cannot offer easy solutions for these contradictions, but it is worth beginning my emphasizing that Ruth found herself in the Haredi world almost by chance. Were it not for her relationship with Rabbi Maizes, whom she met in France in a very specific context, and had her engagement to Rabbi Poliatschek not been cancelled, she would never have become embroiled in the Yossele affair. Her affiliation to Neturei Karta can best be described as the product of circumstances and chance. Her initial connection with Modern Orthodoxy and Religious Zionism was more natural for her, and her son joined her in the journey up to this point. Ruth had close ties to strongly intellectual Jewish circles. Rabbis Leon Ashkenazi and André Zaoui were not only leaders of the French Jewish community but were prolific and important thinkers. Zaoui had connections to Martin Buber and

Gershom Scholem, while Ashkenazi had ties with Emmanuel Levinas and André Neher, who led the French school of modern Jewish thought. Despite her education and erudition, however, Ruth chose the zealots of Meah Shearim in Jerusalem over the intellectuals of the nearby Rehavia neighborhood (it is worth noting that both Zaoui and Ashkenazi ultimately chose to settle in Jerusalem).

Ruth did not decline Rabbi Maizes' request to smuggle Yossele out of Israel. It is important here to recall her general tendency to admire strict men. A careful reading of her autobiography shows that Ruth was not particularly fond of men in general, often describing them in unflattering terms. She offered the opinion that Isser Harel looked like a Nazi while her own father reminded her of Charlie Chaplin. She described her fiancé Rabbi Poliatschek as mentally ill, and the list goes on. Her descriptions of women were far more positive. In broad terms, this dichotomy is maintained throughout her autobiography. However, a series of unusual men are excluded from this generalization: Rabbi Maizes, Nachman Straks, Amram Blau, and Rabbi Yoel Teitelbaum. Their common denominator is a tough and inflexible character, combining strict piety with a combative personality. All four men spent time in prison: Maizes and Straks were incarcerated in the Soviet Union and fought for their right to observe their religion; Ruth described them as modern-day martyrs. Amram Blau was imprisoned in Israeli jails many times for his violent conduct as leader of Neturei Karta. Blau also headed the "Modesty Patrols" in Jerusalem, which used physical force to impose the Haredi code of modesty.[96] Yoel Teitelbaum, the spiritual leader of radical ultra-Orthodoxy, spent five months in Bergen-Belsen concentration camp during the Holocaust.[97] Thus the profile of her preferred Haredi man, for whom she was willing to embark on a dangerous operation to kidnap and smuggle a child, was very different to the stereotypical image of the Haredi man poring over the religious texts – a character Daniel Boyarin has referred to as "feminine man."[98] She admired men who were strong and tough, like her father – the father she hated so much that she was unable even to bring herself to mention him by name in her autobiography; whom she claimed to pity; and who according to her own descriptions was rigid and cold but also the fearless recipient of a medal for his heroism in fighting the Nazi occupation. We can therefore suggest that the qualities she attributes to her father also describe herself, as well as the men to whom she was attracted. Yet while she maintained a fierce hatred of her father, she showed unconditional loyalty to these Haredi men, to the point that she was willing to forgo her liberty for them – since kidnapping is a serious offense that could have led to her protracted imprisonment. Here we see the stark pathological correlation between Ruth's hatred of her father and the motivation for her conversion.

An examination of Ruth's personality reveals a character who enjoyed excitement and was willing to take risks, even to the point of risking her life. She was involved in the French Resistance; she kidnapped a boy and concealed him for about three years. She evidently sought out risk and challenge, and she was excited by the adrenaline created by her involvement in dangerous actions.

Ruth's behavior is consistent with the character of a convert: her passionate hatred for the father was replaced by her unconditional love for Maizes. He exploited her loyalty and love of adventure in order to kidnap Yossele Schumacher and hide him from the world as part of the zealots' struggle against the secular State of Israel. The years preceding Ruth's conversion were traumatic, including imprisonment, an unsuccessful engagement, and depression – a picture that is similar to that painted by psychological research into the biography of converts.

Ruth found in Orthodox Judaism spiritual comfort and psychological redemption. However, conversion does not change the individual's character, as psychological research has proved.[99] As she moved into Orthodox circles, she continued to be afflicted by bad moods. Accordingly, it is reasonable to conclude that she had a tendency to depression. In discussing her motives, however, we must also recall her distaste for modern political ideologies such as nationalism. The world of anti-Zionist Haredi Judaism thus offered a convenient refuge from the political system she hated so fiercely.

Ruth chose to raise her son Uriel by proxy, placing him in the care of foster families and boarding schools and playing very little role in his upbringing. A parental decision to place a child in guardianship reflects a measure of trust, and the expectation that the child will eventually be returned to their parents. Nachman Straks broke the trust placed in him by his daughter Ida when he refused to return Yossele to his parents' custody. Ruth joined the conspiracy and hid the boy for several years. This reflects the depth of the transition she had undergone. It also suggests that her conversion to Orthodox Judaism did not lead her to internalize the basic Talmudic doctrine, "do not do to your fellows what is hateful to you." Ruth was devoted to her son's education but indifferent to the suffering of other parents. Her cruelty toward Yossele and his parents, and her unwillingness to acknowledge her unacceptable behavior, are also evidence of her flawed personality.

Ruth entered the world of Judaism after a surprising spiritual journey that included new religious movements and detailed study of ancient philosophies. Her drift toward Judaism coincided with serious personal crises including financial fraud, expulsion from Switzerland, personal disillusionment with potential intimate and business partners, and time in jail. Her second conversion, embodying her ideological transition to anti-Zionism, came during the kidnapping of Yossele Schumacher. The justifications she offered for her actions obliged her to accept anti-Zionist and ultra-Orthodox ideology. Since her actions were grave in the extreme, the cognitive dissonance created was also substantial, and she was forced to struggle to convince herself of the justice of her actions.

Thus we can see that Rabbi Maizes' influence over Ruth was so great that he not only persuaded her to commit a serious offense but also deflected her from Orthodox Zionism to extreme ultra-Orthodoxy. Maizes served as the archetypical stern father figure so many converts seek during their process of religious transition.

In conclusion, I will return to the question I posed at the beginning of this chapter: who are you, Ruth Ben-David? Ruth was a delicate woman and a fraudster; modest and devious. She was devoted to the truth and was determined to tell her own story without concealing any detail, yet she was also a pathological liar who changed and distorted her own biography. She hated the State of Israel yet loved her soldier son. She was Madeleine Ferraille and she was Ruth Blau. A contradictory and mysterious character, by any standards.

Notes

1 Ruth Blau, *The History of Yossele Schumacher*, Brooklyn: Copy Corner, 1993.
2 Blau Archive, Box 1, author's name unclear, undated.
3 Blau Archives, Box 1. Letter on behalf of Avraham Stenmann, 29 Tevet 5724 (January 14, 1964).
4 Ruth Blau, *Guardians of the City*, Jerusalem: Idanim, 1979 (in Hebrew).
5 Isser Harel, *The Yossele Campaign*, Tel Aviv: Yediot Aharonot, 1982 (in Hebrew).
6 Greer F. Cashman, "No Stranger to Controversy," *Jerusalem Post*, May 24, 2000 https://web.archive.org/web/20010119125400/http://www02.jpost.com/Editions/2000/03/05/Features/Features.3576.html (viewed on September 26, 2017).
7 www.ranaz.co.il/notPublished/article47_19930616.asp (viewed on June 2, 2016).
8 See, for example, William James' concept of a "twice born conversion" and Leo Tolstoy's autobiography: *A Confession*, London: Oxford University Press, 1961.
9 Chana Ullman, *The Transformed Self: The Psychology of Religious Conversion*, New York: Plenum Press, 1989, 1–26.
10 Raymond Paloutzian, James Richardson and Lewis Rambo, "Religious Conversion and Personality Change," *Journal of Personality* 76 (6) (2009): 1047–1079.
11 Ullman, *The Transformed Self*, 1–26.
12 Blau, *The History of Yossele Schumacher*, 10.
13 Ibid., 12.
14 Ibid., 11. Hannah Ullman notes that converts often tend to describe their mothers in positive terms while the father is cast in a negative light. Ullman, *The Transformed Self*, 41–43.
15 Blau, *The History of Yossele Schumacher*, 15.
16 Cashman, "No Stranger."
17 Blau, *The History of Yossele Schumacher*, 18.
18 Ibid.
19 Ibid., 17–18.
20 Ibid., 22–23.
21 Ibid., 29.
22 Ibid., 24.
23 Ibid., 35.
24 Cashman, "No Stranger."
25 Shalom Goldman, *Jewish-Christian Difference and Modern Jewish Identity*, Lanham, MD: Lexington Books, 2015, 24.
26 Blau, *The History of Yossele Schumacher*, 49.
27 Ibid.
28 Ibid., 50.
29 Ibid., 54–55.
30 Ibid., 55.
31 Ibid., 56.
32 Ibid., 50.
33 Ibid., 60.
34 Ibid., 63.
35 Ibid., 78.
36 In her autobiography, Ben-David refers to Zaoui by the pseudonym "Elbaz."
37 Valentin Nikiprowetzky and André Zaoui, *Maimonide. Le livre de la connaissance*, Paris: Presses Universitaires de France, 1961.

38 Menachem Finkelstein, *Conversion, Halakhah, and Practice*, Ramat Gan: Bar Ilan University Press, 2006.
39 Telephone conversation with Bianca Zaoui, June 6, 2016. Mme. Zaoui remarked that Madeleine had a strong personality and was prone to immodest conduct.
40 Email correspondence with Rabbi Jonas Jaquelin, June 2, 2016.
41 Blau, *The History of Yossele Schumacher*, 83.
42 David Ellenson and Daniel Gordis, *Pledges of Jewish Allegiance*, Stanford, CA: Stanford University Press, 2015, 38–69.
43 Blau, *The History of Yossele Schumacher*, 94.
44 www.historicalstatistics.org/Currencyconverter.html
45 Cashman, "No Stranger."
46 "Extradition Agreement Signed with France," *Davar*, November 13, 1958, 2.
47 New York Supreme Court, Appellate Division – First Department, Dutch-American Mercantile Corporation against Corta Corporation and Leon Swergold, file 8432.
48 Blau, *The History of Yossele Schumacher*, 106.
49 http://manitou.org.il/%D7%AA%D7%95%D7%9C%D7%93%D7%95%D7%AA-%D7%97%D7%99%D7%99%D7%95-%D7%A9%D7%9C-%D7%94%D7%A8%D7%91-%D7%90%D7%A9%D7%9B%D7%A0%D7%96%D7%99/ (viewed on June 5, 2016).
50 Blau, *The History of Yossele Schumacher*, 114–115.
51 Cashman, "No Stranger."
52 Blau, *The History of Yossele Schumacher*, 175–176.
53 Yosef Fund, *Separation or Integration: Agudat Yisrael Confronts Zionism and the State of Israel*, Jerusalem: Magnes Press, 1999 (in Hebrew).
54 Ullman, *The Transformed Self*, 59–74.
55 Blau, *The History of Yossele Schumacher*, 122.
56 Menachem Friedman, *Society and Religion: Non-Zionist Orthodoxy in the Land of Israel*, Jerusalem: Ben-Zvi Institute, 1978; Aviezer Ravitzky, *Messianism, Zionism, and Religious Radicalism*, Chicago: University of Chicago Press, 1993, 40–78; Motti Inbari, *Jewish Radical Ultra-Orthodoxy Confronts Modernity, Zionism and Women's Equality*, New York: Cambridge University Press, 2016, 173–202.
57 Blau, *The History of Yossele Schumacher*, 130.
58 Ibid., 193–198.
59 Ibid., 241.
60 The rabbi of the *moshav*, which was established by Young Agudat Yisrael, was Benjamin Mandelson, who adhered to an anti-Zionist ideology.
61 Unsigned, untitled, collection of articles *Mishmeret Chomatenu*, from members of Neturei Karta, vol. 14, 6 Iyar 5722–1962, Blau Archive, Box 1.
62 www.youtube.com/watch?v=5Gr9tIxda_k (viewed on January 3, 2019).
63 Blau, *The History of Yossele Schumacher*, 209.
64 Harel, *Yossele Campaign*, 233–234.
65 "Kanievsky, Jacob Israel," in: *Encyclopaedia Judaica*, edited by Michael Berenbaum and Fred Skolnik (2nd ed., vol. 11), Detroit, MI: Macmillan Reference USA, 2007, 762–763.
66 Blau, *History*, 214.
67 Ibid., 237.
68 The debates were held on June 6, 1960, March 7, 1962, and July 9, 1962. See: Harel, *Yossele Campaign*, 16–20, 43–46, 151–155.
69 https://drive.google.com/file/d/0B_wZ8qKsEas2bWVrMUtTNGFvd1k/view (viewed on November 30, 2018).
70 Harel, *The Yossele Campaign*, 31–39.
71 Blau, *The History of Yossele Schumacher*, 227.
72 Ibid., 233.

73 Ibid., 242.
74 Ibid., 244. In his study, Menachem Keren-Kratz showed that one of the central goals of radical Haredi Judaism was to distinguish itself from the central stream of the Haredi world. See Menachem Keren-Kratz, "Marmaros – The Cradle of Extreme Orthodoxy," *Modern Judaism* 35 (2) 2015, 147–174.
75 Blau, *The History of Yossele Schumacher*, 260.
76 Ibid., 289, 310.
77 Menachem Keren-Kratz, *R' Yoel Teitelbaum – The Satmar Rabbi (1887–1979): Biography*, Tel Aviv: Ph.D. dissertation, Tel Aviv University, 2013, 215–220 (in Hebrew).
78 Harel, *The Yossele Campaign*, 106.
79 Blau, *The History of Yossele Schumacher*, 269–270.
80 Ibid., 271.
81 Blau, *The History of Yossele Schumacher*, 297–299. Harel reached a similar conclusion: *The Yossele Campaign*, 77.
82 Michael Wolf, "The Halakhic Attitude to Din Rodef and Din Moser," in: *Delinquency and Social Deviation: Theory and Practice*, edited by Moshe Arad and Yuval Wolf, Ramat Gan: Bar Ilan University Press, 2002, 215–249 (in Hebrew).
83 Chabad sources claim that the Rebbe supported the resolution of the affair and the child's return to his parents only toward the end of the stage, when it was clear that the Mossad was about to discover Yossele's location. He did so after ensuring that all those involved would be pardoned, including several Chabad Hasidim who had been involved from the beginning, including the child's uncle. See http://chabad.info/magazine/%D7%91%D7%99%D7%AA-%D7%9E%D7%A9%D7%99%D7%97-%D7%A0%D7%9E%D7%A9%D7%9B%D7%AA-%D7%9E%D7%A1%D7%9B%D7%AA-%D7%94%D7%97%D7%A9%D7%99%D7%A4%D7%95%D7%AA-%D7%91%D7%A4%D7%A8%D7%A9%D7%99%D7%99%D7%AA-%D7%99%D7%95/ (viewed on July 28, 2016).
84 Harel, *The Yossele Campaign*, 121.
85 Ibid., 80.
86 Blau, *The History of Yossele Schumacher*, 303.
87 Ibid., 302.
88 Ibid., 340.
89 Harel, *The Yossele Campaign*, 105.
90 Blau, *The History of Yossele Schumacher*, 409.
91 Ibid., 422.
92 Ibid., 424.
93 Ibid., 429.
94 Cashman, "No Stranger."
95 Harel, *The Yossele Campaign*, 262.
96 Inbari, *Jewish Radical Ultra-Orthodoxy Confronts Modernity, Zionism and Women's Equality*, 74–93.
97 Menachem Keren-Kratz, "Hast Thou Escaped and Also Taken Possession? The Satmar Rebbe – Rabbi Yoel Teitelbaum and His Followers' Response to Criticism of His Conduct During and After the Holocaust," *Dapim: Studies on the Holocaust* 28 (2) 2014: 97–120.
98 Daniel Boyarin, *Unheroic Conduct: The Rise of Heterosexuality and the Invention of the Jewish Man*, Berkeley: University of California Press, 2007, 1–29.
99 Paloutzian, Richardson, and Rambo, "Religious Conversion and Personality Change," 1073.

5 The "deconversion" of Haim Herman Cohn

A model of secular religion

Haim Herman Cohn was a central figure in the shaping of Israel's judicial system, serving as an advisor to the state, as attorney general, and as a Supreme Court justice. Cohn was a brilliant man, an autodidact, and a first-rate lawyer. He is considered one of the individuals most responsible for shaping of the State of Israel as a law-abiding liberal democracy.

One of the main chapters of his life was the process of his abandonment of faith in his twenties. This was a traumatic process that entailed disappointment and grief. Cohn was born into a strict Orthodox household and was a descendant of a distinguished rabbinical family, but the home was open to the modern world in the spirit of German Neo-Orthodoxy. His maternal grandfather was Rabbi Shlomo (Salomon) Carlebach from Lubeck (Germany), an important rabbinical figure who left a strong impression on the young boy. His paternal grandfather, Rabbi Yosef Cohn, was a chief rabbi and a scholar of ancient languages. Haim Herman had planned to follow in his grandfathers' footsteps and become a rabbi, but his powerful intellectual drive pushed him outside of the religious world. The story of how Cohn fell out of faith may seem typical of many young men of his generation who abandoned the Orthodox lifestyle. However, Cohn's story has some unique aspects. Over a lifetime as a nonbeliever, a heretic who denies the existence of God, he continued to study and teach religious laws. One of the main tasks he assumed was to adapt Jewish law to the reality of a liberal and modern state so that it could be integrated in the Israeli corpus of law. Though he defined himself as an agnostic who denied God and His eternal heavenly laws, Cohn was paradoxically one of the strongest supporters of adding the Halakhah to the Israeli law system. However, his enthusiasm for Jewish law seemed bizarre to non-Orthodox Jews in Israel, while the Orthodox saw in him a threat, not just because of his undeniable knowledge of Jewish law but also because he was known for his debating prowess – as a lawyer, he almost never lost a case. Thus, Cohn was left virtually alone to wage a lost battle.

The process of his rejection of God began even before the Second World War, but reached its peak after news spread regarding the fate of Jews during the war, and especially after news arrived regarding the fate of his young brother Leo-Yehuda, who was murdered by the Nazis in Auschwitz. The reality he encountered after the war upset him, and as a prosecutor he directed the blame toward

God and His heavenly justice. After his deconversion, he switched his loyalty from the Jewish religion to the State of Israel, which became the focus of gravity of his identity and which he served with devotion. Another lesson he drew from the Holocaust was a firm commitment to human rights.

Two figures who helped Cohn move from one side to another were Rabbi Avraham Yitzhak Kook (1865–1935), the first Chief Rabbi of Mandatory Palestine and Cohn's one-time spiritual mentor, and David Ben-Gurion. Kook was an Orthodox and a Zionist, and through his teachings, Cohn switched his political allegiance from non-Zionist Orthodoxy to pro-Zionist Orthodoxy. The second figure he adored was Ben-Gurion, the leader of the Zionist movement and Israel's first prime minister. Cohn worked under Ben-Gurion as attorney general for ten years, until he had a physical breakdown and he had to retire out of fear for his health. After his resignation, he was appointed to the Israeli Supreme Court, where he was known for his tendency to write minority opinions and to defend the weakest elements of society.

This chapter draws on three main sources. Cohn gave long interviews to the author Michael Shashar that were published in the manuscript *Haim Cohn Supreme Court Justice – Conversations with Michael Shashar* (1989), but Cohn was not pleased with the result and composed an autobiography titled *Personal Introduction – Autobiography* (2005), which was published posthumously. In my opinion, there are no significant contradictions between the two works, although the autobiography is more detailed. Cohn's wife Michal Zemora-Cohn composed another essay on his life that contains some interesting additional anecdotes.

This chapter will describe the course of Cohn's life and the circumstances that led him to change his loyalties. This discussion will enrich our understanding of the role of Halakhah in a the modern State of Israel and of the debate over Jewish identity as a component of Israeli identity. I will being with a discussion of the general term "deconversion" and its application in Israeli society.

Deconversion and *chazara beshe'ela*

The term "deconversion" refers to the loss or deprivation of religious faith and is the product of intellectual doubt, moral criticism, emotional suffering, and disaffiliation from the community. Deconversion may take the form of a sudden dramatic reversal or may be a more protracted and even inconclusive process of doubt and uncertainty.[1]

Research into deconversion suggests that it is seldom a rapid or sudden event; in most cases, this is a slow and gradual process.[2] Individuals who have disaffiliated from one mainline denomination are most likely to affiliate with another slightly more liberal or conservative church. When people change their religious affiliation, it is generally in small steps.[3]

Armand Mauss proposed three categories of religious defection. The first is the intellectual dimension, reflecting disbelief in one religious faith while accepting an alternative for it. Atheism or agnosticism can be acceptable expressions of this intellectual level, which may include statements against the existence of God. The second level is social: a defection can be on the communal or associational level, embodying an unwillingness to confirm to church norms. Mauss connects social ties to disengagement. The third category is emotional defection, which is tied to emotional distress between parents and children or to some negative event involving religion that causes people to deconvert.[4]

Malachi Kranzler examined the process of religious disaffiliation among former religious Zionist Jews. Drawing on Mauss' model, he concluded that this process takes place on three different levels: the conscious, the social, and the practical. The process of *chazara beshe'ela* (the Hebrew term for falling from faith) is slow and moderate. The intellectual aspect of this process is key, and this takes the form of intense wrestling with oneself on questions of faith and reason; the resolution of this dilemma leads many to leave religion. The social aspect includes a disconnection with Orthodox society and the forging of new ties with a less religious community. This stage includes the abandonment of regular religious rituals such as prayer, as well as breaking taboos and religious prohibitions, such as eating non-kosher food. These events serve as milestones in the process. Another important aspect in the process is when there is a change of lifestyle, such as leaving home to serve in the army, going to college, taking long trips outside of Israel, or moving to another town. The process of leaving religion may take between five to ten years and include long deliberations, a dissonance between religion and logic, and ultimately a breaking away from old communities. In most cases, however, there is no forced rupture of the ties with the former community, as it is recorded among those who leave the ultra-Orthodox enclave.[5] Those who leave Orthodox Zionist communities maintain their relationships with family and friends.[6] Haim Herman Cohn underwent a similar process, as will be described below.

Cohn's childhood

Haim Herman Cohn was born into German Orthodoxy, which combined a strict religious lifestyle with considerable openness to all aspects of German culture. Samson Raphael Hirsch (1808–1888) was an Orthodox rabbi and the founder of Neo-Orthodoxy (under the Hebrew slogan *Torah im Derech Eretz* – "Torah with the way of the world"). This approach enjoyed the intellectual endorsement of Rabbi Azriel Hildesheimer. Rabbi Shlomo Carlebach, Cohn's grandfather, was one of the first to be ordained by Rabbi Hildesheimer.

In both the autobiographical essay and the interview with Shashar, Cohn places great importance on his experiences in the household of his grandfather, Rabbi Shlomo Carlebach. Cohn viewed his grandfather as the ideal Orthodox rabbi. In addition to his rabbinical ordination, Carlebach also held a doctorate in German literature. His books reflected his loyalty to both worlds: He wrote three books of Talmudic commentary in Hebrew, as well as books in German on rabbinical matters such as women's purity, the Jewish household, and the history of the Jews of Lubeck. But he also penned a list of books recommended for every Jewish household that included not only religious books but also a long list of non-Jewish poets, playwrights, and novelists.[7]

The rabbi was married to Esther, the daughter of the previous chief rabbi of Lubeck, and the couple had 12 children of their own and six adopted children. Most of their sons became rabbis and most of the girls married rabbis. Cohn did not go to a daycare facility or school, and he studied with his grandfather from the age of three until the rabbi's death six years later. His grandfather taught him Hebrew, prayers, and the Bible, which he later accompanied with German, math, and general education. The days were divided equally between the religious and the secular subjects, and at the end of the day, the rabbi gave the student a candy: "I remember the daily candy, for it had played an important role in my service and diligence."[8]

The grandfather was a fierce anti-Zionist: he was repelled by the idea that Jews might leave their exile, and he believed this transition should take place only with the coming of the messiah. Cohn said that his grandfather described Zionism as arrogant, since it believed could hasten the building of Jerusalem before the right time scheduled by God. He also opposed Zionism due to the secular nature of the pioneers, and he was afraid that the new ideology would lead many to abandon religion (as would indeed be the case with his beloved grandson Haim). Another reason for opposing Zionism was that Carlebach was a proud and patriotic German: he loved his homeland, admired the emperor, and saw German culture as the pinnacle of European civilization.[9]

After the grandfather died in 1919, the family moved to Hamburg, where his father was hired as a senior banker. Cohn described his father as a very rich man, and the family owned a large house with servants. However, according to Cohn, the father educated his children (four boys, of whom Haim was the oldest) to be thrifty and to live in moderation. Thus, for example, during family vacations the parents would stay in fancy hotels while the boys lodged in youth hostels. The father insisted that the boys spend their weekly allowance on buying gifts for their loved ones or donate their money to charity.[10]

With the transition to Hamburg, the paternal grandparents became a more important influence in Cohn's life. He described his grandmother, Miriam Cohn, as a significant figure in his childhood. According to his descriptions, she had a dominant personality: "She was the one and remained the one who made all decisions."[11] She rejected the inherent discrimination against women in Jewish societies[12] and refused to wear a wig, a symbol of modesty, instead wearing a small embroidery on her head. Every Thursday, she went to listen to the opera with her grandchildren, although her husband refused to join her since Jewish law prohibits men from listening to women singing. Cohn described how the grandmother used to intervene in judicial deliberations that took place in her home due to her husband's role as a rabbinical arbiter.[13] The grandmother used to rule on all the rabbinical aspects that did not require her husband's input.[14]

The grandfather, Yosef Cohn, was a philologist who studied the meaning of words in ancient languages. He was ordained from the Jewish Theological Seminary of Breslau in 1875, so that his ordination was non-Orthodox, and he was one of the students of Zecharias Frankel, although in his lifestyle and his religious affiliation he remained an Orthodox Jew.[15] The grandfather taught the child Talmudic traits, and Cohn described how the grandmother used to listen to the lessons, make comments, ask questions, and sometimes make harsh remarks on the words of the sages. Her comments, recalled Cohn, made a strong impression on his little heart. "From her I learned that you take nothing for granted and even absolute truths should be exposed to criticism."[16]

From Cohn descriptions, we can conclude that he grew up in wealth and comfort, and that he was exposed from an early age to dominant figures who were liberal and open to German culture. We can see that his upbringing provided a model for his reversal later in his life, since he had been exposed as a child to an unusual environment that was open to criticism of conventional norms.

His parents sent young Haim to the Talmud Torah School, where secular and religious subjects were studied equally, under the leadership of his uncle Dr. Joseph Zvi Carlebach. Carlebach held a doctorate in math and physics, and the Lemel School in Jerusalem invited him to teach his fields of expertise between 1904 and 1907. The Lemel school was excommunicated by the rabbis of the Old Yishuv, since it offered students both a secular and religious education, and the ban brought the uncle closer to Rabbi Avraham Kook, who was living in Jaffa at the time. Kook was a fierce opponent of the Old Yishuv from within the Orthodox ranks. In 1908, Carlebach returned to Germany, and during the First World War he served as a chaplain in the German military, entering Lithuania with the forces. After the war, Carlebach established the Jewish Gymnasium of Kovno, which offered secular and religious studies.[17] Carlebach was perceived by Cohn as "an ideal type of a German rabbi educator."[18]

After graduating from high school, Cohn enrolled at Munich University. His original plan was to finish his university education and then attend rabbinical school. He took a class on bankruptcy laws and realized that he was interested in studying law. The school year was packed with general and religious studies, while at the weekends he used to travel to the nearby Alps. Cohn recalled that he enjoyed the lectures and the study of secular and religious matters, music and theater, hiking and sightseeing.

During that year he also met Elsa, a young Jewish student; the couple spent much time together and decided to get married. The parents on both sides opposed a hasty marriage, suggesting that Cohn should first go to study in a yeshiva and postpone his marriage by two years. Cohn decided to go to Jerusalem, where he visited Merkaz HaRav Yeshiva, headed by Rabbi Kook, on his uncle's recommendation.

Haim Herman reached Jaffa's shores in 1930, together with his younger brother Alexander. The two had planned to inspect several yeshivot in Jerusalem, but they went first to Merkaz HaRav, and after a short visit they decided to stay:

> I was literally charmed by the glowing and merciful eyes of the Rabbi [Kook], I could not take my eyes out of him. His face projected a certain flesh and blood holiness; the movements of his gentle hands and his quiet and well speaking tone has projected on the nobility of his soul.[19]

There was deep hostility between Kook and the ultra-Orthodox rabbis of Jerusalem due to Kook's support for Zionism.[20] Cohn recalls seeing ultra-Orthodox yeshiva students on Purim burning a doll in the image of Kook while they danced and sang around the fire. After seeing these images, Cohn decided that he should disconnect from their circles.[21] According to Cohn, the Jerusalemite rabbis hated Kook "since they knew he was above them. . . . All hatred is coming from fear, nothing else. Later you put ideology on top of it."[22] I find Cohn's description fascinating, particularly since the members of these exact circles would later come to hate Cohn himself. Michal Zemora-Cohn, Haim's second wife, described how the couple used to receive hate letters written by ultra-Orthodox Jews, and every night they received telephone threats full of vitriol.[23] Cohn concluded that when he arrived in Jerusalem, the teachings of his grandfather that Zionism is forbidden by the Jewish law were still rooted in his heart. "When I saw and heard the Rabbi [Kook] and started reading his essays, my grandfather's theories vanished and cleared the way for Zionist enthusiasm, and the Rabbi made this Halakhically right."[24]

Cohn was a member of Agudat Yisrael, the ultra-Orthodox non-Zionist organization, and had even chaired its local youth chapter in Hamburg.[25] Accordingly, he initially considered Zionism as a "great offence against religion."[26] However, he had an intellectual interest in the subject and wanted to learn more about Kook. After weighing the two sides engaged in the debate on Zionism and noting the tendency of the radicals to show personal hostility and demonize Kook, he disassociated himself from them and rejected their influence.

While studying at Merkaz HaRav, Cohn continued his academic education, traveling to Mount Scopus every afternoon to study at the Hebrew University. He took classes mainly in Jewish law and Jewish history. He wanted to major in law, but since the Hebrew University did not yet offer a degree in law, he decided to return to Germany, marry Elsa, and become a lawyer.

In 1932, Cohn arrived in Frankfurt and registered for a doctorate program in law at the Goethe University Frankfurt. He was able to transfer credit from his two years of study at the Hebrew University, so that he was only required to study for one year. This was the year that the Nazis came to power in Germany, but Cohn emphasizes that he never suffered any particular anti-Semitism. He began to write a dissertation on Jewish law, but never finished the project. Following the rise of the Nazis, he decided to marry Elsa and leave Germany. In September 1933 he returned to Jerusalem, where he would remain for the rest of his life.

Apostasy

Cohn was accepted to a junior position at the law firm of Dr. Mordechai Buxbaum, the legal counsel of Agudat Israel in Palestine. Cohn worked in the office for three years and learned how to run a law firm. Buxbaum's clients were mostly rabbis and Torah students from the Old Yishuv. Over these years, Cohn learned that Torah sages are human and they may engage in criminal acts. "Something moved inside me when I saw the behavior of these great holy men, who study the Torah all day long, and have nothing but God in their mind."[27] He recalls his profound disappointment on learning how rabbis and Torah scholars behaved:

> Piety and righteousness are no guarantee against evilness and corruption. This was a great disappointment for me: I grew up in faith that the fear of God is incompatible with hurting other people, and that keeping the commandments also requires keeping the commandments between fellow men, no less than keeping the commandments between man and God. . . . Many of my Torah scholar clients were cruel husbands who beat their wives and deserted their children. . . . I learned to dislike them, and I was always sorry that the first I learned to dislike were criminal Orthodox men.[28]

Cohn notes that from the late 1930s he began to doubt that the Torah was the word of God. He felt that he needed to explore his doubts, and claims that his wife Elsa supported him.[29] The question that troubled him most was the nature of divine justice, especially in the context of violence toward women. As mentioned, he felt that this problem was prevalent among many of his clients. In addition, he grew up with a grandmother who had spoken out clearly against the discrimination of women, and this sense of injustice was embedded in his character. Cohn quoted Spinoza's declaration that divine justice must be perfect, and contrasted this with the inclusion in the Halakhah of provisions that discriminate against women and regard them as property. He also regarded the biblical law of "an eye for an eye" as cruelty.

The process of deserting the religion of his upbringing was protracted, extending over 12 years. The journey began in Merkaz HaRav Yeshiva, where Cohn studied the Bible with Rabbi Zvi Yehuda Kook. The book that despaired him the most was the book of Job: "The question I could find no answer to was not why God created the world, but why God created Satan, and why he sent him to afflict misery on mankind."[30]

As a result of these doubts, he started learning by himself the laws of the ancient nations, and he saw that ancient kings used to legislate laws but to attribute these to the Gods they believed in.

> Eventually there was no doubt in my mind that like any other ancient systems, in Mosaic Law, too, they (the legislators) saw a need to attribute their laws to an all-powerful and omniscient God, for otherwise there was no chance of enforcing these laws on humans. The threat that sinners would be punished by the gods was stronger than the threat of human punishment. It is not just that you cannot hide anything from the gods: you also cannot predict the severe and cruel punishment that these Gods can inflict upon you.[31]

Over the years, Cohn developed the concept of God as a "legal fiction." Thus, the ancient legislator invented God to rationalize the concept of following the law. According to this theory, God is a myth intended to create respect toward the law.[32] These insights led him to study the anthropology, sociology, and philosophy of law.[33]

Friedrich Nietzsche, one of the most important philosophers of modern times, exerted a powerful influence over the new Hebrew culture that was developing in the Land of Israel. Nietzsche declared the death of God in his book *Thus Spoke Zarathustra*, symbolizing the death of the old world that was chained by religious institutions and the birth of a new man free from these chains. Nietzsche also believed that secular myth would replace God in the creation of a new society. Intellectuals from left and right saw in him a role model for creating a new social order. As historian David Ohana has shown, many Zionist thinkers saw Nietzsche as a source for building a secular and anti-clerical Zionist ideology. Many thinkers viewed Zionism as a secular religion and used the messianic myth to prove that Zionism is the fulfillment of messianic promises of redemption.[34]

Cohn said that by the time he discovered Friedrich Nietzsche, he was already full of doubts. He spend two years studying Nietzsche's writings in depth, modestly dismissing his own apostasy as no more than plagiarism of Nietzsche.[35]

Cohn describes himself as an agnostic:

> I never knew for sure that there is no God in the universe. I stopped believing in His existence, but I may be wrong. . . . Inside my heart I am convinced God does not exist, but I cannot declare his nonexistence as long as there is no clear proof.[36]

Although he stopped believing, he remained a scholar of Torah: "I am very impressed by it – not because it is the work of God, but because it is the work of men."[37]

Cohn said that a human legislator can change or even nullify laws, but divine law is eternal, immutable, and cannot be nullified by men. Times change and new needs arise, but divine law does not move forward, remaining unchangeable for thousands of years. Cohn asserts that if God were indeed the legislator, He would have changed the laws in times when change was required. Cohn lamented the freezing of Jewish law and the fact that Torah scholars have only rarely found the courage to fix wrongs.

> The sacredness of Torah laws lies in their eternalness, and any attempt to change them is considered an affront to God. Whether or not there is a precedent for changing the laws – Jewish law remain frozen, a celebration of the eternal.[38]

Cohn confronts the evidence brought by those who support the existence of God. Cosmological arguments claim it is impossible that the world was created by itself, as something cannot come out of nothing. Cohn responds to this claim by saying that this is not proof of God's existence, but rather an admission on our part that we cannot explain creation.[39] The teleological argument claims that nature is so perfect that there can be no doubt that something created it. Cohn responds that this is not evidence of God but evidence of the fact that our brain is limited and cannot understand everything. The experimental argument claims that many people report that they have witnessed the presence of God, whether He spoke to them or they saw Him in a dream. Cohn responds that no one can prove that such people were wrong, but equally no one can know if they were right. The final argument is moral, according to which God has created justice. Cohn responded that he also once believed that God truly hears prayers, but reality showed him that there is no justice in the world.[40]

The lesson of the Holocaust

Cohn said that he gave up on God during prayer. For many years he used to lead congregations in prayer, but he stopped after having doubts. His despair was not a result of God not listening to his prayers; on the contrary. His personal situation was good: he was married with children, and had a good job. "The source of my despair were the troubles and tribulations of the Jewish community in Palestine and the Jewish people as a whole, but also the deterioration of morals in the entire world."[41]

When news had begun to arrive regarding the situation of the Jews in Europe, Cohn was in a state of doubt. People knew that Nazi Germany had plans to exterminate Jews, but he found it hard to believe that Germans would be able to conduct such atrocities. He read daily news about the transportations to camps and the mass killings and concluded that there was no God to prevent these crimes. He felt that if God had indeed chosen the Jews, He had chosen them to be murdered and annihilated: "I reached an internal conclusion that I acted mercifully toward God by not believing in him; if I had to believe in His existence, I would have hated Him."[42]

Cohn rejected all the theodical explanations that seek to justify God's actions or inactions during the Holocaust. He rejected the argument that God had concealed his face, asking: "Where was God, why did He hide Himself?"[43] He rejected the argument that the Holocaust was a punishment for sin, such as the sin of assimilation or Zionism, as many Orthodox rabbis argued.[44] He also rejected the argument that God broke the covenant for only one time: "This means that His promises are not promises, His oaths are not oaths."[45] He similarly rejected the claim that God tested the Jews in the Holocaust, as if this were a similar instance to the Binding of Isaac. Cohn brought the case of the Reform Rabbi Leo Baeck, himself a Holocaust survivor, who saw the Holocaust as a test he must pass without any challenge to his original faith. Cohn saw Baeck's response as an expression of such pure faith, of love of God that does not surrender and is so obvious that it made a great impression on him.

The case of Baeck led him to describe the death of his brother Leo (Judah), who was incarcerated and murdered in Auschwitz. Leo had been the spiritual leader of a Jewish youth underground cell in the French Resistance, and he used to preach of the merciful God who was about to save and redeem the Jews. From eyewitnesses in prison, Cohn learned that his brother had managed to arrange daily prayers in the mornings and evenings, under the watchful eyes of German wardens.

> The mourning for my beloved brother has intensified ten times more because of the anger over his simple faith that was wasted for nothing, and his innocent trust in illusions. It is not that his beliefs and illusions did not strengthen his spirit, and as such they had a good purpose; I think that from an objective and practical point, his fate and the fate of many others who were slaughtered have removed the halo of divine election or providence from Jewish identity forever, and in my opinion, it has changed Judaism completely. "The final and winning proof" is not for the nonexistence of God – I remained an agnostic without the ability to know the truth – but the proof that if there is a God, He has lost all of the heavenly attributes that the Torah identifies with Him, and He is not anymore the God I grew up to believe in.[46]

His abandonment of faith was not only due to the loss of his precious brother and the extermination of the Jewish community he had known. Cohn was able to feel through his own flesh and blood the persecutions and the deliverance of Jews like lambs to the slaughter, when this became real and not just something you read of in history books: "When you see the spilt blood, it all makes different meaning." Cohn explained that he never was able to overcome the shock of violence and evil. His wife Elsa supported and even encouraged him in this direction.[47]

His grandfather Yosef Cohn lived with the couple in Palestine, and as long as he was alive, they kept a kosher house, and he escorted his grandfather occasionally to synagogue, but only for the grandfather's sake. His grandfather died in March 1948, and on his death, "I was released of all these external things."[48] His first step beyond the fold came when he refused to read the Torah in public during the High Holidays.

Cohn told his biographer Shashar that after the war he came to London and for the first time ordered bacon and eggs – non-kosher food. He was unable to touch the food and returned it, but over the years he learned to like this food. He admitted that he eats pork to prove to himself that he is free of all the commandments, and he refuses to wear a kippa.[49]

By way of comparison, it is interesting to refer to Elie Wiesel's response to the Holocaust as presented in his novel *Night*. According to the novel, Wiesel grew up in a Belz Hasidic family in Hungary prior to the Holocaust. Following the Nazi invasion of Hungary he was deported to Auschwitz, where he lost his entire family and barely managed to survive. His trials and tribulations as a young man in the Holocaust led him to declare that, for him, God died in the death camps: "Behind me, I heard the same man asking: *Where is God now?* And I heard a voice within me answer him: . . . *Here He is – He is hanging here on this gallows.*"[50] Wiesel's response to the dilemma of God's justice was a secularizing exit. After he was liberated, he did not return to the fold of Hasidic

Judaism, for he put the blame on God. However, Wiesel, like Cohn, invested much of his career in teaching and researching rabbinical and Hasidic Judaism and, like Cohn, although an agnostic he has never stopped thinking and speaking about his religion.

Zionism as Jewish identity

Cohn said that the Holocaust erased not only his belief in God but also his belief in men. The rampage of evil shocked him to the core, and he was disillusioned by the world's indifference to the sufferings of the Jews: "I realized that the Holocaust exposed not just the ugliness and evilness of the wicked Nazis and their collaborators; it also exposed the fatal and tragic character of the weak human nature." Cohn felt shamed by the fact that he had managed to survive and could live in comfort while being helpless in front of other human tragedies that we frequently are exposed to through the television screen. After he renounced God, it could have seemed an obvious step for him to replace faith in the divine with faith in men. However, knowing that Nazis made a free choice to be barbaric taught him that he could not trust humankind. Indeed, he came to hate the Nazis and even to view them as subhuman and dangerous animals who do not deserve to live – the same qualities they attributed to the Jews.[51]

Over the years, he learned to overcome hatred. As a judge and as an attorney general, he managed to treat even the worst criminals with humanity and without hatred or revenge. The lesson he learned from the Holocaust was the great danger that comes from a feeling of superiority. The Nazis believed that they were a supreme race and rulers of the world, and this led them to their crimes. By the same token, a Jewish sense of superiority, arguing that the Jews are God's chosen people elected over all the nations, is a dangerous superiority complex.[52]

One of the most vital lessons Cohn drew from the Holocaust was the importance of a Jewish state. Jews cannot trust divine providence or the nations of the world and cannot rely on human advancement or the victory of democracy and humanism.[53]

For Cohn, Zionism is true Judaism: "I do not see authentic Judaism in keeping Torah and commandments."[54] The great mission of the State of Israel, according to Cohn, is to bridge between observant and nonobservant Jews, and to ensure that there is a meaningful Judaism for those who decide to become nonobservant.

> According to my understanding, the nation of Israel and the Land of Israel are one; for if I were not a Zionist I would not be a Jew, and since I am a Zionist I need a Jewish state in the Land of Israel.[55]

According to Israeli lawyer and prosecutor Dina Zilber, Cohn had to have an ideal to follow. Since his Orthodox ideal failed, Zionism filled the hole that developed in his heart. His new idol was Ben-Gurion, whom he viewed as almost a biblical prophet.[56]

Jewish law

During the pre-state period, Cohn wanted to put his knowledge as a lawyer to the service of the Zionist movement. He believed that the new state should adopt a just and enlightened judicial system, but he also felt that this should be a Jewish system; the state should certainly have its own laws, not merely a copy of Ottoman or British ones. Thus he decided to investigate Jewish law and examine the extent to which it could meet the needs of a modern state: "I devoted each and every free hour to that task, and every hour brought new amazements."[57]

He began with family laws, partly because he was more familiar with them as a lawyer, but also because they include the most difficult problems, due to discrimination against women. He believed that he could find solutions based on an approach that would be faithful both to the law and to modern times: "there must be a way to revoke the discriminations without revoking the Halakhah."[58] But his experiment failed:

> It was not long before I became disillusioned of my hope to rewrite the law in a way that would be acceptable to the rabbis. Not only was the view that suggestions made by heretics like me should not be considered, they are considered as vain, or even worse as heresy, by definition. Any attempts to make Jewish law the foundation of secular law was viewed as blasphemy.[59]

Cohn developed a method that while reading judicial discussions in the Talmud, he focused on the minority opinions. The Talmud recorded disputes among the rabbis and sages over almost every judicial or ritual question. The Talmudic text ultimately resolved all these debates, but Cohn suggested that while modern law cannot always adopt the final Halakhic decision, in many cases the minority options may meet the standards of liberal laws.[60] As a Supreme Court justice, Cohn would become known for his expertise in writing minority opinions.

By the end of 1947, while preparing for the transition to an independent state, the Zionist movement established a statutory committee and a legal committee to lay the legal foundation for the new state. Cohn was asked to join the national effort, reporting that it was assumed that Jewish law would serve as the foundation for the Israeli law system.[61] Over a period of four months, the committee was unable to discuss Jewish law, faced with more urgent topics to debate during the transition from the British Mandate to an independent state. Soon after, new institutions such as the government and the Knesset were created. Nevertheless, he remembered these days as the happiest of his life:

> I would have not discussed this episode so much if it were not so important in my life. I assumed this project with immense enthusiasm and with a sanctity that I have never know before. I was privileged to be among the state's builders and to lay the foundations for the rule of law in our Jewish and democratic state. I felt that my wildest dreams and aspirations were being fulfilled in front of my eyes.[62]

Pinchas Rosen, Israel's first Minister of Justice, appointed Cohn Director of Legislation, but soon after, Ben-Gurion summoned Cohn and gave him the position of attorney general.

One of the first issues he had to deal with came after a man was prosecuted and sentenced to death – the first murder case in the young state. After the conviction, Cohn went straight to Ben-Gurion and demanded a temporary provision in the regulations declaring that in the new state no one would be sentenced to death, and any death sentence would be transmuted to a life sentence. To this day, judicial execution has never been used in Israel, with the sole exception of Adolf Eichmann, the Nazi officer.

Jewish law does not present one exclusive position on the death sentence. Genesis 9:6 states: "Whoever sheds human blood, by humans shall their blood be shed." This principle is also mentioned elsewhere (Numbers 35:31). The sages of the Sanhedrin opposed such legislation, and Rabbi Tarphon and Rabbi Akiva emphasized that if they were sitting on the Sanhedrin, "no-one would ever die" (Mishna, Makot 1:10). This example shows the complexities of the Jewish law and the system Cohn adopted, which argues for selective reading of the law. Cohn said that the legislator should look for inspiration in Jewish law whenever considering what to legislate. Legislators must seek inspiration in Jewish law, he explained, whether this is in the minority opinion or the actual ruling. If it seems fit and right to a modern society, "than we should adopt it – not because it is Jewish, but because it is right and just." The same logic applies to the death penalty: "We abandoned the biblical deaths and the laws of evidence and warnings that do not fit a humane and modern state, and we adopted the words of the sages who called for the abolition of the death penalty."[63]

An issue that is often held against Cohn was his support for the system of martial law imposed on Israeli Arabs from the creation of the State of Israel (1948) through 1966. Cohn's support for this regime is especially puzzling due to his well-known commitment to human rights (following his retirement from the Supreme Court, he was appointed president of the Association for Civil Rights in Israel). The military regime denied many rights to Arab Israelis due to their assumed hostility toward the new state. The fear of an Arab underground led Cohn to agree to establish a military regime that included administrative detention, confiscation of property, and restrictions on movement. As attorney general, Cohn was required to represent the state in courts and to defend martial law. Israeli Supreme Court Justice Itzhak Zamir wondered whether Cohn crossed a delicate line between his duty to represent the state and causing injustice to the Arab citizens of the state. It was argued against Cohn that he defended and even formulated governmental decisions that dealt a strong blow to human rights. Zamir said that the legal community understood from the beginning that the military regime was unjust, and it was later considered illegal.[64] Why would Cohn defend such an aggressive system? Zamir offers several explanations: first, Cohn tended to believe the security authorities; he was willing to defend them because he was convinced that their actions were for the good of the state. As a result, he came to be seen as someone who represented the state rather than its citizens. Later, Zamir claimed, Cohn changed his style and supported the public against the system. He also became much more skeptical regarding a military establishment that sought to deny citizens their rights in the name of national security. Second, as attorney general he saw his mission as being to offer objective and reliable counseling to the state. The attorney general, he believed, must serve the government and gain its trust.[65] Michal Zmora-Cohn offered another explanation: "Haim followed Ben-Gurion almost with his eyes closed."[66] She recalls that Cohn was asked many times why he changed from a strict security hawk who wrote the notorious laws of martial law to a humanist and a prominent fighter for human rights. Michal does not accept Zamir's explanations and offers her own interpretation:

> He admired Ben-Gurion, and was willing to do whatever he ordered him. This drove him insane in his early career, but later he recuperated and unleashed a decree from his conscience and released the values of justice that throbbed in his heart.[67]

Michal gave another example to Cohn's admiration of Ben-Gurion. After the prime minister retired, Cohn went to visit him at his home at Sede Boker, and according to Cohn's autobiography, Ben-Gurion expressed his regret that after the establishment of the state he had left the rabbinical courts intact. After the meeting Cohn told his wife that the decision to leave the courts was like "the weeping of generations, but still, we had no-one greater than Ben-Gurion."[68]

Who is a Jew?

Cohn greatest contribution to the Jewish character of Israel is his interpretation of the perennial question "who is a Jew?" which allows us to examine his broader attitudes toward religion, law, state, and identity.

In 1950, the Knesset legislated the Law of Return, which allows every Jew to immigrate to Israel and receive Israeli citizenship. "My part in the formulation of the Law of Return and the legal discussions that came before it remain in my memory as one of the best experiences I have ever had."[69] The law did not define who is a Jew for this purpose. The Orthodox representatives wanted to impose the Halakhic definition of Jewishness, but Ben-Gurion objected. Since Ben-Gurion wanted the law to be approved unanimously, no clear definition was added. The idea behind the law was that the State of Israel should be a refuge for any persecuted Jew, and the Jewish purity of potential immigrants was not the essence.

Cohn emphasizes that even in the early days preceding the legislation he objected to Halakhic definitions, such as the religious principle that a Jew is someone who was born to a Jewish mother, since a normative state should not investigate the beliefs of individuals or their mothers. He also objected to investigations into immigrants' racial origins. The State of Israel was built on the ashes of persecuted Jews who were hunted by racist legislators. How could a state that was supposed to be a safe haven for persecuted Jews hurt their honor by first scrutinizing their Jewishness, Cohn wondered. Accordingly, he suggested that this question be left open for the Supreme Court to decide. His suggestion was accepted, and Yisrael Ben-Yehuda, the Minister of Justice, ordered the authorities to register as a Jew any person who "declared with pure intentions that he is a Jew and not of any other religion." As time passed, cases arose of mixed families arriving in Israel in which the wife was not Jewish but insisted on being registered as such. This led to growing political pressure from the Orthodox parties to amend the law.[70]

By way of a compromise, Ben-Gurion suggested that the government would seek the opinions of "the sages of the people of Israel" in Israel and abroad on this debate and decide based on their response. Ben-Gurion sent a letter of inquiry to 45 people, 30 of whom were Orthodox, and the majority of the responses said that Jewish identity should be determined according to Jewish law.[71]

One of the "sages" was Cohn himself. His principled opinion was in favor of subjectivity: he argued that any person who honestly identifies himself as a Jew is a Jew. According to Cohn, there are many options for Jewish identity: some may become Jews through birth to a Jewish mother or strict conversion; others married Jewish spouses and suffered severe persecution, clearly showing their identification with Jews and their belief in a shared destiny.

> One thing that seems the most important is the free choice that every individual should make in his views for what it means to be Jewish, and this free choice should be guarded in any way possible, so that no-one will presume to reject any claim made with pure intensions to be Jewish.[72]

He rejected the idea of determining who is a good Jew and who is a bad Jew, stressing that every individual is autonomous to make his or her own decisions.

According to Cohn, someone who sees himself as a Jew with pure intentions should be considered as such, even if the person is not Halakhically Jewish. A child of a Jewish father but not a Jewish mother, or a person converted by a non-Orthodox rabbinical court may genuinely consider himself as a Jew. The same is true of people who immigrate to Israel out of identification with the Jewish people and seek to participate in building the land: their actions testify to their pure intentions. The same logic applies to people who followed their spouses to concentration camps and endured persecutions and torture. "The Nazi crematoriums did not distinguish between Halakhic and non-Halakhic Jews, nor between them and their spouses."[73]

Cohn adds that a man with two Jewish parents will most likely consider himself to be a Jew, and no further tests will be needed. When only one of the parents is Jewish, however, the parents and/or the person themselves will have to make a conscious decision that he is a Jew. As for converts, the mere fact that they stood in front of a rabbinical court and declared their desire to be Jewish underscores their choices; it does not matter whether the court is non-Orthodox. Indeed, there may be cases where converts refuse to believe in the God of Israel. Cohn claimed that the number of people who wish to join the ranks of the Jewish people while maintaining a lack of belief in God was growing. However, he noted in this context that there are also many Jews in the Diaspora who have rejected Judaism as a religious creed: is it right that we still call them Jews? Cohn pointed out the Halakhic anomaly that a Jew who rejects this identity is still considered Jewish, even if he or she acts against Jews or against the Jewish state.[74]

In 1962, while sitting on the Supreme Court, Cohn was called on to determine the case of Brother Daniel. Daniel Rufeisen was born a Jew but converted to Christianity and became a Carmelite monk. The State of Israel granted him citizenship, but he wanted to receive his rights according to the Law of Return. As a convert to Christianity, the court ruled against him, but Cohn wrote a strong minority opinion dissenting from this ruling. The decision of the Ministry of Interior was based on the government decision that "a person who declares in pure intention that he is a Jew, and not a member of any other religion, will be registered as a Jew." There was no disagreement that Rufeisen was a Catholic Christian by religion, but he wanted the state to register him as a Jew by nationality, and to secure Israeli citizenship under the Law of Return.[75] In his minority opinion, Cohn acknowledged that Catholicism and Judaism have long been in opposition and there is a long history of Catholic persecution of Jews. One cannot forget the history of Jews who had to pretend to follow the Catholic religion in order to survive, as in the case of the crypto-Jews of Spain. However, times have changed, and a man now arrives at the gates of the State of Israel and wishes to join his fate to that of the state, although his religion is Catholic. "Should we close the gates for him?" Cohn asked. "Does the circle of destiny oblige us to pay him back measure for measure?" Cohn emphasized that the most important aspect defined in the law is subjectivity; in other words, the right to immigrate to Israel is dependent on a person's declaration that he/she is a Jew. Cohn argued that the law does not relate to the raising of religious objections or the scrutinizing of the individual's beliefs. Accordingly, the immigration officer must follow the guidelines and accept the "pure intensions" of the candidates, without making any additional inspections.[76] Cohn was willing to regard a Catholic monk as Jewish since the monk saw himself as such. The monk's religion was irrelevant for Cohn, who argued that a modern state has no right to examine the beliefs of its citizens. Accordingly, being Israeli is tantamount to being Jewish.

Marriage to Michal Zemora

Cohn's second marriage to Michal Zemora raised an interesting dilemma that illustrates Cohn's worldview. Cohn divorced his first wife Elsa in 1952, and in 1966 proposed to Michal Zemora. This would be Michal's third marriage: she was divorced from her first husband while her second husband had passed away. Jewish law prohibits a Cohen from marrying a divorcee, and accordingly the couple could not marry inside Israel but only in a civil union outside the country. Cohn decided to resign his post as a Supreme Court justice in order to marry Zemora, feeling that it would be inappropriate for a justice who was a Cohen to wed a divorcee. His fellow justices refused to accept his resignation, and Cohn decided to consult with Yitzhak Nissim, the Sephardi Chief Rabbi. He suggested he could make a small blemish on his body, such as cutting his finger, which according to the Halakhah would disqualify him as a priest, thereby leaving him free to marry Zemora. Nissim rejected the plan, and the couple decided to marry in a civil union outside of Israel.

While visiting New York City, Edward Sandrow, a Conservative rabbi, agreed to marry them, since he was willing to consider Michal a widow rather than a divorcee. The story was reported in the front page of the *New York Times*.[77]

Cohn died on April 10, 2002, at the age of 91. Although he had been a member of a secular burial organization all his life, his family decided to bury him in Jerusalem according to Orthodox Jewish ritual.[78]

Discussion

The emergence of a secular Jewish culture in the Hebrew language during the first half of the twentieth century has sparked a lively debate concerning the place of religion in the emerging Zionist movement in Palestine. Scholar Yuval Jobani proposed a typological model for Hebrew secularity comprising three categories, each of which is grounded in a different philosophical understanding of the secularization project.

The first is the "radical model," which "strives outspokenly and uncompromisingly to abolish religion, arguing that there is no place for it in the modern era." Speakers of this model argue that its role as a civilization-generating force has terminated, and that it now produces mainly intolerance, violence, oppression, and "holy wars." Speakers of this model can be found among the "Canaanite" movement, whose best-known exponent was Yonatan Ratosh.

The second model of secularity in Hebrew culture in the first half of the twentieth century is the pluralistic model. Unlike the radical model, this approach does not seek to replace religion's monopoly over culture with a secular monopoly. Instead it advocates an ongoing dialogue or open competition in which neither side enjoys a fundamental priority over the other. Pluralist secularists are no less confident in their position than their radical peers, but they refuse, as a matter of principle, to reject the religious position altogether. They respect religious culture insofar as they respect the rights of people to lead their lives according to their values, traditions, and preferences, as long as they do not deny that right to others. Pluralist secularists are willing to acknowledge the existence of virtues even in moral systems that do not revolve around self-criticism and autonomy, because they perceive their own virtue to reside in their openness to otherness and hence support the decentralization of worldviews and lifestyles. One of the first prominent figures to espouse an overly pluralistic model for secular Jewish culture was Ahad Ha'am (Asher Zvi Hirsch Ginsberg). His intellectual enterprise from the turn of the century can be understood as revolving around an attempt to find a theoretical and practical paradigm for mutual recognition and cooperation between secular and religious Jews.

The third model of secularity in Hebrew culture is "the religious model of Jewish secularity." This model offers secular substitutes for religion in order to relocate the religious experience from conventional religious objects to secular objects and ideals. As a result, within this model, originally religious concepts, myths, rituals, and institutional patterns are recruited for the sake of strictly secular ends, such as the nation, the motherland, and the state. Unlike the two previous models, secularization here does not signify the elimination of the religious impulse, but rather its deflection from the transcendent to the imminent realm. A. D. Gordon, one of the prominent thinkers of early twentieth-century Hebrew culture, was a subtle and sophisticated pioneer of secular Jewish culture in its religious version.[79]

This typology can enrich our understanding of Cohn's place in the secularization of Israeli society. Cohn is a clear example of the second pluralistic model. He indeed rejected religion but never became "anti-religious" in the true sense of the term, although some Orthodox circles certainly viewed him as such. He advocated a pluralistic approach according to which every individual has the right to live their life according to their own conscience, as long as they do not break the law. He also believed in a synthesis between a secular modern state and the treasures of Jewish law. In this respect, he drew close to the approach of spiritual Zionism, which saw the state as a spiritual center and a light unto the nations. According to Justice Zamir: "Cohn's Judaism was an open culture, human and merciful, rooted in universalistic values, and yet still with a uniqueness that divides it from any other culture." Zamir labeled Cohn as the representative of such Judaism, which seeks to draw closer Jews who have distanced themselves from Judaism and to bridge the growing gap between Jews and Judaism.[80] According to Cohn, the State of Israel cannot be a state of Jews: it must be a Jewish state. However, the Judaism of the state must be pluralistic rather than Orthodox. In many respects, these ideas complement Ben-Gurion's vision of developing Jewish culture in the Jewish state.[81] However, Ben-Gurion neglected the Halakhic Judaism that had developed in the Diaspora. He adopted the Bible as a national myth for Zionist culture while ignoring the post-biblical Jewish texts.[82] Unlike Ben-Gurion, Cohn sought to blend Zionist culture with Jewish law and make it part of the Israeli law book.

The answer that Cohn gave on the "who is a Jew" issue highlighted his pluralistic tendencies. His answer that being Jewish is a subjective identity that must be accepted if declared with pure intention is today viewed in Israel as naïve. Ruth Gavison, a well-known law professor, has noted that there are many groups in India and Africa that claim Jewish roots. They may indeed seek to immigrate to Israel with pure intentions, but "it would be unwise for the State of Israel to bring them all based on these declarations."[83] Justice Zamir also remarked that a subjective test of identity is unpractical.[84] Nathan Devir, who studied these communities in India and Africa, claimed that they do not intend to immigrate to Israel and their Jewish identity is not a tactic to permit such immigration;[85] nevertheless, suspicions remain.

Cohn's ideas about subjective identity never found support in Israel, but they would seem to be very relevant to American Jews. The Jewish community in America is encountering a new phenomenon in Jewish history, as many outsiders seek to join its ranks. However, many of them do not choose to do so according to the Halakhic conditions. Some convert in non-Orthodox courts and congregations, while others assume a shared destiny with the Jewish people without any formal act of conversion. Many children of mixed marriages subjectively view themselves as fully Jewish. Accordingly, Cohn's vision of Jewish identity has essentially become the norm among American Jews.

As a character trait, Cohn was always open to change, and this helps to explain the transformations in his identity. His openness to self-criticism was expressed in one of the most famous trials in Israeli history: the Amos Baranes affair. In 1976, the court convicted Amos Baranes for the murder of Rachel Heller and he was sentenced to life in jail. The conviction was based on Baranes' own confession, but he later claimed that this had been taken by force, and he appealed to the Supreme Court. Haim Cohn, who wrote the court's decision, rejected the appeal, and Baranes' many requests for a new trial were unsuccessful. Cohn met Baranes in jail, and after the meeting Cohn realized that he had made mistakes in his ruling. He admitted his error and took action to ensure so that Baranes would be pardoned and leave jail after eight years. Baranes demanded a retrial, and in 2002 he was completely exonerated. After the retrial, Cohn wrote to Dalia Dorner, the president of the Supreme Court: "I thank you for correcting the wrong that I have made. May you live a long life."[86]

This story underscores Cohn's personality, his openness to change, and his readiness to reexamine his own positions. The same traits were apparent in his decision to leave religion as in his rulings as a justice. The Baranes affair was not the only instance in which Cohn recognized judicial errors he had made.

To conclude, Cohn experienced a long process of falling from faith, while continuing to admire the wisdom of the Jewish sages and their laws. Throughout his life he continued to study the Jewish texts, and this study formed an important part of his spiritual world. This paradox epitomizes a figure who remained loyal to Jewish identity while undergoing radical changes.

Notes

1 John Barbour, *Versions of Deconversion: Autobiography and the Loss of Faith*, Charlottesville: University Press of Virginia, 1994, 1–4.
2 Stuart Wright, "Leaving New Religious Movements," in: *Falling from the Faith: Causes and Consequences of Religious Apostasy*, edited by David Bromley, Newbury Park, CA: Sage, 1988, 143–165.
3 David Bromley, "Religious Disaffiliation," in: *Falling from the Faith: Causes and Consequences of Religious Apostasy*, edited by David Bromley, Newbury Park, CA: Sage, 1988, 9–25.
4 Armand L. Mauss, "Dimensions of Religious Defection." *Review of Religious Research* 10 (3) (1969): 128–135.
5 Lynn Davidman, *Becoming Un-Orthodox – Stories of Ex-Hasidic Jews*, New York: Oxford University Press, 2015.
6 Malachi Krenzler, "The Process of Religious Disaffiliation Among Former Orthodox Jews (Chozrim Beshe'elah) in Israel: Social Aspects," *Social Issues in Israel* 24 (2017): 66–92 (in Hebrew).
7 Haim H. Cohn, *A Personal Introduction – Autobiography*, Or Yehuda: Kinneret, Zmora-Bitan, 2005, 72–74 (in Hebrew); one of Carlebach's grandchildren was the singing rabbi, Shlomo Carlebach, and an interesting genealogical research has been conducted on the family tree. See http://toladot.blogspot.co.il/search/label/%D7%A7%D7%A8%D7%9C%D7%99%D7%91%D7%9A (viewed on December 14, 2017).

8 Cohn, *A Personal Introduction – Autobiography*, 74.
9 Ibid., 77–78.
10 Ibid., 80.
11 Ibid., 83.
12 Tamar Ross, *Expending the Place of Torah – Orthodoxy and Feminism*, Waltham, MA: Brandeis University Press, 2004.
13 Cohn, *A Personal Introduction – Autobiography*, 84.
14 Ibid., 85.
15 Michael Shashar, *Haim H. Cohn – Supreme Court Judge: Talks with Michael Shashar*, Jerusalem: Keter, 1989, 21.
16 Cohn, *A Personal Introduction – Autobiography*, 85.
17 Naphtali Carlebach, *Joseph Carlebach and His Generation: Biography of the Late Chief Rabbi of Altona and Hamburg*, New York: Joseph Carlebach Memorial Foundation, 1959.
18 Shashar, *Haim H. Cohn – Supreme Court Judge*, 29–30.
19 Cohn, *A Personal Introduction – Autobiography*, 96–97.
20 Motti Inbari, *Jewish Radical Ultra-Orthodoxy Confronts Modernity, Zionism, and Women's Equality*, New York: Cambridge University Press, 2016, 173–202.
21 Cohn, *A Personal Introduction – Autobiography*, 101.
22 Shashar, *Haim H. Cohn – Supreme Court Judge*, 61.
23 Michal Zmora Cohn, "Epilogue: 'Here is the Man,'" in: *A Personal Introduction – Autobiography*, edited by Haim H. Cohn, Or Yehuda: Kinneret, Zmora-Bitan Publishers, 2005, 366.
24 Cohn, *A Personal Introduction – Autobiography*, 101.
25 Shashar, *Haim H. Cohn – Supreme Court Judge*, 34.
26 Ibid., 45.
27 Ibid., 133.
28 Cohn, *A Personal Introduction – Autobiography*, 108–109.
29 Ibid., 211.
30 Shashar, *Haim H. Cohn – Supreme Court Judge*, 126.
31 Cohn, *A Personal Introduction – Autobiography*, 125.
32 Haim H. Cohn, *Being Jewish*, Or Yehuda: Kinneret, Zmora-Bitan, Dvir Publishing House, 2006, 44–59.
33 Cohn, *A Personal Introduction – Autobiography*, 129.
34 David Ohana, *Zarathustra in Jerusalem – Friedrich Nietzsche and Jewish Modernity*, Jerusalem: Bialik Institute, 2016 (in Hebrew).
35 Shashar, *Haim H. Cohn – Supreme Court Judge*, 126.
36 Cohn, *A Personal Introduction – Autobiography*, 130–131.
37 Ibid., 135.
38 Ibid., 139.
39 Ibid., 149.
40 Ibid., 148–154.
41 Ibid., 154.
42 Ibid., 159.
43 Ibid., 161.
44 Aviezer Ravitzky, *Messianism, Zionism, and Jewish Religious Radicalism*, Chicago: University of Chicago Press, 1993, 10–39.
45 Cohn, *A Personal Introduction – Autobiography*, 165.
46 Ibid., 168–169.
47 Shashar, *Haim H. Cohn – Supreme Court Judge*, 127–128.
48 Ibid., 128.
49 Ibid., 130.
50 Elie Wiesel, *Night*, New York: Bantam Books, 1982, 60–61.
51 Cohn, *A Personal Introduction – Autobiography*, 174–178.
52 Ibid., 179.

53 Ibid., 181.
54 Shashar, *Haim H. Cohn – Supreme Court Judge*, 131.
55 Ibid., 138.
56 Dina Zilber, *In the Name of the Law*, Or Yehuda: Kinneret, Zmora-Bitan, Dvir – Publishing House, 2012, 34–51 (in Hebrew).
57 Cohn, *A Personal Introduction – Autobiography*, 184.
58 Ibid., 185–186.
59 Ibid., 186.
60 Ibid., 188–190.
61 Ibid., 192. On the failed attempt by Chief Rabbi Isaac Herzog to establish the Jewish law as the constitution of State of Israel, see Alexander Kyle, *The Invention of Jewish Theocracy*, Oxford University Press (forthcoming).
62 Cohn, *A Personal Introduction – Autobiography*, 194.
63 Ibid., 207.
64 Itzhak Zamir, "Preface: The Man and the Spirit," in: *A Personal Introduction – Autobiography*, edited by Haim H. Cohn, Or Yehuda: Kinneret, Zmora-Bitan, 2005, 40–41.
65 Ibid., 60–64.
66 Zmora-Cohn, "Epilogue," 430.
67 Ibid.
68 Ibid., 431.
69 Cohn, *A Personal Introduction – Autobiography*, 243.
70 Ibid., 245–247.
71 Eliezer Ben Refael, *Jewish Identities: Fifty Intellectuals Answer Ben-Gurion*, Leiden: Brill, 2002.
72 Haim Cohn, *Being Jewish*, Yehuda: Devir, 2006, 203.
73 Ibid.
74 Ibid.
75 Ruth Gavison, "Preface," in: Haim H. Cohn, *Being Jewish*, Yehuda: Devir, 2006, 144–145.
76 Cohn, *Being Jewish*, 180–186.
77 Lisa Hammel, "Israeli Judge Wed Divorcee Here," *New York Times*, March 24, 1966, https://mobile.nytimes.com/1966/03/24/archives/israeli-judge-weds-divorcee-here.html (viewed on May 7, 2018).
78 Zmora-Cohn, "Epilogue," 390–391.
79 Yuval Jobani, "The Lure of Heresy: A Philosophical Typology of Hebrew Secularism in the First Half of the Twentieth Century," *Journal of Jewish Thought and Philosophy* 24 (2016): 95–121; Yuval Jobani, "Three Basic Models of Secular Jewish Culture," *Israel Studies* 13 (3) (2008): 160–169.
80 Zamir, "Preface," 25–26.
81 David Ohana, *Political Theologies in the Holy Land: Israeli Messianism and Its Critics*, London: Routledge, 2010, 17–53.
82 Uriel Simon, *The Status of the Bible in Israeli Society: From National Commentary to Existential Literalism*, Jerusalem: A. Hess, 1991.
83 Gavison, "Preface," 148, note 14.
84 Zamir, "Preface," 25–26.
85 Nathan P. Devir, *New Children of Israel – Emerging Jewish Communities in an Era of Globalization*, Salt Lake City: University of Utah Press, 2017.
86 Zmora-Cohn, "Epilogue," 372–373.

6 Avraham (Avrum) Burg between Religious Zionism and post-Zionism

Avraham (Avrum) Burg gained public attention in Israel when he made his first steps in the early 1980s as a leading activist in the Peace Now movement and one of the organizers of the mass demonstrations against Israel's Lebanon War (1982–1985). Burg is the son of the late Dr. Yosef Burg, one of the leaders of the National Religious Party, but his politics differ starkly from those of his father. During the 1970s, the young generation of Religious Zionists adopted right-wing positions emphasizing the Greater Israel ideology and demanding the annexation of Territories conquered by Israel in the Six Day War of 1967. Though he grew up in a Religious-Zionist home, Avrum Burg was not attracted by this ideology. Indeed, he moved in the opposite direction, opposing the Israeli occupation in the Territories and advocating a solution based on the formula of "Land for Peace."

When Avrum Burg joined the Knesset in 1988, he was part of a group of eight young politicians (known as "The Eight") who promised to make changes in Israeli society and to pursue peace with the Palestinians. "The Eight" were able to fulfill many of the items on their political agenda, although none of them reached the position of prime minister. Between 1988 and 2004, Burg secured impressive political achievements, serving as a Member of Knesset and as chairman of the Knesset Committee on Education, Culture, and Sport. Later he became the chairperson of the Jewish Agency and subsequently the Speaker of the Knesset. In the primaries to lead the Labor Party in September 2001, he lost to Benjamin (Fuad) Ben-Eliezer by a small margin in a heated election that raised numerous accusations of fraud.

Although Burg had a successful political career with many achievements, he decided to quit politics. In an interview with me, he compared himself to a salmon swimming against the stream. A close study of his biography shows that he is an open-minded person who does not fear change and self-examination. His personality explains and informs his ideological transitions: leaving Religious Zionism as an ideological home and joining the Labor Party, and leaving Orthodoxy as a religious structure while accepting the idea of religious pluralism as embodied in Reform and Conservative Judaism, along with a stubborn struggle to separate religion from state (an uncommon idea among the Orthodox in Israel). Later he also departed from mainstream Zionist ideology, adopting post-Zionist ideas and abandoning the two-state solution as the basis for a compromise between Israel and the Palestinians.

Burg should be viewed as a vanguard in the sense that he experienced trans-formations that were later accepted by a larger number of people. In this chapter I will discuss the process that led Burg to leave his ideological home in Religious Zionism and Orthodoxy. This change took place during the 1970s and the 1980s, a period when other notable left-wing voices could also be heard within the Reli-gious Zionist movement, such as Rabbi Yehuda Amital and Professor Yeshayahu Leibowitz. But these were lone voices, while the mainstream of Religious Zion-ism was attracted to the Gush Emunim movement on the hard right.

The political defeat to Fuad (Ben-Eliezer) in 2001, a strong personal blow, marked the beginning of the end of Burg's political career. If we position the first transformation in his ideology at the point when he decided to leave Religious Zionism, the second came when he realized that he would not be able to lead his party and had reached a political dead-end. Only then did he undergo a further transformation from a mainstream politician into a post-Zionist "prophet of rage." One of the symbolic actions he took during this period was to apply for French citizenship (thereby becoming a dual national) so that he could vote for the French presidency.

Burg has had two important role models in his life. The first is his late father, Dr. Yosef Burg, the "eternal" politician and a master of compromise. Yosef Burg served as a Member of Knesset and as a senior cabinet minister in numerous governments over a period of more than four decades, leading to jokes about his everlasting career. The other was the Orthodox maverick Yeshayahu Leibowitz, a philosopher and political theorist who warned of the moral dangers of the Israeli occupation in the Territories and demanded the separation of state and religion. Torn between these two very different influences, Burg ultimately drew his pro-phetic vision from Leibowitz, but adopted his approach for reaching this vision from his father. Only when his political career ended in 2004 was he able to free himself from this dialectical model and assume the position of a prophet who warns of an impending day of reckoning.

The change from a mainstream Zionist to a post-Zionist revolves around the tension between the categories Jew and Israeli. The classic Zionist "Sabra" was depicted as a tough man who disdains the bourgeois Jew of the Diaspora. The Zionist revolution sought to take the Jews out of Europe and to transform their national identity. Accordingly, the Sabra sought to transform the observant bour-geois Jew into a secular, national farmer; at least, this was the image Zionists wanted to present. This model was always more of an ideal than a reality, but the State of Israel of the twenty-first century bears no resemblance to these early Zionist images. When Burg speaks about the option of a new Israeli identity, he essentially seeks to retrieve and revive the "old" pre-Zionist European Jew. His model is that of German Jews prior to the Holocaust, when German-Jewish iden-tity adopted positions along an axis between universalism, progress, and moder-nity on the one hand, and their particularistic Jewish identity on the other. This axis was complex and German Jews were torn between its poles, resulting in the emergence among them of movements of assimilation and acculturation, such as Reform Judaism and Modern Orthodoxy.

The axis between the particular and the universal, between acculturation and assimilation, created several new options for Jews. Modern Orthodoxy, in which Burg grew up, was open to modern lifestyles and education, but resolutely committed to Orthodox practice.[1] Reform Judaism took a step further toward assimilation and universalism yet still maintained a particularistic character in the synagogue and worship.[2] Some Jews developed strong assimilationist and universalist tendencies without the element of Jewish worship or ritual. The philosopher Hannah Arendt is a good example of this approach: she supported the idea of world government and she was indifferent, if not hostile, toward the Jewish national movement.[3] Converts from Judaism to Christianity were usually motivated by the desire to improve their professional opportunities and social status.

My assessment is that Burg has moved along this axis through his various transformations. As long as he saw himself as part of the Zionist consensus, his religious position was similar to his father's brand of moderate Modern Orthodoxy, during the period before the movement swung sharply to the right after the Six Day War. He later moved to a position closer to that of Yeshayahu Leibowitz: an Orthodox Jew who was far more critical of the State of Israel. Following his retirement from politics, he stepped outside the Israeli consensus and developed a sympathy for pre-Zionist Reform Judaism. In particular, Burg came to admire Rabbi Julian Morgenstern (1881–1977), the president of the Reform movement's Hebrew Union College from 1921 through 1947. Burg was attracted by Morgenstern's vision of assimilation of American Jews and his opposition to Jewish nationalism. I should emphasize that Reform Judaism itself has since moved away from this approach (as presented in the introduction), as Burg is well aware. In his last shift (to date, at least) he adopted Hannah Arendt as his role model, dedicating his book *The Holocaust Is Over* (2007) to her memory.

In order to explain the political transformation he chose, this chapter will examine the main stages of Burg's life: his departure from Religious Zionism, his entry into and abandonment of professional politics, and his eventual adoption of post-Zionism. I will seek to highlight dissonances that pushed him to adopt unusual ideological stands and to consider the personal dimensions of these transformations. This chapter draws on Burg's autobiography, published in Hebrew in 2015,[4] and an ideological book he published in 2007 that also includes autobiographical aspects.[5] In addition, I reviewed newspaper articles and conducted an interview with Burg in July 2016.

Childhood and deconversion

Avraham (Avrum) Burg was born in 1955 to a Religious Zionist family in Jerusalem, an only son with three sisters. His mother Rivka (née Slonim) was born in Hebron to a distinguished Ashkenazi rabbinical family. By good luck, she survived the pogrom against the Jews of Hebron in 1929, when 69 Jews were murdered by nationalist Arabs.[6] His father Yosef (1909–1999) immigrated to

Mandatory Palestine from Germany in 1937, just before the Nazis prevented Jews from leaving. Yosef Burg had not been in a rush to leave Germany; before doing so, he completed a doctorate in the teachings of Kant at Berlin University, and he also was ordained as a rabbi by the Hildesheimer Rabbinical Seminary. Yosef Burg was born in Dresden in East Germany to a family of immigrants from Galicia with a Hasidic background. Native German Jews referred to such newcomers as "Ostjuden" and considered them their inferiors.

The Burg family chose to make a home in the Rehavia neighborhood of Jerusalem, an area known for its concentration of German-Jewish intellectuals and where the German language was commonly heard in the streets. Avrum Burg raises an interesting question regarding his parents' decision to live in Rehavia, rather than in Bayit VaGan, the "enclave" of the Religious-Zionist community. It is possible that his parents considered themselves different from the mainstream of Religious Zionism and felt more comfortable living among other German Jews rather than an exclusively Orthodox environment.

Yosef Burg published a partial memoir entitled *Chapters of an Autobiography* (2000) that provides extensive information about his Jewish identity. As noted, Yosef Burg was both an academic and a rabbi. He recalls that during his rabbinical training in the Neo-Orthodox seminary in the early 1930s, students did not cover their heads on a regular basis:

> In our appearance we looked like any other students in Germany. We did not look any different. No-one in the seminary grew a beard or sidelocks. We wore a hat in the streets, and at home, when we studied, we put a kippa on our head. . . . We always carried a kippa in our pocket for prayer, or for occasional blessing over food.[7]

Avrum Burg also commented in surprise that he found a photograph of his father from 1951, when Yosef Burg was serving as Minister of Health, in which his father was not wearing a kippa. Avrum was surprised that his father had not felt it necessary to cover his head in an official portrait.[8] This behavior does not imply that Burg Senior was lax in his Orthodoxy. Rather, he maintained the Neo-Orthodox approach of German Jews and distinguished between religious activities that require covering the head and secular activities for which this is not necessary.[9] However, Yosef Burg abandoned this practice at a certain point: his son identifies the Six Day War as the turning point after which his father began to cover his head whenever he was in public.

Avrum Burg described his childhood as happy; the turning point came with the transition to high school, which he describes as "terrible."[10] His parents decided to transfer him to Nativ Meir Yeshiva, a prestigious Religious-Zionist boarding school. He felt like a foreign implant in the school and experienced a sense of continuous failure. He recalls that his grades dropped and he became wild and unruly. According to his testimony, the boarding school was a depressing place for him, and he hardly had any friends. He was not disciplined, but his parents refused to take him out of the school since "people like us do not leave such a school," meaning that social norms required him to stay in the institution.[11]

It is important to mention the educational processes that occurred during the 1960s and 1970s in the elite Religious-Zionist schools. These processes were the product of the inferior status of Religious Zionism, which found itself torn between two conflicting worlds: secular Zionism and ultra-Orthodoxy. Religious Zionists were not pioneers like the secular Zionists, since most of them were urbanites employed in bourgeois professions; neither were they regarded as the religious equals of the ultra-Orthodox, since they did not produce significant Torah scholars from among their ranks. The solution for this inferiority came in the form of students educated at Religious-Zionist boarding schools, who eventually went on to fill the benches of Merkaz HaRav Yeshiva, headed by Rabbi Zvi Yehuda Kook.

Burg recalls that the boarding school did not have any of the Halakhic flexibility he was used to from his own home, since many of its teachers were ultra-Orthodox. Indeed, at this stage many of the Religious-Zionist schools could not find teachers from their own community to teach religious subjects, so they hired Haredi teachers instead. These teachers encouraged a trend to religious radicalization, like in the ultra-Orthodox world, and the youth who grew up in these schools became more pious in their lifestyle. Another trend was nationalist radicalization, which emerged due to the desire to mimic or surpass the pioneering ethos of secular Zionists. Burg says:

> We tried to copy the practices of Zionist pioneers: we wore our shirts out hanging down outside our pants, we preferred . . . khaki pants. . . . We sang the youth movement songs and we knew the epic war poems by heart. We admired their cultural leaders, Meir Har Zion and the brave paratroopers, the 'Stockade and Tower' pioneers, the illegal immigration (during pre-state period), and the Palmach warriors. All theirs, none of ours. We didn't have even one private and intimate hero for ourselves, until 1967.[12]

Research into Religious-Zionist youth indeed shows how these dilemmas were manifested. Gideon Aran's study of the Gahelet youth movement portrays a group of young Religious-Zionist adults who rebelled against what they perceived as weak and soft parents. The members of this youth movement later would join Merkaz HaRav Yeshiva and eventually went on to lead the Gush Emunim movement. They include such figures as Moshe Levinger, Hanan Porat, Eliezer Waldman, and Haim Druckman. The model they developed placed a much greater emphasis on Torah studies, something that had been less important for their parents, and on the value of pioneering, which also was not a key priority for their city-dwelling parents.[13] Yoel Bin Nun, who would become one of the leaders of Gush Emunim but was not a member of Gahelet, described a similar pattern in his own childhood in Haifa, where the Religious-Zionist youth suffered beatings and humiliations from the secular members of the Socialist youth movements. Bin Nun decided to join Merkaz HaRav in 1963 since he found in it a model that combined religious education with nationalism.[14]

Avrum Burg described how the anti-Zionist ultra-Orthodox Neturei Karta used to mock those who went to the Religious-Zionist youth movement Bnei Akiva, adding that they faced exactly the same scorn from the youngsters who went to the Hashomer Hatzair Socialist youth movement who met nearby. Both these other groups saw Bnei Akiva as a product of compromise, and it is indeed true that the movement was torn between the two poles: "There was nothing total that could identify us."[15]

The solution that was reached by the Religious-Zionist youth was also supposed to influence the young Burg, who was no different from the other youngsters who studied in these institutions. Burg indeed describes listening to Zvi Yehuda Kook's Torah sermons at Merkaz HaRav. However, he mentions two apparently trivial anecdotes that sparked his doubts about the boarding school and eventually led him to rebel.

In his autobiography, he recalls that as a teenager he loved playing volleyball and wanted to join a club. "The worst of decrees then fell on my head. One of the rabbis, who was not even my own teacher, prohibited me to attend the club."[16] The rabbi in question described ball games as "idolatry," and according to religious tradition one should give one's life rather than commit this sin. As a counter-reaction, Burg declared that if this is the God of that rabbi, "how can you believe in Him, in this petty thing that is supposed to rule the world?" In his youthful rebellion, Burg found revenge by harboring agnostic thoughts: "I lost my God and my volleyball." I should explain that many ultra-Orthodox rabbis began to prohibit ball games due to their central place in the modern lifestyle.[17] The rabbi presumably hoped that Burg would focus on his Torah studies, but in fact he only drove him to rebellion.

Another trivial fact that he mentioned as crucial was that when he was 16 he met a girl called Yael and developed a romantic relationship with her; the couple eventually married. The religious institution he grew up in was a single-sex enclave that imposed strict gender separation. During adolescence, the boys' contacts with the opposite gender were limited and supervised. His rebellion against the domineering institution was to meet a girl and enter into a romantic relationship. Burg mentioned that the other boys in the Yeshiva did not meet girls, gaining their sex education from the Talmud and from moralizing books.[18] Burg concludes that their attitudes toward women developed in a way that promotes discrimination and exclusion, with an excessive emphasis on modesty. He mentioned that the school looked unfavorably on his relationship with Yael; he resented the fact that he was forced to hide his affair.

Burg was very critical toward the yeshiva, which he saw as inflexible: "From a child I turned into a robot of the rabbis."[19] After graduating from high school, most former students go to mandatory military service. Most of Burg's friends went on to a Hesder Yeshiva, which combines military service with Torah studies. Burg reports that he also faced pressure to follow this path, but instead decided to sign up for regular military service. Thus we can see a seminal milestone in the course of his life, when what he saw as the excessive rigidity of the yeshiva led him to rebel. In our interview, Burg emphasized that he was always an outsider, so that he does not see any specific breaking point. However, a study of the narrative presented in his memoirs reveals several points of friction.

Avrum Burg joined the army in 1974, two months after the end of the Yom Kippur War, which exposed the surprising weakness of the Israeli military compared to its Egyptian and Syrian adversaries. Although the war eventually ended with a partial Israeli victory, public opinion in Israel was devastated by the military weakness Israel had shown, at least at the beginning of the war, and by the high number of casualties. The tragic end of the war opened Israeli society to various changes that would later lead to the victory of the right-wing Likud in the 1977 general elections. The extra-parliamentary group Gush Emunim (the "Block of the Faithful") also emerged as a counter-reaction to talks about territorial compromises that began after the end of the war with Kissinger's visits to the region.[20]

An important point in Burg's biography came during his military training, when his platoon was sent to evacuate the illegal Gush Emunim settlement of Sebastia in the West Bank (1974). Gush Emunim was established in 1974 as a coalition of groups and public figures from diverse backgrounds. Led by young Religious-Zionist activists, Gush Emunim was supported both by the Orthodox bourgeois urban circles and by secular supporters of the Whole Land of Israel movement.[21] Gush Emunim sought to prevent territorial concessions and to advocate the application of Israeli sovereignty to Judea, Samaria, the Sinai Peninsula, and the Gaza Strip. The movement attempted to advance its objectives by establishing Jewish communities in the occupied Territories.

At the time of its formation, Gush Emunim did not convey a messianic vision. The first settlement action undertaken by activists from the organization came when, without official permission, they established a makeshift settlement at Sebastia in Samaria. The Israeli authorities evicted the settlers several times, but eventually they reached a compromise with Defense Minister Shimon Peres in which they instead agreed be housed on a neighboring IDF (Israel Defense Forces) base – a decision that effectively led to the establishment of the settlement.

That evening, just before Burg and his platoon were sent to evacuate the settlers in Sebastia, there was a break in the training, and the solders watched the movie *The Graduate* with Dustin Hoffman. Again, this seems to be no more than an amusing aside, but Burg describes the film in so much detail that it clearly played an important role for him at this point, representing another step in his journey away from Religious Zionism. The movie famously tells the story of a young man who was seduced by his mother's friend and later entered into a relationship with her daughter. Burg recalls that he was hypnotized by the movie and impressed by the sexual permissiveness of the plot. He could not have watched such a movie in the religious institutions he grew up in: only during military service was he exposed to a different world outside the religious enclave. As mentioned, the rabbis had indeed insisted that he attend a Hesder Yeshiva where he would continue to be protected from the secular world, but his rebellion against their authority led him to be open to other worlds: "I have never seen such explicit films. I sat fascinated and sexually stimulated in the dark."[22]

The movie was turned off before its end and the soldiers were sent to prepare to evacuate the settlers in Sebastia. As he reached the location the next morning, he realized that his assignment was effectively to evict his own friends from the yeshiva. The situation was dominated by a harsh dissonance: "All the evacuators wore uniform like me, and all the evacuated wore kippot." Burg did not understand the situation at that point. He obeyed the order to evict the settlers, but he recalls that he had no political opinions at this time, and did not even vote in the elections of 1974 and 1977.[23] He met Yossi, a settler whom he knew personally from high school, who explained the situation to him:

> "We are returning to Samaria, to our land, we are renewing the Jewish settlement" [said Yossi]. I did not understand what was he talking about. "Who told you to come here?" I wondered. "The Rabbi," he said and pointed. On the other side of the compound I saw students, soldiers, and police officers surrounding the admired Rabbi Zvi Yehuda Kook.[24]

Burg had to make a quick decision. Settling the land was the epitome of the education he had received at boarding school. On the other hand, his commanders expected him to follow his orders and evacuate the trespassers. This is a situation that would repeat itself over the years to come, when a tension emerges between military orders and the worldview of soldiers who oppose territorial compromises.[25] Burg decided to follow the military orders, in another step away from Religious Zionism.

> Here is my friend, and here is my commander, what should I do? "Burg!" Me and the commander, both of us, grabbed Yossi and evacuated him. At that moment my youth ended. The last piece that connected me to these worlds was torn. Between the rabbi and the state, I chose the state. Between man and land I chose man.[26]

For Burg, it was critical to distance himself from boarding school and from the enclave of those shaped by the Religious-Zionist educational approach. This distance, which was a product of choice, reached its height when he was required to confront physically his past worlds. It is possible that the disconnection would have come anyway, albeit at a slower pace, had it not been for this confrontation. But the violent and jolting confrontation certainly forced him to pick a side. This is how he was able to be released from duality and doubt.

Getting into politics

After completing his military service, Burg opened a new page in his life. He exchanged all of his friends and began to study at university. In 1977, Egyptian President Anwar Sadat visited Israel in order to make peace. The visit moved Burg, and it was during this optimistic period that he decided to marry his girlfriend Yael: "This was the right time to make a new family and raise kids in a world that is all good."[27] These good years ended for Burg with a major crisis.

According to the peace deal, Israel was required to withdraw from Sinai and to grant the Palestinians functional autonomy in the occupied Territories. Yosef Burg was appointed by Prime Minister Menachem Begin to lead the negotiation team for the autonomy talks (this component of the peace treaty was never honored due to the murder of Sadat and the outbreak of the Lebanon War in 1982). The peace treaty with Egypt enjoyed the support of most Israelis, but those who opposed it came mainly from the ranks of Religious Zionism and Gush Emunim. They formed the Movement to Stop the Withdrawal from Sinai, which opposed territorial compromises in Sinai and rejected the autonomy plan.[28] Menachem Begin invited Moshe Dayan to lead the negotiations, but he refused, and instead Burg assumed the role. Shortly after, Dayan resigned from the government due to the lack of progress in the negotiations. At this point, Yosef Burg's main role was to appease US President Jimmy Carter while explaining Israeli opposition and procrastinating with the help of word plays and biblical quotations – in short, to use some of the skills for which he was best known.[29]

Although Yosef Burg, a representative of the National-Religious Party, did not oppose the peace treaty, and was a man of compromise on the principled level, the peace deal nevertheless collapsed under his watch. Avrum Burg levels hard accusations against his father in this context: "Begin appointed Dad to this role so he would fail. Dad fulfilled his assignment with astonishing failure."[30] Another anecdote Avrum Burg mentions is that every time his father went to negotiations, he would change the kippa on his head from black to a knitted kippa.[31] The knitted kippa is the symbol of the Gush Emunim movement. This gesture symbolized his mood during the negotiations, as he stood in the middle between his national duty to bring peace and the grim mood against peace in his own party, particularly among the young generation.

This is how Avrum Burg describes the attitude of the young generation in the party toward his father: "He knew they were destroying his dream. He did not believe in their way, but he also did not stand in their way."[32] Avrum Burg sharply criticizes his father for failing to confront Gush Emunim:

> They offered an alternative to the passivity of my father and the rest of their leaders. Their knitted kippot expelled the black Diaspora kippot from places of power and influence in the party. Their masculine mustaches withdrew the full cheeks, and their strong hands pushed out those who had played classical music in their childhood.[33]

We can see here a double insult: Burg Junior was complaining about the depressing years he had spent in the yeshiva, and he was insulted by the humiliating treatment of his father and the other veterans of the party at the hands of the younger generation – his own generation. Burg felt that these young and aggressive men had made a laughingstock of his father, but equally he was convinced that his father must make a decision: although he supported the peace treaty, he decided to become the servant of the worst of worst, those who hate peace and admire war. At that moment, when Burg Junior saw his father ruining the chances for peace due to outside pressure, he decided to create counter-pressure, and he joined the *Peace Now* movement.

Israel launched the Lebanon War (1982–1985) following the assassination of the Israeli ambassador in Great Britain. However, many Israelis opposed the conflict, which they saw as a "war of choice" or even a "war of deception." A true nadir came with the massacre in Sabra and Shatila, where 3,000 Palestinians were murdered by Christian militias who were supported by Israel. These tragic events pushed Avrum Burg outside his comfort zone, and he decided to become a political player.

> Many times I told myself that I will not turn to be like my father, I will not engage in politics. However, now, in front of the enemy – the government of Israel – I was sucked in by powers I could not resist. We started raising signatures, and we established a movement called Soldiers against Silence.[34]

Avrum Burg was one of the organizers of the "demonstration of the 400,000" (1982), which was organized by Peace Now to protest the Sabra and Shatila massacre and to demand the establishment of a national commission of inquiry. Such a commission was duly established and recommended that Ariel Sharon, Minister of Defense, should resign. Sharon refused to leave office, and at another demonstration in February 1983, a grenade was thrown into the crowd by the right-wing activist Yona Avrushmi, killing Emil Grunzweig, one of the protestors. Burg was present at the demonstration and was injured by a grenade fragment that perforated his lungs. Avrum Burg identifies his activities as one of the leaders of Peace Now as crucial to his decision to become a politician.[35]

Shimon Peres, one of the leaders of the Labor Party, was impressed by Burg Junior's activism and asked him to join the party. Burg has recounted the story of his encounters with Peres several times, invariably in an unflattering manner. Burg claims that Peres promised that he would be allowed to shape the Labor Party's platform on the subject of religion and state, but as the classic Israeli political joke adds, he never promised to keep his promise, and of course he indeed did not do so. Similar descriptions can be found at subsequent points of friction between religion and state.

Burg's political agenda comprised two goals: to pursue peace and to promote the separation of religion and state. He was inspired by Yeshayahu Leibowitz, a thinker who gained influence following the Six Day War, though he never became a mainstream figure in the Religious-Zionist movement. Leibowitz saw the observance of commandments as the essence of Judaism: a legalistic religion that requires solely technical obedience to the law. Accordingly, Leibowitz can certainly be characterized as a strict Orthodox Jew who opposed any type of change in Jewish religious law, despite his maverick status. In an article from 1943, at an early stage in his philosophical career he supported the establishment of the State of Israel as a theocracy, where the laws of the Torah would be the laws of the land.[36] He later changed his mind, recognizing that the Halakhah cannot offer significant answers to the challenges of a modern state. He feared that changes in the law would be required in order to adjust to the new situation of a state, but he vehemently opposed such changes. Accordingly, he concluded that the two realms must be kept separate.[37] Since he regarded the Halakhah as the essence of Judaism, he opposed any type of mediation between God and humans. Holy sites can be used as a mediation, because people believe that the presence of God is stronger in such locations. Thus he responded coolly to the conquest of the Western Wall in 1967, even referring to the site as the "Discotel" (a combination of "disco" and *Kotel* or "Wall"). Perhaps paradoxically, he was also a humanist and a universalist, opposing the Israeli occupation of the Territories and rejecting the view that associated full redemption with the Whole Land of Israel as claimed in Merkaz HaRav circles.[38] Leibowitz was direct and blunt and did not shy away from verbal confrontations, or indeed provocations. He was one of the few Israeli figures who was not swept along by the euphoria the followed the Six Day War, warning with considerable prescience of the ramifications of Israel's occupation of the Palestinian people.

Avrum Burg told me in our interview that he was exposed to Leibowitz and his ideas after finishing his military service, during which he worked for a military college and arranged many meetings between Leibowitz and the soldiers. His attitude toward Leibowitz is clearly one of admiration:

> From my childhood until his death he was like light and shadow for me, part of my life. . . . Over the years I became closer to him, I learned him and learned from him, therefore I considered myself as his representative in the Knesset. Still then I lived like an Orthodox and I ignored the contradictions which are rooted in his views: his wonderful openness and the halakhic rigidity he was committed to.[39]

As noted above, Avrum Burg arrived in the Knesset in 1988, joining a national unity government headed by Yitzhak Shamir of the Likud. Burg was one of a group of young politicians from the Labor Party who promised to shake up the system and to introduce groundbreaking changes in peace, economics, and the relations between state and religion. The so-called Gang of Eight included Chaim Ramon, Yossi Beilin, Amir Peretz, and Yael Dayan. Only Peretz later went on to become the head of the party. Beilin is best known for his role as the architect of the Oslo Accords, the peace treaties signed with the Palestine Liberation Organization (1992–1995). Ramon is known for his work to disconnect the party from the Histadrut (labor union) and from the Clalit HMO (health maintenance organization), which was once closely linked to the party. Burg's role was to revise the party's policy on religion and state, but he learned the hard way that this might be the hardest task of all.

The Labor Party held a general meeting in 1990, following the failure of the so-called Dirty Trick, when Shimon Peres unsuccessfully attempted to depose Shamir as prime minister with the help of the Shas Party. Burg recalls that his proposal to separate state from religion was adopted with a large majority: "This was a great moment, maybe the highest point I ever reached in my public life."

Burg subsequently won first place in the primaries for the party's list in the Knesset elections.

Burg goes on to explain that Shimon Peres and Yitzhak Rabin, the leaders of the party, were terrified by the decision, anticipating that after the elections they would need to sign coalition agreements with Orthodox parties that oppose the separation of state and religion. Peres reconvened the party's leadership and initiated a new vote on the issue, effectively neutralizing the original vote. "I looked toward the mighty Shimon Peres, and not for the first time I saw how blunt his opportunistic hypocrisy could be."[40]

Burg describes his defeat in this second vote as a personal nadir, particularly because he made peace with his defeat and gave up:

> I applied many mechanisms of self-deception to myself in order not to do what was required and to run away as far as I can. . . . The many background noises caused me to stop listening to myself. I accepted the quasi-democratic verdict and lowered my head. This was the point where I told myself one of the two political lies that shaped my life. The separation of religion and state was not just "another issue"; it was not just a compromise, one of many, that every man has to make in his life, especially if he is a political figure who understands that that politics is the art of compromise with the given possibilities. Once I gave in to Peres's tricks, I stopped being a man of substance and I turned into a professional politician. I gave up on my mission in order to pursue a career. I compromised on my internal identity for my public appearance.[41]

From this quote we can see that Avrum Burg marks 1990 as the year of his entrance into real politics – meaning the art of compromise. The tension between the values that brought him to be a public emissary and his inability to fulfill them created a cognitive dissonance. According to his testimony, when he was a soldier, he was able to overcome the dissonance he faced at the time and leave Religious Zionism, but in 1990 he chose compromise and political hypocrisy. He may well have hoped to return to the issue of religion and state in the future, but between vision and politics, between Yeshayahu Leibowitz and Yosef Burg, he chose his father's path – the path of professional politics. According to his testimony, it was only when he chose to leave the political world in 2004 that he found his real truth.

Leaving politics

Burg suffered a further blow in 2001 when he lost in the Labor Party leadership election to Benjamin (Fuad) Ben-Eliezer. These results were very close: at first it was announced that Burg won, but Fuad appealed to the court due to allegations of fraud, and after a legal battle, repeat elections were announced in 40 polling stations, and it was eventually declared that Fuad had won the elections.[42]

Burg describes the defeat as an earthquake: "I won the primaries, but then all the corrupted establishments with their political bullies moved against me, and stole the victory from my voters and me."[43] He entered into a period of deep introspection that lasted several months, and recalls telling his son that he had realized that he no longer wanted a political career. He acknowledges that as a political man he derived satisfaction from power, but he recognized that politics had become a profession. He also became convinced that his key political objectives of making peace and separating state from religion could not be achieved within the political establishment. He tacitly admitted that walking in his father's shadow had led him to a dead end:

> Politics is like prison: the constant compromises, the careful maneuvers, the endless balance . . . are bars that are very hard to break. When you are inside, you are so used to the agenda, to the lifestyle, to the warden and the menu, that you do not even see that you are in prison.[44]

He could have chosen to stay and wait for another opportunity, but the party was in bad shape, winning just 17 seats in the 2003 elections. Burg was left on the back benches of the opposition. New figures joined the party and seemed destined to become its leaders. Thus, for all practical purposes, the 2001 defeat ended his political career. Burg went on a five-week trek in the Appalachians, and after returning announced that he was resigning from political life. He moved into business and also began to write memoirs and prose.

Burg recalls that when he was a young man he had a conversation with Leibowitz, who indirectly mocked his father and called him a man with no opinion.[45] Burg was offended, but he later felt that Leibowitz had a point. Yosef Burg was a man of establishments and compromises. Leibowitz, by contrast, was a prophet of rage who rejected compromise and always spoke his mind. Burg Junior felt that he had turned into a copy of his father and of Shimon Peres: "I evaded fully expressing my opinions as much as I could."[46]

It might seem that leaving politics was not the best solution for Burg, since he has claimed on several occasions that he is in a state of "cruel personal and public isolation,"[47] and that he desires to return to politics. In an interview for *Haaretz* in 2007, he suggested that he might play a role in the 2010 Israeli elections,[48] and indeed in 2010 he established a new party, but eventually he chose not to run.[49] In 2015 he announced that he would join Hadash, the Jewish-Arab far-left party. Although Hadash represents a universal vision, in practical terms it is a predominantly Palestinian party. In our interview, he told me that he has chosen not to pursue this connection further.

Political transformation

The move from politician to prophet has clarified Burg's political ideas, which may be presented in brief. His current vision is to establish a state based on the concept of equal citizenship and a Jewish-Arab confederation. According to his new approach, there must be complete equality for all citizens, in contrast to the current situation, where the State of Israel is defined as a Jewish nation-state.

Although the State of Israel offers equal rights to its Arab citizens, still there is much discrimination against them in various fields, including immigration rights, military service, and housing benefits, and there is unequal distribution of funds toward the Arab minority.

His practical solution to the Arab-Israeli conflict is to establish a single democratic state between the Mediterranean Sea and the Jordan River where all citizens will be equal. This state would be a confederation of a Jewish entity and an Arab entity, with an overall government for both. He proposes to abolish the Jewish character of the State of Israel and to turn it into a multinational state.[50] On the question of the Arab refugees, he proposed that a symbolic number of Palestinians be allowed to return to the Jewish federation.

In his book *The Holocaust Is Over* (2007), Burg explored the traumatic impact of the Holocaust on Israeli society, arguing that it led to the conviction that "the entire world is against us." He remarked that the Holocaust has become a central theme in Israeli education, as reflected in the almost obligatory high school trips to the death camps in Europe. Studies have shown that these trips encourage a strong national identity among the young participants.[51] Burg argues that the unparalleled death toll in the Holocaust and in Israel's wars has turned the country into a "modern Sparta" that understands only the language of force. He compares Israeli militarism to that in Germany under Otto von Bismarck (1862–1890): the centrality of the military, the sliding to the right of the mainstream, and the indifference of the majority toward the minority. All of these allow the "virus of the radical right" to infect the mainstream. Because of the Holocaust, Burg continues, Israeli society allows itself to engage in unacceptable and dangerous behavior toward the Palestinians. Moreover, he claims that this trauma also leads Israelis to prefer generals as their leaders, creating a symbiosis between the military and the political leadership. According to Burg, the lesson of the Holocaust should have been universal: that humanity must never again allow another genocide. Israel, he concluded, drew a profoundly particularistic lesson from the trauma, encouraging Jewish militarism.

Israel's relationship with Germany and the West brought the benefits of reparations and financial support, and allowed the Jews to develop a military power they had never before possessed. But by the same token, Burg noted, Israel continued to regard itself as weak. Faithful to its pledge never to forget, it "reincarnated" Hitler into the Arab body. His conclusion is that

> on the day we release the Arabs from the role we gave them as Nazis, it will be much easier to speak with them and to solve two existential problems: the constant war between the children of Israel and the children of Ishmael, and the healing of the national soul that is required for remembering the events of Holocaust.[52]

Burg is critical of the Israeli left, which he feels does not aspire to universal values. The Israeli left does not demand peace from the standpoint of justice, he argues, but is instead motivated by the desire for "the Palestinians to get the hell out of our eyes." For him, the left represents a holistic perspective that believes in the value that all humans were born equal. The Israeli left, by comparison, is chauvinistic and fake.[53]

A further conclusion Burg reached concerns the universalist message he found in the German Jewish experience. He praises Julian Morgenstern, the president of the Hebrew Union College, who as early as 1904 criticized Zionism as an attempt to escape from the traditional obligation to "repair the world" (*Tikkun Olam*) while creating a reclusive Jewish ghetto in the Middle East. Reform Judaism was a movement that supported the assimilation of Jews as equals in their gentile environment, and accordingly Reform scholars saw Zionism as an isolationist movement. According to Burg, their fears have proven to be justified: "The structure of the political establishment of the Jewish people would become a laboratory for the creation of narrow nationalistic feelings that would change the [Jewish] historical character beyond recognition."[54] It must be noted, however, that Reform Jews, including Rabbi Morgenstern himself, changed their positions radically after the Holocaust, where most Reform rabbis turned to support political Zionism, Reform Judaism joined the Zionist Congress, and during the 1970s opened institutions in Israel.

The establishment of the State of Israel united virtually all American Jews. Among the few who continued to harbor reservations were several German-Jewish intellectuals with socialist tendencies, such as Hans Kohn and Hannah Arendt. "At the point where Leibowitz ended for me, Hannah Arendt began," said Burg, stressing that he was particularly impressed with her idea of outcasts by choice – people who chose to be alienated because of their opposition to the idea of Jewish nationalism and their choice to remain loyal to the concept of the emancipation of Jews in humanity.

Burg explains that his mission now is to assimilate Jews into the Arab civilization they despise, but at the same time he wants to prevent the rupture between Jews and the universalistic West.[55] He repeated several times his conviction that Israel has deteriorated to the point that the vision it embodied on its establishment differs vastly from the actual results. However, he readily acknowledges that Arab civilization is also far from perfect, in particular due to its chauvinistic and antidemocratic tendencies, as he discussed in his book *God Has Returned*.[56]

Burg is striving to find balance "between Jerusalem and Tel-Aviv, between sacred and profane, between east and west, between Israel and Europe, between tradition and progress. Between this place and the wide world, between lost and hope. And between Israel and Judaism."[57] I found in these statements a deeper openness to the art of compromise that continues to be rooted in his personality, even if he refuses to admit it. In his identification with Arendt, who represented a very unpopular view in her opposition to Jewish nationalism, he seeks to depict himself as a similar radical on the left. However, his admission that he is torn between different worlds shows that he is more like his father than Leibowitz or Arendt, who were known for their unequivocal opinions.

The Holocaust Is Over came under sharp criticism in Israel. Hebrew University philosopher Elhanan Yakira described the book as a "parody" and as an "outstanding patchwork – pretentious, pompous, self-righteous, utterly confused, and at times self-contradictory; it is also deeply false in most of the claims it makes." Yakira wrote a powerful book showing how Holocaust deniers and anti-Israeli critics have manipulated the memory of the Holocaust into an argument against Israel. Yakira concluded that the picture of Israel that emerges from Burg's narrative almost constitutes a victory to Hitler. Yakira claims that Burg grew up with a Zionist silver spoon in his mouth. The fact that he comes from the most Jewish-Zionist of backgrounds, was Speaker of the Knesset and head of the Jewish Agency – an institution that is known for the very generous way it treats its executives – apparently grants his utterances extra force. No wonder, Yakira remarks, that anti-Zionist critics such as Tony Judt cite him as a reliable source.

Yakira also attacked the way in which the son viewed his father as a model of old Jewish wisdom, common sense, and religion – a symbolic counterpart to the present Israeli political and moral bankruptcy.

> The truth of the matter, however, is that Burg the father was one of Israel's most opportunistic and mediocre politicians ever. His greatest gift was his endless capacity to survive. . . . His most notable display of lack of integrity was perhaps, the way he [*sic*] – depicted by his son as a man of peace and compromise – remained the head of his party while it was becoming nationalist, messianic, and the political expression of the most extreme "greater Israel" religious ideology.[58]

Jewish identity

Whereas Leibowitz was a strict Orthodox Jew who opposed any changes in the Halakhic way of life, Avrum Burg is no longer Orthodox; he supports religious reforms and espouses agnostic views. His public work aims to break the monopoly power of Orthodoxy in Israel by separating state from religion.

In his book *The Coming of Days*, he writes: "I don't know if there is a God in the heavens. If there is a creator." He described the Bible as a wonderful work, human but aspiring to the divine.[59] In his opinion, the collusion between religion and politics is devastating and will lead to destruction. Therefore separating the two is crucial: "Any attempt to expand the place of God beyond His borders, to contain Him, and to force Him on a secular establishment such as the state means disrespect for the eternal and will end in spiritual disaster."[60]

Burg regards the Orthodox establishment as xenophobic, mentioning rabbis such as Yitzhak Ginsburg, Ovadia Yosef, and Menachem-Mendel Schneerson as the worst examples.[61] By contrast, he sees in American Judaism the right model for Israel. During the 1980s he visited San Francisco, where he met for the first time with Reform rabbis. He was initially dismayed and alarmed by their approach, but over three decades he has learned to appreciate this spiritual movement and has become a partner in its efforts.[62] His commitment to pluralistic Judaism is reflected in the fact that he has begun to officiate at non-Orthodox marriage ceremonies in Israel. He also advocates amending the Orthodox prayer book to remove expressions of xenophobia, discrimination between man and woman, and prayers for the renewal of the Temple sacrifices.[63]

He is often asked: if these are your opinions, why do you still wear a kippa? Burg responds that the kippa is for him "a basic instinct. . . . I was never forced to wear it, it was always there." Nevertheless, he no longer identifies with Orthodoxy: "I want a different meaning to my Judaism."[64]

Discussion

Historian Michael Brenner said that German Jews developed the acculturation model, which allowed them to maintain their Jewish identity while assimilating into the surrounding culture, whereas Eastern European Jews adopted a more separatist and insular approach. With hindsight, Brenner concluded, the German-Jewish model became the model for American Jews, whereas the Eastern European model was adopted by the Zionist movement and later by the State of Israel. American Judaism includes three main streams: Reform, Conservative, and Orthodoxy, all of which originated in Germany. In Eastern Europe, by contrast, Orthodoxy competed against secular or even anti-religious Judaism. In general terms, Brenner explains, this is what we see in Israeli society today. Jewish Eastern European writers wrote in Yiddish or Hebrew, whereas in Germany they wrote in German. Although the background of most Jewish writers in North America is Eastern European, they all have adopted the German model of acculturation.[65] Burg is fascinated by the pluralistic model of American Jews and he writes about it in length.[66] He believes that the future of Israeli society depends on its ability to adopt the pluralistic model and to renew Jewish culture accordingly.

Another model that Burg copies from North America is the confederative system as a solution for the Arab-Israeli conflict. The Oslo Accords (1993–1995) attempted to create two states for two peoples, with a joint border, whereas each state has its own ethnic identity. The failure of the Oslo Accords and the inability to impose separation has led Burg and others to think creatively and propose a confederative model. This model is certainly not consensual in Israel, however, and raises worries concerning security and the maintenance of a distinct Jewish identity. It is interesting to mention that in the pre-state period, the Brit Shalom movement supported a Jewish-Arab confederative model. Its members included several distinguished German Jews, such as Judah Leib Magnes (the first president of the Hebrew University of Jerusalem and a Reform rabbi), Martin Buber, Gershom Shalom, and Hans Kohn.[67]

I found it interesting that Burg devotes little attention to the Oslo Accords in either of his books. Whereas he discusses other periods of his life in detail, he remains quiet regarding his period of activity as a politician, particularly during the period when peace seemed to be within reach. He devoted his life to pursue peace between Israel and the Palestinians, and the Oslo Accords were an attempt to make it happen. Is he now embarrassed by his support for a peace deal based on a two-state model? In his book he mentioned that he found Rabin's insistence on passing the agreement with a Jewish majority deplorable and anti-democratic.[68]

Burg describes how personal traumas have led him to change his politics. The repressive lifestyle in the yeshiva pushed him to agnosticism, while his personal political failure led him to post-Zionism. He writes in detail and in a negative tone about the way in which Israeli society has become introverted due to the trauma of the Holocaust. However, Burg almost completely deletes from his memoirs the trauma that was left after the failure of the Oslo Accords, which initially aroused high expectations. Extensive Palestinian violence and suicide attacks that led to the death of hundreds of Israelis created a lack of confidence among many Israelis in the Palestinian leadership and the ability to reach peace. The Palestinians certainly do not bear all the blame for the collapse of the peace process: During the period of the Oslo Accords, Israel continued to develop the settlements, while the financial situation for Palestinians in the Territories deteriorated sharply. The outburst of the Al-Aqsa Intifada (September 2001) created a state of war between the two nations and eliminated whatever remained of the Oslo Accords. The suicide terrorist attacks by the Palestinian organizations, including the Fatah movement, led to the deaths of 1,100 Israelis and the injuring of some 8,000 people, dealing a serious blow to the chances for peace. Israel built the Separation Barrier around much of West Bank as the result of the Second Intifada, while the IDF launched Operation Defensive Shield (2002) against terrorist organizations. The conflict continued until 2004, and since then there have also been three rounds of combat between Israel and Hamas in Gaza. The resulting trauma in Israeli society changed the country's political landscape. The peace camp has collapsed, and as of the time of writing there is nothing to suggest that any change in public opinion is likely for the foreseeable future. I would therefore suggest that Burg may be mistaken in his analysis. The Israeli preference for right-wing governments may have less to do with the long-term influence of the Holocaust and more to do with the brutal conflict that erupted between the two sides following the collapse of the Oslo Accords.

To conclude, the political changes Burg has undergone were the result of his open-minded character and his ability to reconsider his own position following personal crises. These were processes that took years to develop.

Regarding the question of the possibility of an Orthodox left, Burg's case tends to refute such a possibility. Yeshayahu Leibowitz was a respected figure but always considered a "lone wolf." Burg's leaning to the left not only pushed him beyond Religious Zionism but ultimately led him out of Orthodoxy. A compromise that would keep him inside was unreachable, and as much as this reflects on him, it also reflects on the world he left.

Even after quitting parliamentary politics, Burg still maintains a presence in the political arena, leaving room for a possible return in the future. His story is one of duality and detachment. Standing between two worlds can lead to paralysis or to action. Clearly, Burg has identified himself as alienated, but this has led him to action. Burg's case illustrates the power of cognitive dissonance to shape political and personal opinions. Breaking the circles after crisis situations allowed Burg to achieve ideological renewal and positive change.

Notes

1 David Ellenson, *Rabbi Esriel Hildesheimer and the Creation of a Modern Jewish Orthodoxy*, Tuscaloosa: University of Alabama Press, 1990; Adam Ferziger, *Exclusion and Hierarchy: Orthodoxy, Nonobservance, and the Emergence of Modern Jewish Identity*, Philadelphia: University of Pennsylvania Press, 2005; Jacob Katz, *A House Divided: Orthodoxy and Schism in Nineteenth-Century Central European Jewry*, Hanover, NH: Brandeis University Press, 1998.
2 Michael Meyer, *Response to Modernity: A History of the Reform Movement in Judaism*, New York: Oxford University Press, 1988.
3 Idith Zertal, "A State on Trial: Hannah Arendt vs. the State of Israel," *Social Research* 74 (4) (2007): 1127–1158.
4 Avraham Burg, *The Coming of Days*, Or Yehuda: Dvir, 2015 (in Hebrew).
5 Avraham Burg, *Defeating Hitler*, Tel Aviv: Yediot Aharonot, 2007 (in Hebrew).
6 Hillel Cohen, *Year Zero of the Arab-Israeli Conflict, 1929*, Waltham, MA: Brandeis University Press, 2015.
7 Yosef Burg and Meir Hovav, *Chapters from an Autobiography*, Jerusalem: Yad Shapira, 2000, 38 (in Hebrew).
8 Burg, *The Coming of Days*, 137.
9 Mordechai Breuer, *Torah with Derech Eretz: The Movement, Its People, Its Ideology*, Ramat Gan: Bar Ilan University Press, 1987.
10 Burg, *The Coming of Days*, 39.
11 Ibid., 41.
12 Ibid., 57.
13 Gideon Aran, *Kookism: The Roots of Gush Emunim, Jewish Settlers Sub-Culture, Zionist Theology, Contemporary Messianism*, Jerusalem: Carmel, 2013, 29–110 (in Hebrew).
14 Yossi K. Halevi, *Like Dreamers: The Story of the Israeli Paratroopers Who Reunited Jerusalem and Divided a Nation*, New York: HarperCollins, 2013.
15 Burg, *The Coming of Days*, 57.
16 Ibid., 42.
17 Motti Inbari, *Jewish Radical Ultra-Orthodoxy Confronts Modernity, Zionism and Women's Equality*, New York: Cambridge University Press, 2016, 158–160.
18 Burg, *The Coming of Days*, 48.
19 Ibid., 55.
20 On the rise of Gush Emunim on the background of Kissinger's visit, see Motti Inbari, *Messianic Religious Zionism Confronts Israeli Territorial Compromises*, New York: Cambridge University Press, 2012, 15–37.
21 Dov Schwartz, *Religious Zionism: History and Ideology*, Boston: Academic Press, 2009.
22 Burg, *The Coming of Days*, 69.
23 Interview with Burg, July 2016.
24 Burg, *The Coming of Days*, 70–71.
25 Inbari, *Messianic Religious Zionism Confronts Israeli Territorial Compromises*.
26 Burg, *The Coming of Days*, 71.
27 Ibid., 74.
28 Michael Feige, *Settling in the Hearts: Jewish Fundamentalism in the Occupied Territories*, Detroit, MI: Wayne State University Press, 2009, 196–211.
29 Yehuda Avner, "Burg the Statesman," *And Joseph Was Liked – The Biography of Rabbi Joseph Burg Z"l*, edited by Yehudah Azrieli, Jerusalem: Renanim Congregation, 2000, 51–57.
30 Burg, *The Coming of Days*, 75.
31 Burg, *Defeating Hitler*, 271.

32 Ibid., 79–80.
33 Burg, *The Coming of Days*, 71.
34 Ibid., 88.
35 Ibid.
36 Yeshayahu Leibowitz, "Teaching Torah in a Modern Society," in: *Judaism, The Jewish People and the State of Israel*, edited by Yeshayahu Leibowitz, Jerusalem: Schocken, 1976, 37–50 (in Hebrew).
37 Yeshayahu Leibowitz, "Outline for the Problem of the Jewish Religion in the State of Israel," in: *Judaism, The Jewish People and the State of Israel*, edited by Yeshayahu Leibowitz, Jerusalem: Schocken, 1976, 85–87 (in Hebrew).
38 David Ohana, *Political Theologies in the Holy Land: Israeli Messianism and Its Critics*, London: Routledge, 2010, 76–92.
39 Interview, July 19, 2016.
40 Burg, *The Coming of Days*, 98.
41 Ibid., 105–106.
42 www.nrg.co.il/online/1/ART1/610/978.html (viewed on June 28, 2016).
43 Burg, *The Coming of Days*, 111.
44 Ibid., 113.
45 Ibid., 140.
46 Ibid., 117.
47 Ibid., 108.
48 Ari Shavit, "Divorce," *Haaretz Supplement*, June 6, 2007, www.haaretz.co.il/1.1416131 (viewed on June 28, 2016).
49 Shalom Yerushalmi, "Remember Me? The Comeback of Avrum Burg," *NRG*, June 8, 2010, www.nrg.co.il/online/1/ART2/141/660.html (viewed on June 28, 2016).
50 Burg, *The Coming of Days*, 229–232.
51 Jackie Feldman, *Above the Death Pits, Beneath the Flag: Youth Voyages to Poland and the Performance of Israeli National Identity*, New York: Berghahn, 2008.
52 Burg, *Defeating Hitler*, 132.
53 Ibid., 172.
54 Ibid., 65.
55 Burg, *The Coming of Days*, 266.
56 Avraham Burg, *God Has Returned*, Tel Aviv: Yediot Aharonot, 2009.
57 Burg, *The Coming of Days*, 266.
58 Elhana Yakira, *Post Zionism, Post Holocaust – Three Essays on Denial, Forgetting, and the Delegitimation of Israel*, New York: Cambridge University Press, 2010, 217–218.
59 Burg, *The Coming of Days*, 26.
60 Burg, *Defeating Hitler*, 303.
61 Ibid., 290–298.
62 Burg, *The Coming of Days*, 140.
63 Burg, *Defeating Hitler*, 325.
64 Burg, *The Coming of Days*, 119–139.
65 Michael Brenner, "German Jews as a Model for Modernity?" *Two Homelands: The Jekkes Between Central Europe and the Near East*, edited by Moshe Zimmerman and Yotam Hotam, Jerusalem: Merkaz Shazar, 5786, 32–34.
66 Burg, *The Coming of Days*, 146–151.
67 Shalom Ratzabi, *Between Zionism and Judaism: The Radical Circle in Brith Shalom, 1925–1933*, Leiden: Brill, 2002.
68 Burg, *The Coming of Days*, 173.

Concluding remarks

I opened the book with the following questions: "What leads a person to make fundamental changes in his or her ideology? What are the social conditions that affect change?" I will now seek to offer a tentative answer to these questions, based on the six case studies we have discussed and the accumulated knowledge in the literature.

The first aspect I want to raise is the personal nature of ideological change. All the subjects of our study decided to change due to specific personal situations; we may assume that if circumstances had been different, their transformations would also have been different. Ideological change is no doubt a product of an intellectual process, but the triggers that push toward a transformation tend to be personal in nature; later, people may add an intellectual rationalization to explain their decisions. For example, if it were not for Koestler's imprisonment, the poor reception of Podhoretz's book, Ben-David's failed engagement, Teichtel's tribulations as a refugee, the murder of Cohn's brother in Auschwitz, and Burg's education in a strict yeshiva, it is possible that these individuals would never have decided to change, or that their transformations would have headed in different directions. Ideological change begins with a personal course.

Second, the process of transformation is slow and gradual. All the cases discussed in this book reveal a pattern of progressive change. The literature on religious conversion has also identified this trend. It is true that we can also find narratives describing rapid and sudden change; a classic example is the story of the conversion of the Apostle Paul. However, most cases do not follow this type of scenario.

All the individuals discussed in this book are highly intelligent and unique; they are also extreme. All wanted to share their life insights with others. With the exception of Rabbi Teichtel, they all wrote autobiographies, and in several cases more than one (Koestler, Podhoretz, Ben-David, Burg, and to some extent even Cohn). This fact suggests that these individuals had a high level of self-awareness and concluded that it would be interesting and important for others to learn from their life history and insights. In that respect, we can see that all of the subjects of this study saw themselves as leaders who paved ways for others to follow. They wrote autobiographies and books for the purpose of explaining their changes and proselytizing others to join their path.

It is important to pay attention to the exit decision that marked all the figures discussed in this book. In many cases, people may feel discomfort with a certain ideology and community, but nevertheless decide not to exit. They may claim that they prefer to fix things from inside. In this regard, I believe that the analysis of this phenomenon can be enriched by drawing on another psychological theory concerning consumers' behavior in the markets. In his book *Exit, Voice and Loyalty* (1970), Albert Hirschman argues that when consumers are unhappy with merchandise, they can either stop buying the firm's products (the exit option) or express their dissatisfaction directly to management (the voice option). He stressed that the very act of voicing a protest is an expression of loyalty to the firm/institution.[1] Conversely, exiting is an expression of disloyalty. As consumer research has shown, there are cases in which protest can be channeled in a way that does not affect loyalty. However, even the most committed may have their breaking point. In this book, I examined the boundaries between voicing a protest and exiting.

All the figures discussed in this book had open personalities and a highly developed sense of curiosity to examine what society considers "heresy." This curiosity and openness eventually turned them into "heretics" by the standards of their original community and "apostates" from the standpoint of their new social group. In some cases, the process of transformation included an attachment to role models, figures greater than life, who helped them transform. Yeshayahu Leibowitz, Rabbi Kook, and Rabbi Maizes served as such figures. For Rabbi Teichtel, however, the Munkacser Rebbe served as the anti-figure, so that Teichtel's ideological transformation was narrated against Shapira.

The role of family is important in the decision to change any may be applied from positive or negative perspectives. In the cases of Podhoretz, Cohn, and Burg, we saw that the support of wives was essential for the bold decision to change. Thus we can conclude that the support of spouses, or immediate family members, is crucial. Koestler and Ben-David were single when change took place, and we have no information about Teichtel's marital status. However, a careful reading of Ben-David and Burg's narratives reveals a complex father-child relation that eventually might influence a decision to change in the direction of counter-reaction and youth rebellion.

Ideological change is a process that contains several stages: doubt, followed by a revelation, exit from community, and acceptance of a new social group with different political values. The change of community is important as well; all the figures in this research moved from one community to another. Thus we can conclude that the socialization process, the support one might find in his or her community (including family), is an essential factor.

I chose to conclude the case studies with Avraham (Avrum) Burg, and I believe his case represents the most significant ideological change that is taking place among Jews in Israel and the United States at the beginning of the twenty-first century. As argued in the book, Jewish identity during the twentieth century was understood as standing between the poles of ethics and piety on the one hand, and ethnicity or nationality on the other. Following the Holocaust and the establishment of the State of Israel, most Jews gravitated toward viewing their Jewish identity from a national perspective. Through this process, the ultra-Orthodox anti-Zionist movement became marginal and Reform Judaism changed its platform to acknowledge the importance of the State of Israel and Jewish peoplehood. Standing beside Israel was an important pillar of identity among Diaspora Jews – an act that came to signify Jewish unity.

However, with the turning of the centuries, unqualified and undisputed support for Israel can no longer be taken for granted among a growing section of the American Jewish elite. Their dissatisfaction with Israel's policies in the occupied Territories is expressed mostly through the ethical and religious language of *Tikkun Olam* (the mystical Hebrew term "repairing the world," which has come to refer to the concepts of social justice). Sociologist Shlomo Fischer argued, for example, that "liberal American Jews tend to talk about 'Jewish values' without further qualification. By that, they generally mean progressive or liberal values connected to ideas about social justice." Fischer quoted Rabbi Rick Jacobs, leader of the Reform movement, who said at the 2017 Union of Reform Judaism Biennial that Israel's settlements in the West Bank "run counter to higher Jewish values."[2] Jewish Voice for Peace, a pro-Palestinian American Jewish organization, explained its mission on its website as "to build Jewish communities that reflect the understanding that being Jewish and Judaism are not synonymous with Zionism or support for Israel."[3] Speakers of this ideology tend to negate the idea that all Jews have a shared destiny and are subject to binding mutual solidarity. They also tend to express a distaste for the concept of nationalism in general, and Jewish nationalism in particular, while narrating their concerns through the language of ethics and religious values. This represents, in my opinion, a shift of the pendulum toward the understanding that Judaism is a religion, or a set of ethical imperatives, rather than a national collective.

A movement in the pendulum can also be seen in Israel in the form of a phenomenon among Israeli Jews who grow up secular and even anti-religious. There is a growing trend among secular Israeli Jews to take an interest in the Jewish bookshelf, together with a growing New Age movement. This does not imply that more Israelis are becoming Orthodox; it means that many Israelis feel emptiness regarding their heritage, and that the secular egalitarian Israeli ethos cannot fill their needs. This aspect of Jewish renewal is manifested in the large number of participants at educational events on the night of Shavuot (*Tikkun Leil Shavuot*) and the growing number of Israelis joining educational events and classes on Jewish texts, ethics, and mysticism.[4]

I hope that this book has added another layer to our understanding of modern Jewish identities and the process of transformation. "Who is a Jew in our days?" As we have seen, this is a question that can yield some diverse and surprising answers.

Notes

1 Albert Hirschman, *Exit, Voice, and Loyalty: Responses to Decline in Firms, Organizations, and States*, Cambridge, MA: Harvard University Press, 1970.
2 Shlomo Fischer, "Israelis are Divided Over Whether They Are 'Jewish' or 'Israeli,'" *Forward*, October 25, 2018. https://forward.com/opinion/412732/israelis-are-conflicted-about-whether-they-are-jewish-or-israeli-heres/ (viewed on October 29, 2018).
3 https://jewishvoiceforpeace.org/mission/ (viewed on October 29, 2018).
4 Shai Feraro and James R. Lewis, eds., *Contemporary Alternative Spiritualties in Israel*, New York: Palgrave Macmillan, 2017.

Bibliography

Aaron, Daniel. "A Decade of Convictions: The Appeal of Communism in the 1930's." *Massachusetts Review* 2 (4) (1961): 736–747.

Abrams, Nathan. *Norman Podhoretz and Commentary Magazine: The Rise and Fall of the Neocons*. New York: Continuum, 2010.

Applebaum, Ann. "Yesterday's Man." *New York Review of Books*. January 11, 2010. www. anneapplebaum.com/2010/01/11/yesterdays-man/ (viewed on November 17, 2016).

Apter, David. "Political Religion in New Nations." In: Greetz, Clifford (ed.). *Old Societies and New States*. New York: Free Press, 1963, 57–104.

Aran, Gideon. *Kookism: The Roots of Gush Emunim, Jewish Settlers Sub-Culture, Zionist Theology, Contemporary Messianism*. Jerusalem: Carmel, 2013 (in Hebrew).

Avishai, Bernard. "Koestler and the Zionist Revolution." *Salmagundi* 87 (1990): 234–259.

Avner, Yehuda. "Burg the Statesman." In: Azrieli, Yehudah (ed.). *And Joseph was Liked – The Biography of Rabbi Joseph Burg Z"l*. Jerusalem: Renanim Congregation, 2000, 51–57.

Bacon, Gershon. "Birth Pangs of the Messiah: The Reflections of Two Polish Rabbis on Their Era." In: Frankel, Jonathan (ed.). *Studies in Contemporary Jewry* 7: *Jews and Messianism in the Modern Era: Metaphor and Meaning*. New York: Oxford University Press, 1991, 86–99.

Baldwin, Barry. "Two Aspects of the Spartacus Slave Revolt." *Classical Journal* 62 (7) (1967): 289–294.

Balfar, Ella. *The Kingdom of Heaven and the State of Israel*. Ramat Gan: Bar Ilan University Press, 1991 (in Hebrew).

Barbour, John. *Versions of Deconversion: Autobiography and the Loss of Faith*. Charlottesville: University Press of Virginia, 1994.

Batnitzky, Leora. *How Judaism Became a Religion*. Princeton, NJ: Princeton University Press, 2011.

Beck, Richard. "Communion and Complaint: Attachment, Object-Relations, and Triangular Love Perspectives on Relationship with God." *Journal of Psychology and Theology* 34 (1) (2006): 43–52.

Bellah, Robert N. *The Broken Covenant: American Civil Religion in Time of Trial* (2nd edition). Chicago: University of Chicago Press, 1975.

Ben Refael, Eliezer. *Jewish Identities: Fifty Intellectuals Answer Ben-Gurion*. Leiden: Brill, 2002.

Berkowitz, Roger. "Approaching Infinity: Dignity in Arthur Koestler's *Darkness at Noon*." *Philosophy and Literature* 33 (2) (2009): 296–314.

Blau, Ruth. *Guardians of the City*. Jerusalem: Idanim, 1979 (in Hebrew).
———. *The History of Yossele Schumacher*. Brooklyn: Copy Corner, 1993.
Bloom, Maureen. *Jewish Mysticism and Magic*. London: Routledge, 2007.
Bloomstock, Robert. "Going Home: Arthur Koestler's Thirteenth Tribe." *Jewish Social Studies* 48 (2) (1986): 93–104.
Boyarin, Daniel. *Unheroic Conduct: The Rise of Heterosexuality and the Invention of the Jewish Man*. Berkeley: University of California Press, 2007.
Brenner, Michael. "German Jews as a Model for Modernity?" In: Zimmerman, Moshe and Yotam Hotam (eds.). *Two Homelands: The Jekkes between Central Europe and the Near East*. Jerusalem: Merkaz Shazar, 5786–2006, 32–34.
Breuer, Mordechai. *Torah with Derech Eretz: The Movement, Its people, Its Ideology*. Ramat Gan: Bar Ilan University Press, 1987.
Bromley, David. "Religious Disaffiliation." In: Bromley, David (ed.). *Falling from the Faith: Causes and Consequences of Religious Apostasy*. Newbury Park, CA: Sage, 1988, 9–25.
Brown, Benjamin. "'As Swords to the Earth's Body': The Opposition for East European Rabbis to the Idea of Congregational Schism." In: Goldstein, Yossi (ed.). *Yosef Daat*. Beer Sheva: Ben Gurion University Press, 5770–2010, 215–244 (in Hebrew).
———. "The Two Faces of Religious Radicalism: Orthodox Zealotry and 'Holy Sinning' in Nineteenth-Century Hasidism in Hungary and Galicia." *Journal of Religion* 93 (3) (2013): 341–374.
Burg, Avraham. *The Coming of Days*. Or Yehuda: Dvir, 2015 (in Hebrew).
———. *Defeating Hitler*. Tel Aviv: Yediot Aharonot, 2007 (in Hebrew).
———. *God Has Returned*. Tel Aviv: Yediot Aharonot, 2009 (in Hebrew).
———. Interview on July 2016.
Burg, Yosef and Meir Hovav. *Chapters from an Autobiography*. Jerusalem: Yad Shapira Publishers, 2000 (in Hebrew).
Burgess, Glenn. "The Divine Right of Kings Reconsidered." *English Historical Review* 107 (425) (1992): 837–861.
Carlebach, Naphtali. *Joseph Carlebach and His Generation: Biography of the Late Chief Rabbi of Altona and Hamburg*. New York: Joseph Carlebach Memorial Foundation, 1959.
Carroll, Peter N. "The Spanish Civil War in the 21st Century: From Guernica to Human Rights." *Antioch Review* 70 (4) (2012): 641–656.
Cashman, Greer F. "No Stranger to Controversy." *Jerusalem Post*, May 24, 2000. https://web.archive.org/web/20010119125400/http://www02.jpost.com/Editions/2000/03/05/Features/Features.3576.html (viewed on September 26, 2017).
Cesarani, David. *Arthur Koestler: The Homeless Mind*. New York: Free Press, 1999.
Cohen, Hillel. *Year Zero of the Arab-Israeli Conflict, 1929*. Waltham, MA: Brandeis University Press, 2015.
Cohn, Haim H. *Being Jewish*. Or Yehuda: Kinneret, Zmora-Bitan, Dvir Publishing House, 2006 (in Hebrew).
———. *A Personal Introduction – Autobiography*. Or Yehuda: Kinneret, Zmora-Bitan, 2005 (in Hebrew).
Cohn, Norman. *The Pursuit of the Millennium*. London: M. Secker and Warburg 1957.
Cooper, Levi. *The Munkaczer Rebbe Chaim Elazar Shapira the Hassidic Ruler – Biography and Theology*. Ramat Gan: Ph.D. Dissertation, Bar Ilan University, 2011.
Davidman, Lynn. *Becoming Un-Orthodox – Stories of ex-Hasidic Jews*. New York: Oxford University Press, 2015.

Davies, Ioan. "The Return of Virtue: Orwell and the Political Dilemmas of Central European Intellectuals." *International Journal of Politics, Culture, and Society* 3 (1) (1989): 107–129.

Dawson, Lorne. "Clearing the Underbush: Moving Beyond Festinger to a New Paradigm for the Study of Failed Prophecy." In: Tumminia, Diana and William Statos, Jr. (eds.). *How Prophecy Lives*. Leiden: Brill, 2011, 69–98.

Devir, Nathan P. *New Children of Israel – Emerging Jewish Communities in an Era of Globalization*. Salt Lake City: University of Utah Press, 2017.

Eburne, Jonathan P. "Antihumanism and Terror: Surrealism, Theory, and the Postwar Left." *Yale French Studies* 109 (2006): 39–51.

Ellenson, David. *Rabbi Esriel Hildesheimer and the Creation of a Modern Jewish Orthodoxy*. Tuscaloosa: University of Alabama Press, 1990.

Ellenson, David and Daniel Gordis. *Pledges of Jewish Allegiance*. Stanford, CA: Stanford University Press, 2015.

Endelman, Todd. "Jewish Self-Identification and West European Categories of Belonging." In: Gitelman, Zvi (ed.). *Religion or Ethnicity? Jewish identities in Evolution*. New Brunswick, NJ: Rutgers University Press, 2009, 104–130.

Erikson, Erik. *Young Man Luther: A Study in Psychoanalysis and History*. New York: W. W. Norton, 1962.

Exline, Julie J., Kalman J. Kaplan and Joshua B. Grubbs. "Anger, Exit, and Assertion: Do People See Protest Toward God as Morally Acceptable?" *Psychology of Religion and Spirituality* 4 (4) (2012): 264–277.

"Extradition Agreement Signed with France." *Davar*, November 13, 1958, 2.

Feige, Michael. *Settling in the Hearts: Jewish Fundamentalism in the Occupied Territories*. Detroit, MI: Wayne State University Press, 2009.

Feldman, Jackie. *Above the Death Pits, Beneath the Flag: Youth Voyages to Poland and the Performance of Israeli National Identity*. New York: Berghahn, 2008.

Feraro, Shai and James R. Lewis (eds.). *Contemporary Alternative Spiritualties in Israel*. New York: Palgrave Macmillan, 2017.

Ferziger, Adam S. *Exclusion and Hierarchy: Orthodoxy, Nonobservance, and the Emergence of Modern Jewish Identity*. Philadelphia: University of Pennsylvania Press, 2005.

———. "Hungarian Separatist Orthodoxy and the Migration of Its Legacy to America: The Greenwald-Hirschenson Debate." *Jewish Quarterly Review* 105 (2) (2015): 250–283.

Festinger, Leon, Henry W. Reicken and Stanley Schachter. *When Prophecy Fails: A Social and Psychological Study of a Modern Group That Predicted the Destruction of the World*. Minneapolis: University of Minnesota Press, 1956.

Finkelstein, Menachem. *Conversion, Halakhah, and Practice*. Ramat Gan: Bar Ilan University Press, 2006.

Fischer, Shlomo. "Israelis Are Divided Over Whether They Are 'Jewish' or 'Israeli.'" *Forward*. October 25, 2018. https://forward.com/opinion/412732/israelis-are-conflicted-about-whether-they-are-jewish-or-israeli-heres/ (viewed on October 29, 2018).

Fishkoff, Sue. *The Rebbe's Army: Inside the World of Chabad-Lubavitch*. New York: Schocken Books, 2003.

Fleming, John V. *The Anti-Communist Manifestos: Four Books that Shaped the Cold War*. New York: W. W. Norton, 2009.

Friedman, Menachem. "Messiah and Messianism in Chabad – Lubavitch Hasidism." In: Ariel-Joël, David et al. (eds.). *War of Gog and Magog: Messianism and Apocalypse in Judaism – Past and Present*. Tel Aviv: Yediot Achronot, 2001, 161–173 (in Hebrew).

————. *Society and Religion – Non-Zionist Orthodoxy in the Land of Israel, 1918–1936*. Jerusalem: Ben Zvi Institute, 5738–1978 (in Hebrew);

Fund, Yosef. *Separation or Integration: Agudat Yisrael confronts Zionism and the State of Israel*. Jerusalem: Magness Press, 1999 (in Hebrew).

Gavison, Ruth. "Preface." In: Cohn, Haim H. (ed.). *Being Jewish*. Or Yehuda: Kinneret, Zmora-Bitan, Dvir Publishing House, 2006, 141–148 (in Hebrew).

Gerson, Mark. *The Neoconservative Vision: From the Cold War to the Culture Wars*. Lanham, MD: Madison Books, 1996.

Gillespie, Michael A. *The Theological Origins of Modernity*. Chicago: University of Chicago Press, 2009.

Goldman, Shalom. *Jewish-Christian Difference and Modern Jewish Identity*. Lanham, MD: Lexington Books, 2015.

Goldstein, Moshe. *Tikun 'Olam*. Mukacevo: Druck H. Gutmann, 5696–1936 (in Hebrew).

Gordis, Daniel. "Conservative Judaism, Zionism and Israel: Commitments and Ambivalences." In: Ben-Moshe, Danny and Zohar Segev (eds.). *Israel, the Diaspora and Jewish Identity*. Portland: Sussex Academic Press, 2007, 67–80.

Gordon, Louis A. "Arthur Koestler and His Ties to Zionism and Jabotinsky." *Studies in Zionism* 12 (2) (1991): 149–168.

Gough, Maria. "Paris, Capital of the Soviet Avant-Garde." *October* 101 (2002): 53–83.

Greenberg, Gershon. "Elhanan Wasserman's Response to the Growing Catastrophe in Europe: The Role of Hagra and Hofets Hayim upon His Thought." *Journal of Jewish Thought and Philosophy* 10 (2000): 171–204.

————. "Foundations for Orthodox Jewish Theological Response to the Holocaust: 1936–1939." In: Eckardt, Alice (ed.). *Burning Memory: Times of Testing and Reckoning*. Oxford: Pergamon Press, 1993, 71–94.

————. "Hasidic Thought and the Holocaust (1933–1947): Optimism and Activism." *Jewish History* 27 (2013): 353–375.

————. "Menahem Mendel Schneersohn's Response to the Holocaust." *Modern Judaism* 34 (1) (2014): 86–122.

HaCohen, Malachi. "The Liberal Critique of Political Theology: Political Messianism and the Cold War." In: Schwarz, Werner M. and Ingo Zechner (eds.). *Die helle und die dunkle Seite der Moderne*. Vienna: Turia and Kant, 38–50.

————. "'The Strange Fact That the State of Israel Exists'": The Cold War Liberals Between Cosmopolitanism and Nationalism." *Jewish Social Studies* 15 (2) (2009): 37–81.

Halevi, Yossi K. *Like Dreamers: The Story of the Israeli Paratroopers who Reunited Jerusalem and Divided a Nation*. New York: HarperCollins, 2013.

Hammel, Lisa. "Israeli Judge Wed Divorcee Here." *New York Times*. March 24, 1966. https://mobile.nytimes.com/1966/03/24/archives/israeli-judge-weds-divorcee-here.html (viewed on May 7, 2018).

Harel, Isser. *The Yossele Campaign*. Tel Aviv: Yediot Aharonot, 1982 (in Hebrew).

Hart, Mitchell (ed.). *Jews and Race*. Waltham, MA: Brandeis University Press, 2011.

Hartman, David. *Leadership in Times of Distress: On the Maimonides' Letters*. Tel Aviv: Hakibbutz Hameuchad, 1985 (in Hebrew).

Herf, Jeffery. *Undeclared Wars with Israel: East Germany and the West German Far Left, 1967–1989*. New York: Cambridge University Press, 2016.

Hershkovitz, Itzhak. "Em HaBanim Semekhah: From Canonic Treatise to a Dialectic Completion." *Alei Sefer – Studies in Bibliography and the History of the Hebrew Book Printed or Digital* 22 (2011): 115–127 (in Hebrew).

———. "The Halakhah as a Tool for Policy Makers: The Freedom of Ruling and the Responsibility of the Ruler in the Teachings of Rabbi Yissachar Shlomo Teichtel." *Dinei Israel* 26–27 (5769–70/2009–10): 67–88 (in Hebrew).

———. *The Redemption Vision of Rabbi Yissachar Shlomo Teichtel, HY"D: Transitions in His Messianic Perception during the Holocaust.* Ramat Gan: Ph.D. Dissertation, Bar Ilan University, 2009 (in Hebrew).

Hirschman, Albert. *Exit, Voice, and Loyalty: Responses to Decline in Firms, Organizations, and States.* Cambridge, MA: Harvard University Press, 1970.

Hood, Ralph W. "Where Prophecy Lives: Psychological and Sociological Studies of Cognitive Dissonance." In: Tumminia, Diana and William Statos, Jr. (eds.). *How Prophecy Lives.* Leiden: Brill, 2011, 21–40.

Hotam, Yotam. *Modern Gnosis and Zionism: The Crisis of Culture, Life Philosophy and Jewish National Thought.* London: Routledge, 2013.

http://chabad.info/magazine/%D7%91%D7%99%D7%AA-%D7%9E%D7%A9%D7%
99%D7%97-%D7%A0%D7%9E%D7%A9%D7%9B%D7%AA-%D7%9E%D7%
A1%D7%9B%D7%AA-%D7%94%D7%97%D7%A9%D7%99%D7%A4%D7%95%
D7%AA-%D7%91%D7%A4%D7%A8%D7%A9%D7%99%D7%99%D7%AA-%
D7%99%D7%95/ (viewed on July 28, 2016).

http://entertainment.time.com/2005/10/16/all-time-100-novels/slide/all/ (viewed on July 26, 2017).

http://manitou.org.il/%D7%AA%D7%95%D7%9C%D7%93%D7%95%D7%AA-%D7%97%
D7%99%D7%99%D7%95-%D7%A9%D7%9C-%D7%94%D7%A8%D7%91-%D7%
90%D7%A9%D7%9B%D7%A0%D7%96%D7%99/ (viewed on June 5, 2016).

http://toladot.blogspot.co.il/search/label/%D7%A7%D7%A8%D7%9C%D7%99%D7%
91%D7%9A (viewed on December 14, 2017).

https://chomsky.info/19670223/ (viewed on July 26, 2017).

https://drive.google.com/file/d/0B_wZ8qKsEas2bWVrMUtTNGFvd1k/view (viewed on November 30, 2018).

https://jewishvoiceforpeace.org/mission/ (viewed on October 29, 2018).

https://ry4an.org/readings/short/student/ (viewed on July 26, 2017).

Inbari, Motti. *Jewish Radical Ultra-Orthodoxy Confronts Modernity, Zionism and Women's Equality.* New York: Cambridge University Press, 2016.

———. "Messianic Activism in the Works of Chaim Elazar Shapira, the Munkaczer Rebbe, Between Two World Wars." *Cathedra* 149 (2013): 77–104 (in Hebrew).

———. *Messianic Religious Zionism Confronts Israeli Territorial Compromises.* New York: Cambridge University Press, 2012.

———. "Religious Zionism and the Temple Mount Dilemma: Key Trends." *Israel Studies* 12 (2) (2007): 29–47.

James, William. *The Varieties of Religious Experience.* New York: Modern Library, 1902.

Jeffers, Thomas L. *Norman Podhoretz: A Biography.* New York: Cambridge University Press, 2010.

Jobani, Yuval. "The Lure of Heresy: A Philosophical Typology of Hebrew Secularism in the First Half of the Twentieth Century." *Journal of Jewish Thought and Philosophy* 24 (2016): 95–121.

———. *The Role of Contradictions in Spinoza's Philosophy: The God-Intoxicated Heretic.* London: Routledge, 2016.

———. "Three Basic Models of Secular Jewish Culture." *Israel Studies* 13 (3) (2008): 160–169.

Kadosh, Refael. *Extremist Religious Philosophy: The Radical Religious Doctrines of the Satmar Rebbe*. Cape Town: Ph.D. Dissertation, University of Cape Town, 2011 (in Hebrew).

Kanievsky, Jacob Israel. *Encyclopaedia Judaica* 11 (2nd edition). In: Berenbaum, Michael and Fred Skolnik (eds.). Detroit, MI: Macmillan Reference USA, 2007, 762–763.

Katz, Jacob. *A House Divided: Orthodoxy and Schism in Nineteenth-Century Central European Jewry*. Hanover, NH: Brandeis University Press, 1998.

———. *Out of the Ghetto: The Social Background of Jewish Emancipation 117–1870*. Cambridge, MA: Harvard University Press, 1973.

Kellner, Menachem. "'And the Crooked Shall be Made Straight': Twisted Messianic Visions, and a Maimonidean Corrective." In: Morgan, Michael and Steve Weitzman (eds.). *Rethinking the Messianic Idea in Judaism*. Bloomington: Indiana University Press, 2014, 256–273.

Keren-Kratz, Menachem. "Hast Thou Escaped and also Taken Possession? The Satmar Rebbe – Rabbi Yoel Teitelbaum and His Followers' Response to Criticism of His Conduct During and After the Holocaust." *Dapim: Studies on the Holocaust* 28 (2) (2014): 97–120.

———. *Marmaros-Sziget: 'Extreme Orthodoxy' and Secular Jewish Culture at the Foothills of the Carpathian Mountains*. Jerusalem: Magness Press, 2013 (in Hebrew).

———. "Marmaros – The Cradle of Extreme Orthodoxy." *Modern Judaism* 35 (2) (2015): 147–174.

———. *R'Yoel Teitelbaum – The Satmar Rabbi (1887–1979): Biography*. Tel Aviv: Ph.D. dissertation, Tel Aviv University, 2013 (in Hebrew).

Koestler, Arthur. "Arthur Koestler." In: Crossman, Richard (ed.). *The God that Failed*. New York: Harper Colophon Books, 1949, 11–76.

———. *Arrow in the Blue*. London: Vintage, 2005.

———. *Darkness at Noon*. New York: Scribner, 1968.

———. *Promise and Fulfilment: Palestine 1917–1949*. New York: Macmillan, 1949.

———. *The Invisible Writing*. London: Vintage, 2005.

Kraus, Itzhak. "The Theological Responses to the Balfour Declaration." *Bar Ilan* 28–29 (5761–2000): 81–104 (in Hebrew).

Krenzler, Malachi. "The Process of Religious Disaffiliation Among Former Orthodox Jews (Chozrim Beshe'elah) in Israel: Social Aspects." *Social Issues in Israel* 24 (2017): 66–92 (in Hebrew).

Kyle, Alexander. *The Invention of Jewish Theocracy*. New York: Oxford University Press, forthcoming.

Leibowitz, Yeshayahu. *Judaism, the Jewish People and the State of Israel*. Jerusalem: Schocken, 1976 (in Hebrew).

Liebman, Charles and Eliezer Don-Yehiya. *Civil Religion in Israel: Traditional Judaism and the Political Culture in the Jewish State*. Berkeley: University of California Press, 1983.

Livni, Michael. "The Place of Israel in the Identity of Reform Jews: Examining the Spectrum of Passive Identification with Israel to Active Jewish-Zionist Commitment." In: Ben-Moshe, Danny and Zohar Segev (eds.). *Israel, the Diaspora and Jewish Identity*. Portland: Sussex Academic Press, 2007, 86–101.

Mauss, Armand L. "Dimensions of Religious Defection." *Review of Religious Research* 10 (3) (1969): 128–135.

Melton, Gordon. "Spiritualization and Reaffirmation: What Really Happens When Prophecy Fails." *American Studies* 26 (2) (1985): 17–29.

Meyer, Michael. *Response to Modernity: A History of the Reform Movement in Judaism*. New York: Oxford University Press, 1988.

Muffs, Yochanan. *Love & Joy: Law, Language and Religion in Ancient Israel*. New York: JTS, 1992.

Myers, Jody E. *Seeking Zion: Modernity and Messianic Activism in the Writings of Tsevi Hirsch Kalischer*. Oxford: Littman Library of Jewish Civilization, 2003.

Nadler, Allan. "The War on Modernity of R. Hayyim Elazar Shapira of Munkacz." *Modern Judaism* 14 (3) (1994): 233–264.

Nelson, Eric. *The Hebrew Republic*. Cambridge, MA: Harvard University Press, 2010.

New York Supreme Court, Appellate Division – First Department, Dutch-American Mercantile Corporation against Corta Corporation and Leon Swergold, file 8432.

Niditch, Susan. *War in the Hebrew Bible: A Study in the Ethics of Violence*. New York: Oxford University Press, 1993.

Nikiprowetzky, Valentin and André Zaoui. *Maimonide. Le livre de la connaissance*. Paris: Presses Universitaires de France, 1961.

Nikkel, David. "William James: The Mystical Experimentation of a Sick Soul." unpublished paper.

Ohana, David. *Nationalizing Judaism: Zionism as a Theological Ideology*. Lanham, MD: Lexington Books, 2017.

———. *Political Theologies in the Holy Land: Israeli Messianism and Its Critics*. London: Routledge, 2010.

———. *Zarathustra in Jerusalem – Friedrich Nietzsche and Jewish Modernity*. Jerusalem: Bialik Institute, 2016 (in Hebrew).

Paloutzian, Raymond, James Richardson and Lewis Rambo. "Religious Conversion and Personality Change." *Journal of Personality* 76 (6) (2009): 1047–1079.

Pianko, Noam. *Jewish Peoplehood: An American Innovation*. New Brunswick, NJ: Rutgers University Press, 2015.

Piekarz, Mendel. *Ideological Trends of Hassidism in Poland During the Interwar Period and the Holocaust*. Jerusalem: Bialik Institute, 1997 (in Hebrew).

Podhoretz, Norman. *Breaking Ranks: A Political Memoir*. New York: Harper and Row, 1979.

———. *Ex-Friends: Falling Out with Allen Ginsberg, Lionel and Diana Trilling, Lillian Hellman, Hannah Arendt, and Norman Mailer*. New York: Free Press, 2000.

———. *Making It*. New York: Random House, 1967.

———. *My Love Affair with America: The Cautionary Tale of a Cheerful Conservative*. New York: Free Press, 2000.

———. "My Negro Problem – And Ours." In: Jumonville, Neil (ed.). *The New York Intellectuals Reader*. New York: Routledge, 2007, 327–340.

———. *Why Are Jews Liberals?* New York: Doubleday, 2009.

———. *Why We Were in Vietnam?* New York: Simon and Schuster, 1982.

Polak, Avraham. *Khazaria: History of a Jewish Kingdom in Europe*. Tel Aviv: Mosad Bialik, 1951 (in Hebrew).

Popper, Karl. *Conjectures and Refutations: The Growth of Scientific Knowledge*. New York: Harper and Row, 1965.

Poulain, Martine. "A Cold War Best-Seller: The Reaction to Arthur Koestler's 'Darkness at Noon' in France from 1945 to 1950." *Libraries & Culture* 36 (1) (2001): 172–184.

Pritchett, Wendell E. *Brownsville, Brooklyn: Blacks, Jews, and the Changing Face of the Ghetto*. Chicago: University of Chicago Press, 2003.

Ratzabi, Shalom. *Between Zionism and Judaism: The Radical Circle in Brith Shalom, 1925–1933.* Leiden: Brill, 2002.

Redman, Ben. "Radical's Progress." *College English* 13 (3) (1951): 131–136.

Reiser, Daniel. "Aspects in the Thought of Rabbi Yisachar Shlomo Teichtal and a Study of New Documents." *Yad Vashem Studies* 43 (2) (2015): 143–190.

Ross, Tamar. *Expending the Place of Torah – Orthodoxy and Feminism.* Waltham, MA: Brandeis University Press, 2004.

Sarna, Jonathan. *American Judaism: A History.* New Haven, CT: Yale University Press, 2004.

Scammell, Michael. "Arthur Koestler in Civil War Spain." *AGNI* 54 (2001): 86–104.

———. *Koestler.* New York: Random House, 2009.

Schatz-Uffenheimer, Rivka. "Confession on the Brink of the Crematoria." *Jerusalem Quarterly* 34 (1985): 126–141.

Schindler, Pesach. "Tikkun as Response to Tragedy: Em HaBanim Smeha of Rabbi Yissakhar Shlomo Teichtal – Budapest, 1943." *Holocaust and Genocide Studies* 4 (4) (1989): 413–433.

Schmitt, Carl. *Political Theology: Four Chapters on the Concept of Sovereignty* (trans. George Schwab). Cambridge, MA: University of Chicago Press 1985.

Scholem, Gershom. *Kabbalah.* Jerusalem: Keter Publishing House, 1974.

Schwartz, Dov. *Faith at a Crossroads – A Theological Profile of Religious Zionism.* Leiden: Brill, 2002.

———. *The Messianic Idea in Israel.* Ramat Gan: Bar-Ilan University, 1997 (in Hebrew).

———. *Religious Zionism: History and Ideology.* Boston: Academic Press, 2009.

Schweid, Eliezer. "A Happy Mother of Children: The Theodicy of the Zionist God of Rabbi Yissachar Shlomo Teichtel." In: Idel, Moshe, Deborah Diment and Shalom Rosenberg (eds.). *Minkhah LeSarah – Studies in Jewish Philosophy and Kabbalah.* Jerusalem: Magness Press, 1994, 380–398 (in Hebrew).

Shamir, Ruth. *Who Are We?* Herzelia: Milo, 2012 (in Hebrew).

Shapira, Anita. "The Bible and Israeli Identity." *AJS Review* 28 (1) (2004): 11–42.

———. *Walking toward the Horizon.* Tel Aviv: Am Oved, 1988 (in Hebrew).

Shapira, Chaim E. *Minchat Elazar* 5. Jerusalem: Torah Muncas, 5756–1995 (in Hebrew).

Shashar, Michael. *Haim H. Cohn – Supreme Court Judge: Talks with Michael Shashar.* Jerusalem: Keter, 1989.

Shavit, Ari. "Divorce." *Haaretz Supplement.* June 6, 2007, www.haaretz.co.il/1.1416131 (viewed on June 28, 2016).

Simon, Uriel. *The Status of the Bible in Israeli Society: From National Commentary to Existential Literalism.* Jerusalem: A. Hess, 1991 (in Hebrew).

Spence, Donald. "Narrative Smoothing and Clinical Wisdom." In: Sarbin, Theodore (ed.). *Narrative Psychology.* New York: Praeger Special Studies, 1986, 211–232.

Stone, Jon R. (ed.). *Expecting Armageddon: Essential Readings in Failed Prophecy.* London: Routledge, 2000.

———. "Prophecy and Dissonance: A Reassessment of Research Testing the Festinger Theory." *Nova Religio* 12 (4) (2009): 72–90.

Streib, Heinz, Ralph W. Hood Jr., Barbara Keller, Rosina-Martha Csöff and Christopher Silver. *Deconversion: Qualitative and Quantitative Results from Cross-Cultural Research in Germany and the United States of America.* Germany: Vandenhoeck and Ruprecht, 2009.

Talmon, Jacob. *The Origins of Totalitarian Democracy.* London: Secker & Warburg, 1952.

Teichtel, Issachar S. *Em HaBanim Semekhah*. Budapest: Druck von Salamon Katzburg, 5703–1943 (in Hebrew).

———. *Faith Tempered in Holocaust Furnace*, 1. Jerusalem: Unclear publisher, 1994 (in Hebrew).

———. *Mishne Sachir*. Jerusalem: Machon Keren Re'em, 5769–2009 (in Hebrew).

———. *Tov Igal*. Slovakia: Unknown publisher, 1926 (in Hebrew).

Tolstoy, Leo. *A Confession*. London: Oxford University Press, 1961.

Ullman, Chana. *The Transformed Self: The Psychology of Religious Conversion*. New York: Plenum Press, 1989.

Unsigned, Untitled, Collection of Articles *Mishmeret Chomatenu*, from Members of Neturei Karta, vol. 14, 6 Iyar 5722–1962, Blau Archive, Box 1.

Varon, Jeremy. *Bringing the War Home: The Weather Underground, the Red Army Faction, and Revolutionary Violence in the Sixties and Seventies*. Berkeley: University of California Press, 2004.

Weingarten, Shmuel. "Miyvan metzula liyerushalaim shel maala." *Or Hamizrach* 19 (1970): 235–245 (in Hebrew).

Wiesel, Elie. *Night*. New York: Bantam Books, 1982.

Williams, Leonard. *American Liberalism and Ideological Change*. DeKalb: Northern Illinois University Press, 1997.

Wolf, Michael. "The Halakhic Attitude to Din Rodef and Din Moser." In: Arad, Moshe and Yuval Wolf (eds.). *Delinquency and Social Deviation: Theory and Practice*. Ramat Gan: Bar Ilan University Press, 2002, 215–249 (in Hebrew).

Wright, Stuart. "Leaving New Religious Movements." In: Bromley, David (ed.). *Falling from the Faith: Causes and Consequences of Religious Apostasy*. Newbury Park, CA: Sage, 1988, 143–165.

www.historicalstatistics.org/Currencyconverter.html

www.myjewishlearning.com/article/evil-eye-in-judaism/ (viewed on July 26, 2017).

www.nrg.co.il/online/1/ART1/610/978.html (viewed on June 28, 2016).

www.ranaz.co.il/notPublished/article47_19930616.asp (viewed on June 2, 2016).

www.youtube.com/watch?v=5Gr9tIxda_k (viewed on January 3, 2019).

Yadgar, Yaakov. *Sovereign Jews: Israel, Zionism and Judaism*. Albany: SUNY Press, 2017.

Yakira, Elhana. *Post Zionism, Post Holocaust – Three Essays on Denial, Forgetting, and the Delegitimation of Israel*. New York: Cambridge University Press, 2010.

Yerushalmi, Shalom. "Remember Me? The Comeback of Avrum Burg." *NRG*, June 8, 2010. www.nrg.co.il/online/1/ART2/141/660.html (viewed on June 28, 2016).

Zamir, Itzhak. "Preface: The Man and the Spirit." In: Cohn, Haim H. (ed.). *A Personal Introduction – Autobiography*. Or Yehuda: Kinneret, Zmora-Bitan Publishers, 2005, 11–68 (in Hebrew).

Zertal, Idith. "A State on Trial: Hannah Arendt vs. the State of Israel." *Social Research* 74 (4) (2007): 1127–1158.

Zilber, Dina. *In the Name of the Law*. Or Yehuda: Kinneret, Zmora-Bitan, Dvir Publishing House, 2012 (in Hebrew).

Zmora-Cohn, Michal. "Epilogue: 'Here is the Man.'" In: Cohn, Haim H. (ed.). *A Personal Introduction – Autobiography*, Or Yehuda: Kinneret, Zmora-Bitan, 2005, 359–440 (in Hebrew).

Zygmunt, Joseph F. "Prophetic Failure and Chiliastic Identity: The Case of the Jehovah's Witnesses." *American Journal of Sociology* 75 (6) (1970): 926–948.

Index